So I'm God ...

Now What?

So I'm God ...

Now What?

by Steve Rother and the group

Lightworker
Publications

So I'm God ... Now What?
by Steve Rother and the group

Published by: **Lightworker Publications**
a subsidary of **Lightworker**

www.Lightworker.com

ISBN: 978-1-928806-24-0

The authors and publishers of this book do not dispense medical advice or prescribe any technique as a form of treatment for physical or emotional problems and therefore assume no responsibility for your actions. The intent of this material is to provide general information to help your quest for emotional and spiritual growth. We encourage you to seek professional assistance for all areas of healing.

Lightworker Books CD's and DVD's can be purchased in retail stores, by telephone, or on www.Lightworker.com.
Lightworker 702 871 3317 in Las Vegas, Nevada

Editing, Layout and Design: Tony Stubbs (www.tjpublish.com)
Cover Photo: Steve Rother

Lightworker is a non-profit corporation dedicated to spreading Light through human empowerment.

Printed in the United States of America

Contents

Acknowledgments

It's not always easy working with the group. They choose their own team when it comes time to put together a project like this book. We wish to thank those directly responsible for the production of this book. These are the people the group chose to help get this book out:

Janee Vere   Mary Jones
Meg Gour   Gevera Bert
Margarita Walter   Tony Subbs
Jon Carl   Charmaine Lee

I would also like to thank some very important members of the Lightworker family who have been very inspirational and supportive of our work. Without their light and encouragement, none of this would be possible.

Ronna Herman   Lee and Patty Carroll
Geoff and Linda Hoppe   Rev. Fred Sterling
Isha Lerner   Jean Adrienne
Keith Smith   Janelle Collard
Cynthia Sue Larson   Tyberonn (James Tipton)
Jim Self   Sonia Bos
Stephen Lewis   Michael Ananda

From Steve:

I present two to four channels a month from the group. During some, if we have time, they like to interact with the audience on a very personal basis. When that is possible, we offer a question-and-answer period at the end of the channel. Many times the group uses these Q & A sessions to introduce new ideas and concepts not spoken of anywhere else. Other times, they take a subject they have spoken of at length and recap it in a very concise way. The audience really enjoys this time as it shows them on a very personal basis how this information applies to their lives and lets them interact personally with the loving presence we call the group.

This book is composed of these questions and answers arranged by topic. This was difficult at times as they tend to cover many different topics in one answer. You can read it front to back, use it as a reference book or use it as you would a deck of cards to see what spirit wants you to know in that moment. You will also notice that each channel is listed by a number. These correspond to the master channel number we use to catalog all of the live channels presented at the seminars. The monthly Beacons of Light ~ Re-minders from Home messages from the group are presented live on the VirtualLight broadcast, transcribed and sent out as a monthly re-minder from the group. Those channels are not cataloged in this way. They can all be found on the Lightworker.com/ beacons site. The master channel numbers that do not contain a 'D' mean the entire channel is available as a DVD and CD from our online store at Lightworker.com. They are also listed there by the master catalog number. Here you can watch the entire channel including the Q & A session.

You will hear the group speak of me almost as if I'm not in the room. Believe me, I am in the room and very much aware of what's going on. Often there is an internal dialog going on between me and them that is never heard. It usually goes something like this: "You want me to say that out loud?"

They call me "the Keeper" for they say I am the Keeper of the Hearts and they love to embarrass me whenever possible. I should also say here that the group never gave me the name "the group." They never began a channel with "Greetings from the Group." As many of you know, when they first came to me, they refused to identify themselves all together. They said their message was about true empowerment and that we easily give our power away to labels and they were not going to give us one. It was early in the second or third month of channeling that I became aware that they were multiple entities and I mentioned that in the monthly message I sent out. Someone wrote back and asked a question and closed it with: "What does your group think of that?" From that point on, they were known as the group. Many of you reading this book will note that "the group" is never capitalized. Even though I use it as a proper name that should normally be capitalized, they have asked me to use a small "g." This came from the Beacons of Light for July 2006: "God with a little 'g'," where they talked about a new relationship of empowered humans to spirit (see http://lightworker. com/beacons). Although the group has not said this, it is my belief that these higher level entities really have no need to tell you how high they are. Their work embodies the use of discernment whereby you run everything through your own filters and take only that which resonates within your own heart. They have no judgment of us, and love each of us for our unique beauty. Everything offered in this book is offered for your own discernment. Take only that which resonates deep within your own heart as your truth.

The reason I chose the title *So I'm God . . . Now What?* is because of a very special question asked by a young man at one of these Q & A sessions. That question and the group's response is the first message in this book and will explain the entire focus of a new age of empowerment facing all of humanity.

We are in a very magical time as we now step into possibilities that have never before been seen on Earth. You have waited eons of time and many, many lifetimes hoping that, one day, humanity would evolve to a high enough level to take the step that is right before us now. As we take this next giant step in our evolution, the group likes us to re-member that we are never alone on this journey, as we are all in this together and that this time, none of us moves to the next level unless all of us go together. Reaching out that hand to others is the act of the Human Angel. They also want us to know that the destination is not at all important; enjoying the journey is what the game is all about. As the group loves to say: "Enjoy the ride."

From the beginning of these messages, they always close with three re-minders. Since there are no complete channels in this book, this is the only place in this book these words appear. I thought it important to re-mind you to:

- Treat each other with respect.
- Nurture one another, and
- Play well together.

ESPAVO
Steve Rother
Spokesman for the group.

So I'm God ... Now What?

Many times I have heard the group say that we are actually god and that we all have the same powers of creation as god. My question is simple. What are we supposed to do with that? Okay, So I'm God ... now what?

The group:

Such an interesting question. But the truth is, we are asking you the very same question ... now what? Let us clarify. When you first began the game, there was only one rule you placed in effect: Free choice in all matters. There were many who said it would never work and that at least some pre-direction was needed to guide the human experience. But you decided there would be none, and so the game began. For eons of time, the game of free choice was what you would call the underdog of all games. Yet now, all of that has changed and you are leading the way in evolution. All eyes are upon the inhabitants of Earth as they lead the way in vibrational advancement.

You began the game with one intent – to find god. All of your experiences on earth up to now have been an attempt to find and define the indefinable – the heart of creation or what you call god. Now you are effectively removing a part of the veil, which will let you see the greatest secret of all time – that you are god. The cosmic joke is on you, dear ones, for what you have been searching for outside of yourself has been inside you all the time.

That brings us back to your question ... now what? Dear ones, although you are evolving at an unprecedented rate, you are still playing the game with the solitary rule of free choice in all matters. That means you may use this power of creation for anything you desire. Now, you ask if you should use it to bring you personal gratification or to manifest world peace and end hunger. We tell you it makes no difference what you create, only that you step into your powers of creation. If you ended hunger on your planet, you would only have to create new ways to learn mastery.

That is why we ask you the very same question you have asked us. Now what? Please understand that the paradigms have changed. We are no longer here to lead, educate or tell you what to do. Your days of "follow the leader" are over. Now you are learning to follow yourselves ... and that is infinitely more difficult. Yet that is what holds the key to your next step. You line up to ask us questions but you must see what is happening from our perspective. Our greatest task is to help the creators re-member that they are creators. Therefore we tell you we are here not to answer your questions but to help you re-member your questions. In this way, we give you form that you will use to create. There is no longer a grand plan for humanity. You all want to know if you are on your path. Dear ones, there is no path any longer. This is a new time and a new dawn for empowered humans to now walk the Earth, in intentional creation. The answer to your question: "Now what?" can only be answered with another question: What makes your heart sing, dear ones? Enjoy the ride.

ESPAVO

ABUNDANCE

Receiving Abundance

In the Beginning, #003 Cortez, CO

Question:

My question is, how do I step into the knowledge of the gratitude to receive the abundance?

The group:

Ah, such a wonderful question. It is shared by no less than three-fourths of the people in this room and almost five-sixths of the entire planet. So let us tell you about one of the most difficult lessons humans can learn. You are finite, and because of the fact that you are finite, you have a beginning and an end. Because of that structure you have put yourself in, because of the fact that you have built the veil so incredibly complete and working so perfectly well, it makes you believe that you, in fact, have a beginning and an end. That is an inbred belief in lack. That tells you that you are not a never-ending being, and that when this life is over, you have to give up this body and everything else along with it.

That is the normal belief. That translates out into everything you do. And everything you do that expresses infinite energy helps to rejuvenate you. In fact, that will be the essence of the rejuvenation you will see in your physical form. For, as the Children of Crystal Vibration come in, they will bring some of these energies with them and very easily help you translate them. And in the meantime, things are changing. In the meantime, each of you sitting here is trying to figure out, "How am I going to be a Human Angel? How am I going to give something to someone when I cannot even pay my own mortgage? Spirit, help me pay my mortgage."

Oh, we love that one. We think that is so humorous. Even more humorous was the time the Keeper started channeling the group. He loves to call us and say, "Well, I've got this group of entities on my shoulder so I'll ask a question about my own abundance." In fact – he is very imaginative – and one of his first questions to us directly was, "Dear Group, can you tell me about the stock market?"

Oh, the laughter in this room was not equaled by our laughter that day. No, no. We thought it was absolutely hilarious that here you have built a game within a game within a game within a game that is built on a perception of a perception of a perception, and you want us to tell you where it is going? We think that is hilarious. So it is not about the shortcuts. It is about principles of allowing endless, infinite energy into your field and we will tell you that, even though you believe you are finite, even though you believe the things around you are finite, they are not. And the more you can treat them as infinite, the more you will experience true abundance, for abundance is not a thing you have; abundance is a flow of energy through you.

Express the energy of your own abundance outward and you make space for it to come in. We have given many, many opportunities. One we will share with you this day is Merlin's Law. Yes, there was a time when King Arthur wanted to make a rule that everyone in his land would experience the same wonderful abundance that he experienced. So he made a law that all monies would be divided equally. "Oh, that is such a brilliant thought," he said. So he would distribute all the wealth to everyone, including his own. He literally distributed the wealth really well; he put it all out there … and it failed miserably. He got very discouraged so he went to his friend Merlin and asled, "Merlin, what am I doing wrong? Why cannot people in Camelot experience abundance?"

Merlin, being the very wise man that he was, said a few very interesting things. First, he said, "The expression of abundance can never be mandated, for it has to be an individual choice. You are on the planet of free choice, so each and every one must choose it. It starts not as the receiving of abundance, but the expression of abundance. And second, no law can be made that will ever distribute abundance throughout your world because each person must find their own comfort level with abundance. But I will give you a suggestion."

Here is the interesting piece. Merlin's suggestion spread throughout the land. It was very, very successful and all of Camelot became much more abundant, even though there were still pockets of poverty. Of course, poverty is a choice. Poverty sometimes is a drama we get wrapped up in because humans love their dramas, do they not? So here is part of Merlin's suggestion: he said, "Start with the expression of abundance and express the extra you have created in your life, for that is what true abundance is. It is having more than is minimally needed. And as you express abundance, you create a vacuum that draws more abundance into your life."

The funny part is, even though Merlin said no laws could ever be passed to increase abundance for all, the custom spread throughout all the land and soon became known as Merlin's Law. The suggestion was simple. In all relationships, in all business dealings, in all exchanges of any type, you make your best deal possible. In every deal you make, you find a way to give a little bit more. And when it comes time to complete that deal, you give a little bit more in that deal because that is the extra. That is abundance, and expressing your belief in infinite energy in that form sets it into motion and creates the flow of abundance through you. It is only one of the many examples but it is a beautiful one.

You live abundance. Do you really want to learn about abundance? Look at the dolphins. They never own anything yet they are the most abundant creatures upon the planet. They are so abundant they have a gift to give to humans now. They give you laughter. They give you play. They are here to teach you how to play. But if you look at dolphins, they are all about swimming through even the murkiest waters. Nothing ever sticks to them because they have no belief in lack, so they simply go right through and they have everything at any time they want.

Understand that abundance is a flow through energy and not about holding anything or counting anything, because that is when it becomes finite and you are expressing infinite energy. Your economists know it; at least the smarter ones do. For if you have fifty people in this room and we give each one of you one of your dollars, you would think that if one person here gave that dollar to this person here, then there were only forty-nine dollars left in the room. That is not true. If everybody holds onto their dollar, there are only fifty dollars in the room but if you circulate the dollars, there is the equivalent of five thousand dollars in the room. Interesting. It is an expression of infinite energy. That is the best we can offer you in this short time and we thank you for asking the question.

Making Enough Money

Human Angel Tools #034, Elspeet, Holland

Question:

About my financial situation, I am not able to find a way to make enough money. I try this and I try that, and it's not working. I am always worrying about money and I went to the Eight Rooms of Creation and thought, "Now things are going to change."

The group:

And they did change.

Question:

Yes. They got worse.

The group:

Actually you got your wish; they did change. What you are working with is actually the art of graceful acceptance. The rooms on the web site are arranged to help you understand the flow of creation energy. In your case, it would have been best to start with the last room first — the room of Acceptance. Acceptance is the art of allowing energy to flow through you comfortably, even with the restrictions in place of your own pains and your own energy stamps on the tubes that run through you to carry that energy. Even when that comes into the form of money, there are different ideas you place upon that. You have spent so many lifetimes in vows of poverty, on your knees, thinking that being without gave you more capabilities to bring in spirit. In the lower vibrations of who you were, it worked. Here, it does not pay the rent. It does not allow you to live in the comfort you deserve as a Human Angel. Therefore, the biggest piece of this has a lot to do with acceptance. You notice now that this word has been used five times. It means allowing that energy to flow completely through you and getting comfortable with the art of graceful acceptance even in the form of money.

If you view money as a tool from which you can do your work, the more you allow to flow through you, even in the form of money, the more you have in order to do things unique for other people. That is the difference between being self-first and being selfish. Those who allow this to flow through them comfortably have a larger flow.

The other challenge is that you have previously, up to this point, made your living in certain areas that are no longer a vibrational match. The truth is, it was necessary for you to be motivated to change and that is why you seemingly had a setback when things got worse. Your own higher self is motivating you. Now with the higher vibration you carry, as you work with this energy, you no longer have the tolerance to do this and you begin the self-sabotage of not allowing yourself to receive money. This is what is really happening at this stage more than anything else. You have pulled away and gone through a Phantom Death, and reset your energy. Then you stepped right back into the workplace you left, but you are not the same person and it is not possible for you to do the same work. Every time you try to set something up, every time you try to find work, you quietly pull the rug out from under yourself. You do so because you are very afraid of the mismatch of energy. Now is the time to find your passion, dear one.

Know there are no vibrational mismatches you cannot change, and you will find more support. Accept where you are. Do not worry about it, and find love and beauty in the things you do have, instead of focusing on the pieces that are missing. You will change that slight perception between having money and not having money, for it is a very slight perception change that makes the difference. It is not about anything big or anything important. 'Very slight' makes all the difference in the world. Please understand also, there is a huge difference in being poor and not having money at the moment. Poor is a state of mind that you do not have. Not having money at the moment is a temporary situation.

The Need for Money

Christopher Falls In Love, #D1002, Oostmalle, Belgium,

Question:

This is so difficult for us to believe that the money game is needed to survive. I believe all creation has always come from God. Could you please comment on this?

The group:

Oh dear ones, you are the creators. You have no idea who you are. You have no idea of your own abilities. Yet we tell you, even as most of you look back in your life, you see you have created things sometimes through other people, but you have created most of what you already wanted in your life. The Game we love to watch, the one you have devised yourself, is the one you call money. You are so imaginative and play some wonderful Games. And we will embarrass the Keeper here, for we love to do that.

The Game we call money is a Game within itself. It is a form of exchange. The challenge comes with money when you treat it as energy, for it is not. It is only a reflection of energy, much the way you could walk into a carnival and see the twisted mirrors, the convex and the concave mirrors. You could walk in front of them and find yourself fifteen feet tall and very, very skinny, or you could see yourself two feet tall and very fat.

Money can be manipulated in much the same way. Is it wrong? Of course not; it is a Game you are playing. It is just like the other Game, only this is what you have devised. For us, the funny part is when you equate your belief systems of spirituality and money. For you have made your restrictions from times past when you learned to not trust yourselves, so you believe instantly that if you are to be spiritual, money will not be a part of it. You somehow will not need money.

We challenge you to do this: If you are creators, there is nothing beyond your reach. Money is simply one Game you have learned to play. It is not evil. It is a Game you devised. Learn how to work with it. You are the creators. You have done so much more than that. Move past your own belief systems into accepting abundance. For we tell you, if you are going to create Home on your side of the veil, you had better get comfortable with abundance. There is no greater place of abundance than Home. If you are going to emulate all that is here at Home and bring Home to your side of the veil, you will experience the greatest of abundance of All That Is. Ah, the energy of money. It will be no problem.

To go to the next level, if you are of God, will God take care of you? We take you back to the teachings of the one we call Jesus. He looked upon the coin and he saw Caesar's face, and he said, "That which is Caesar's, render unto Caesar." You took it to mean, "I am spiritual and do not need money." That is not what he was saying. What he simply meant was, "This is Caesar's game. Let us play this game here."

Dear ones, do not fear those things you have created yourself. You have full control over much more than you think. You have spent so many lifetimes in sacrifice, for that was the global lesson you were learning as a collective. If this vibration way down here was your truth, now we have this new vibration, so have the courage to release some of the old truths you have gotten as you grasp new, higher truths that support your higher vibration. It is challenging sometimes. Allow yourself the oneness. Yes, allow yourself the money to come in, as well. For when you are fully in the state of abundance, you can reach out to people. We ask you to value yourself, for no one else can value for you. Set your own value of what you need in your lives to be comfortable.

Dear ones, we wish to re-mind you of Home. If you are Home, you are extremely comfortable. You have spent so many times on your knees in sacrifice, taking vows of poverty, for that is necessary for lower vibrations you are in now. Dare to raise your own standard of living. Dare to be comfortable. You are the Human Angels. You will use this touch of an angel. You will use this in many ways. For it is not the flow of money that is a problem; it is the hoarding of money that is the problem. Find a way to let that flow through you, and you will find your happiness.

Such an important question and we thank you for asking.

Money vs Passion

Christopher Falls In Love, #D1002, Oostmalle, Belgium,

Question:

I was recently gifted with an abundance of time to do what I want, and I am trying to look into my passion, but it seems that if I choose to be in my passion, I won't have any money. So it seems I have to make a choice. I don't want to leave my passion but I don't want to be poor. Any advice?

The group:

First, we will say simply that, in the higher vibrations of the new planet Earth, it is not possible to separate your passion from your abundance. The more passion you experience on a daily basis, the more abundance you will experience. The misdirection of energy lies in a belief that you must release all worldly goods to find spirituality. This is a direct result of the many lifetimes you have spent on your knees with vows of poverty in order to find spirituality. In the lower vibrations of the older times, this was a truth that helped you to release your attachment to worldly goods and find a higher meaning in life. Humans have a habit of finding a truth and then taking it to extremes, only to lose the true meaning. Such was the case here. As your vibrations rise, you reach for higher truths to support your higher vibrational rate. Now the collective of humanity is beginning to redefine truth about the relationship of spirituality and abundance. It is still true that if you carry an attachment to worldly goods, it will restrict you. Yet, you must know abundance to create Heaven on Earth.

Attachment is not abundance, and there lies the heart of the issue at hand. We tell you, unless you can understand true abundance, the creation of Heaven on Earth will not be possible, for Heaven is the most abundant place of all. Dare to rewrite this script and allow yourself to be spiritual and abundant in all areas. Know too that being without money is a temporary condition, while being poor is a state of mind rooted deeply with a belief in lack. Heaven has no lack. Move into your passion, and the money and abundance in all areas will follow. We can complicate it further if you like, but it really is that simple.

Spiritual Investment

Christopher Falls In Love, #D1002, Oostmalle, Belgium,

Question:

I am about to make a big investment and start a spiritual business with my partner, yet the big investment has me more than a little concerned. Still I feel that my whole future is what I now see on the horizon. Can the group tell me if I am on the right track with this investment?

The group:

First, let us remind you that the horizon is actually an imaginary line that recedes as you approach it. Know that your real future is happening this very day. The Game you play with money is a manmade Game. Thus it must be approached accordingly.

You humans are so imaginative! You have made the Game of money as an exchange of representing energy. The challenge comes quite often and you think it is energy, so you use it accordingly and treat it as energy.

Just like the distorting mirrors at the carnival, the Game you call money has been manipulated in a very similar fashion. You intended to have the same spiritual implications and the same spiritual integrity that you have in your heart but sometimes, you have difficulties receiving it for that very reason. You have spent so many lives on your knees as monks in vows of poverty, thinking that releasing your abundance in the form of money would help you gain spirituality and help you rid yourself of your possessions so you had nothing holding you. That worked well in the lower vibrations of who you were then, but it does not serve you up here.

We remind you that you are playing a Game. What if we told you that you not only choose the game piece you move around the Gameboard but you also choose your level of comfort in relationship to abundance? You may choose to play the game on any level of abundance you like. Ahh yes, we can see you doubting the words we just gave you. Still, most people do not fully understand the flow of energy in the form of money. It is easy to see that people who have a lot of money still have money problems. They just have a different set of problems associated with money. Please understand, what level of abundance you choose to play the Game matters very little. Those who do not have money think that once they do have it, all will be right in their world. Those who do have money often find a disappointing emptiness in that which they have. True abundance is a flow of energy and not an amount of energy that one has acquired.

You are the Human Angels. You are the ones re-creating Heaven on Earth as we speak. Well, we tell you, if you expect to re-create Heaven, you had better get very comfortable with the idea of abundance, dear ones, for there is no greater place of abundance than Heaven – abundance in all areas including money. Money is not something static you can count; money is a flow, for energy is not stationary enough to be calculated in the way you try to deal with money. Instead, we ask you gradually to increase the flow of money through you. That is your abundance in the form of money.

Even if you step into your passion and move right into your work, there will come the time when you will be called from your own higher self to be at a certain street corner at a certain time, and you will meet a very dear friend who is desperate for money. Many of you in this room have no problem with creating abundance in your life. Own it, dear ones. Do not be ashamed of that, for there are others who have spent many lifetimes in poverty and need your assistance. Write the books. Teach the classes. Help the money flow to all who choose to flow through them, for it is only a reflection of energy.

The other restriction many of you experience having to do with money is not anything about creation at all. Many of you are wonderful creators, and create all sorts of things. You all simply have a problem with acceptance. So accept your creations, especially when they come back to you in the form of money.

The way you formulated your question made it sound as if you had a choice of either being in your passion or being in the money. We tell you that is not the case. By putting yourself in your passion, you will release the belief systems that tell you it's an either/or choice. Putting yourself in your passion will draw the abundance in all areas of your life.

There is only one secret to success in the higher vibrations of the New Planet Earth: Your success in all areas, including money, is directly proportional to the joy and passion you can experience every single day of your life. Simply put, in your grandparents' day, the work paradigm was "Work Hard," and in the lower vibrations of that time, this actually produced positive results. Then came your parents' day and the work paradigm changed to: "Work Smart," where the pace quickened and creations came faster than ever before. Today, even as you try to apply these paradigms, neither of them produce results. Today, the work paradigm is: "Work Passionately," and the real results come when you do the things you love to do the most.

Move forward; accept abundance. You do not need to quit what you are doing in order to accept it. You simply need to re-think your acceptance process. Oh, many of you have had so many lifetimes where money was evil. We think that is so humorous. Number one, the idea of evil is humorous, for evil does not exist; that is pointing to a shadow and giving it power. You are so imaginative; we would not have thought of that one, yet we had to re-create it here in Heaven with the Lucifer Experiment. You guys are good. And now we ask you to hold all those things that are dear to you, and envision the money that comes into your field not as something that has caused you greed or something you need, for you do not need anything.

Envision it as a resource. Envision it as a possibility to do more good on this planet. For, as you experience abundance in your life, you can help others to experience it and you can pass it on. Look at it as a flow going through. Look at it, work with your acceptance of it, and look at it as a resource for the Human Angel ... you will be in your passion. We hope that has helped.

ANGER

Dealing with Anger

A Theory of Reality #D0202, Toronto, Ontario, Canada,

Question:

Hi. I have a question about my son who is nine. His name is Sam and he is very talented and creative, but he has difficulty dealing with his anger and I would like to know if there's a way I can better help him.

The group:

Yes, there is. We will tell you there is much you can do and you have already done it. Number one: Identifying the anger is perhaps the most important part. Now the difficult part: You must hold him responsible for healing himself, for he finds comfort sometimes in the pain. And that becomes very difficult to watch, for all of you humans have experienced that to some degree. The life lesson of adaptation is all about learning how to change, and sometimes the pain is so familiar that you will not allow yourself to move into change just so you can stay with the familiar. You can identify parts of the fear. You can find places for this anger or frustration level to come up. We tell you, your son has tremendous creative abilities. If you could find ways for him to create, you would relieve the pressure. It is the frustration of not being perfect to him that comes across as difficulties, rubs the energy, turns the energy backwards and throws it into a reverse polarity, where in later life, he may actually experience depression because of that. You believe you are already aware that it is in your genetic line. We tell you, dear one, he can do well here. He is carrying extreme, creative abilities, so if you can find any way for him to connect to creativity, it will start relieving some of this pressure. Hold him responsible for his anger, for the law of cause-and-effect is very important for him to understand. Let him see the results of what he is doing. Give him the space to create and to change it in himself. That is where the magic lies.

All anger is a building of stress and frustration. If one learns to flow that energy through them and release it, then there is no build-up to later explode into anger. Anger is a short circuit in the emotional system when it is overloaded with stress and frustration. What we are offering you are ideas to help him flow the stress through him rather than hold it inside. Since one of the biggest stresses in life is when a person feels he has no control over his situation, then the easiest way to deal with anger is to find ways of giving him more control over his own life.

There is much you can do here with unconditional love, yet he is the only one who can shift this for himself. Part of the problem here is that the one of whom you speak never found his energy role model. Without the energy role model, he has a little less sense of direction and feels lost more often than most of you. This is a real frustration and lack of feeling in control. We suggest that you place him in a situation where he can be around other males, older males whenever possible, for he will see other male attributes he is uncomfortable with in himself right now, and that is part of the source of his frustration. Let him speak to his father unrestrained and as often as possible, and some of this will start to clear. If that is not feasible, place him around others of older male energy so he may find someone with the same energy matrix as himself. When he sees how the energy matrix is used, when he sees the role model of his own energy matrix, it will suddenly click and he will start using some of his creative abilities. When that happens, the resulting relationships can be very special.

Place him in anything he likes to do, for creativity is not only found in art or music or computers. It can be found in a number of different areas – in sports, in communication, in a number of different ways. Find where the passion is with him, encourage him to do it, and let him get good at making mistakes. For sometimes, the perfectionism, the feeling of not being able to do something good enough, keeps him from doing it. And if you can allow him to paint outside the lines as often as possible, he will get comfortable with making mistakes; he will find there is no such thing as a mistake.

This takes patience and you are doing well. Trust yourself. Create what you can and hold him responsible for healing himself. He has abilities you have not seen yet. Wait until he gets to thirty-five and you will be so incredibly proud.

ANIMALS AND PETS

Animals to Humans?

Do You Know Who You Are? #D0203 Atlanta, GA

Question:

This is probably silly, but what is your feeling on being an animal in another life, because my sister is convinced she was a shark?

The group:

We love silly questions. What we will tell you about that is the connection between levels of dimension is much thinner than you imagine. You have been told by some of your great teachers that the division between the animal world and the human world is great indeed. And yet many of you know that is not true. Many of you who communicate with animals regularly know they are so very close to you. Some of you look in the eyes of your cat and you see a great Chinese man who once was a great healer, and you are trying to figure out how he got there. Is it true? Of course it is. Do you need to explain in intimate detail how that happened and how that worked? We tell you, it is done by choice. Literally there are times when some of the masters themselves will take a step into animal world, to be there as an animal in a different dimension to complete a contract or multiple contracts with humans. It happens much more than you are aware. Can it be that a human can step backward in the evolutionary line into an animal form? Not only can we tell you they can do that, but also they can take five steps back and actually take a step into mineral form. It happens more than you know. And when they are complete with that incarnation, they are allowed to come back and pick up where they left off.

The lines that divide those realities are much thinner. On your side of the veil, they seem very thick; they can seem very inseparable, like totally different dimensions and totally different realities. From our perspective, those lines are very thin indeed. And when you are Home, you have the capabilities of moving backwards very readily with no problem at all, and sometimes great things can be accomplished by a small step backwards. And, of course, at Home, you do not have the judgment: "Backwards means bad and forward means good." That does not exist anyway; it is an illusion of polarity on your Gameboard. So understand that whatever you can do to make these connections to step forward or step backwards, it is very similar to the step souls take when they actually choose to sit on your shoulder as guides during an entire incarnation. And that happens all the time.

Dear loved ones of yours, those who may have been your brothers in previous lifetimes choose to sit on your shoulder during an entire lifetime, to be there to whisper in your ear even though you do not hear it, to tell you that you are loved beyond your understanding even though you do not hear it; to tell you to turn right when you turn left. It is a challenge sometimes, but they do so willingly because that way, they are a part of their own evolutionary process. They are not less than you; they are not higher than you. They are the same as you. Such a joy it is to have them. Such a joy it is to look in the face of your cat. Such a joy it is for you to pet your horse. Such a joy it is for you to talk to your dogs and have them talk back. Understand, some of those are new souls. Most of your animals are new souls that have not been human, but it is entirely possible for that to happen, and it does so more than you realize. There is a progression. We will tell you that you do not evolve to the top of the mineral kingdom and then move into plant life. That is not the way it happens. All of the mineral kingdom moves into plant life at once. All humanity moves into angelic realm at once. That is why you are right on the edge of this movement now and we tell you, it is happening in the blink of an eye. And that is the reason you are becoming the Human Angels and taking that step forward. And when one moves, all move. But the lines are much thinner than you can imagine. Enjoy it. Enjoy it.

Relationships with Animals

TRIALITY #009, Zeist, Holland

Question:

I would like to ask about relationships with pets, animals and nature.

The group:

Let us speak first about some of the misconceptions that do not prevail outside of this room but which you will fall into as you try to take your beliefs outside. There is a belief that a vibrational level segregates animals and humans. And yes, it is a different expression of the infinite energy. It is a different expression on a different level. But we tell you, this flies in the face of many of your teachers. It is entirely possible for a human to take a limited form in an animal to play out karma or contracts. It is entirely possible for you to look your dog in the face and see your grandfather, although the entire being does not fit into the animal, for that is a different vibrational level. However, there are aspects of that person that come in and work with that vibration; therefore, you make connections very, very quickly even if you have not had past life connections. Sometimes, these become more real than your own children. And you wonder, "Why am I so attached to my animals?" We tell you, it's because they are attached to you. They are real to you.

Please do not confuse this with the other contracts taking place even at this time. Some contracts are in place for animals to come in to be assimilated into higher vibration through the food process. Please understand, there are some animals that literally come in with the greatest desire of having a human expression as a hamburger. Ahh, not what you expected from us. It does not mean you need to eat meat to be spiritual. What it means is, different animals come in for different purposes and those that come in look you in the eye and make a connection one spirit to another, and sometimes this is set up way ahead of time. Sometimes, this is set up as the greatest of possibilities, and sometimes you have the opportunity to see things from a different perspective and change that perspective as you move forward. Sometimes, it is an opportunity to develop an entirely new matrix of energy. Sometimes, it is an opportunity to bond in a whole new way.

This is quite often the case with dolphins, for they bridge the gap between human and animal. The whales will do so as well, but in a different area. Dolphins will become a very important part of your life from this day forward. Those who choose to stay will become part of the new energy matrix on Earth that is a part of who you are. The dolphins will play a very important part by bridging the gap for those of you who wish to form organizations to honor the animals, whether it be in Holland and Belgium or the rest of the world. For we tell you, it goes far beyond that. The dolphins will play. Those who choose to stay as dolphins will come to play. That is who they are. That is why they are here.

Question:

I ask because I learned so much from a dog.

The group:

He came in as your teacher. Very wise. Absolutely. He was to be here for a very short period actually, but he chose to stay much longer. He found an opportunity to go, for he had what he needed to go to the next level. Being a dog worked very well for him. We call him a 'he' because he was a teacher in a male form and that was your last connection with him in physical form. He returned as your dog.

Contracts with Pets

Cosmic Winks, Mt. Charleston, NV, 07/14/05

Question:

My question is: Could you talk a little bit about animals like our pets? Can they be Lightworkers?

The group:

There are many vibrational energies on this planet, and many different vibrational levels that congregate together in what we call a bandwidth. One of these bandwidths is human, one is animal, another is insects, then plants, and finally rocks. Depending on where they are in the animal bandwidth, much has to do with resonance to where you are in your bandwidth. In other words, certain animals that are in a low stage of their own bandwidth will resonate with humans in a low stage in their bandwidth. And please understand, low is not worse or bad compared to high. It is simply a different vibrational range. And yet we tell you, most humans working in these areas are in a fairly high state of the bandwidth. They raise their vibration slightly ahead of the norm. You are the ones at the tip of the arrowhead who are changing the paradigms of everything else. As such, you also receive the most resistance, for you are the ones beginning the change. Therefore, your vibration is a bit higher. For this very reason, you resonate with higher things in different bandwidths.

For instance, if we give you a piece of granite and ask you to hold it in one hand and a crystal in another hand, you would want to talk to the crystal before you would talk to the granite, for the crystal is in the higher vibrational range of the mineral kingdom bandwidth.

Actuarial tables will tell you there are more women on the planet, and that traditionally, women live longer because of war. We tell you, this is not the reason. Women traditionally live longer because they are more comfortable than men with putting crystals next to their heart and wearing crystals. That is the reason we asked the Keeper to find the green crystal. Literally it helps to amplify you in a harmonic, and the same is true with animals. You can have a contract with a crystal, but you can also have a contract with an animal. Animals are even a little different because they are closer in your vibrational ranges to your own. You understand them a little better. It is more likely for you to put human attributes on animals than on plants or crystals. However, all of them do have names, spiritual names, as do you.

Different vibrational ranges of what you call animals will take form as different families of animals and have different purposes, much the way the angels in Heaven are also a bandwidth and have a different purpose. We love it when humans put human attributes on Home, for it gives us a chance to play your Game. And you call the angels by name and say, "This angel has this personality and he is a great archangel and I am going to channel him alone." We tell you there is no singular person who is an archangel. There is something we call "angelic purpose," so when you think of an archangel, it is because of that purpose. You give it a human attribute and call it a name, putting 'EL' at the end of it most times. Part of what happens here is that you literally put the connection of that on there for that very reason.

We have even told stories that give US personality to the Keeper. We do not have personality in that sense. We do not have gender. We do not have the disconnections that you deal with in human form so there is no need to try to re-connect in many of those ways.

We make contracts with you, as we have done with the Keeper for the past twelve lifetimes. You, too, have contracts with many of the angels on your shoulders or the guides that are around you. So too will you make contracts with your animals. Humans always think animals are here to help you do something because you wear the veil, whereas often, you are there to help them evolve. Please keep that in mind, and you will understand that even more as you take the form of Human Angel. Animals are here to give you an opportunity for you to do that, and to re-mind you of your divinity and your magnificence. And they come in with such love. The ones you call dog, that little bandwidth within that vibrational range, are simply unconditional love. Isn't it wonderful? You can mistreat them, you can kick them, you can yell at them, and they come back to you, wagging their tail and licking your hand. And humans learn that.

You teach them a higher vibrational range, as you also do for plants and crystals. The crystals you wear add to your own longevity, and help you stay in this bubble of biology. In their world, they are jumping up and down saying, "Look at me! I am carrying the energy of such and such. Is it not grand? I am no longer a crystal. I am a human." And for a short time, they get to play your Game as well. Animals do the same thing.

There is a bandwidth you call cats. Oh, cats are wonderful beings, for they are the reverse energy, and they reflect you in reverse, the same way trees do. They will balance you, and so will the trees if you do not cut them all down. But the reality is, these bandwidths have a huge connection to you, as do we, for we are simply another bandwidth. We are simply another vibrational range in what you call Heaven, or Home. And our greatest job is not to teach you unconditional love, for the dogs do really well at that. It is not to take your negative energy, because the cats are doing a marvelous job. It is to re-mind you of your magnificence. Our wings are not for flying. They are to spread in your presence to help you feel your own energy, and help you see how special you are.

And we thank you for asking the question.

Animals Who Have Crossed Over

The Smile of Spiritual Confidence #012 Edmonton, Alberta, Canada

Question:

Greetings with all my love. Yesterday, you mentioned people who had lost people in the previous year and I wondered if that included someone who lost a soul in animal form?

The group:

Ah, let us speak of the animals. You are so fascinated. Would you like to see different dimensional realities? They go from these very simply. One time, the Keeper asked us for a simple explanation of inter-dimensional realities and we said, "Go fill your bathtub full of water and stick your head in, and you will understand what it is like to have a different dimensional reality where things move a little bit differently." Some of the laws of physics are a little different. Sound and light travel differently. That is what dimensional reality shifts do. The beings you are calling animals – and please keep in mind, you are one yourself – are simply in a different dimensional reality, one step removed from you.

There are many dimensional realities, many more than you are aware of. That is part of what you have begun to see as your own advancement changes. Nowadays, you walk into a room and see the cute little shadow figures in the corner. You are starting to see some of these other things, for we divide them in many more categories than you do. We see humans on one level, we see your pets and your animals on another level. Furthermore, we see large animals – horses, cows, and some of the larger animals – which have different energy needs even in another category than you would see your dogs or your cats. We see the insects in a totally different category than you do, for each one is divided by a different harmonic vibration and they travel up and down that scale. And they are on part of the evolutionary scale for they are evolving, too. Their greatest desire once was to lower their vibration much like yours was, but their greatest desire at this time is to raise their vibration and move as a collective to the next. If you can simply imagine that the insects want to be cats, the cats want to be large animals, and the large animals want to be humans. And it is more than the animals – it is also plants and minerals; it is all the different dimensional realities.

In addition, there is a whole vibrational range you cannot perceive that exists within the same time and space that you do. You see only little glimpses of it. You may think they are hauntings or ghosts, but really they are just playing with you. Whole other levels of things are happening in there. Certain things cross those boundaries with no problem, and unconditional love is one. And many of your household pets are sent in to teach unconditional love. Each animal on this planet, and each range of animal, has a certain particular "flavor" they bring in. There is something that each is particularly good at sending out, and they teach it not only to humans but also to plants and rocks. They even teach it to us, the angels, for we are part of your vibrational level, as well. It is easy to say, for instance, that a cat is here to exchange energy. It is easy to say that a dog is here to teach unconditional love, for you understand those. But there are many more and if you understood what they came in for, you could facilitate that and use it to its highest.

Different animal groups work with different levels. Some are simply here to help entertain, such as the beautiful, exotic birds in the world that do a wonderful job of that. There are many levels in different areas just for your interactions, and as you evolve, they evolve. So, everyone goes together. This is part of what we mean when we talk about the evolutionary ladder and everyone finding their place on the ladder. When the collective is high enough, everyone has an opportunity, including the rocks. And if you do not believe that, ask your crystals. They know.

Learn from Pets

The Color Clear #D0502 St. Louis, MO

Question:

What can we learn from animals, especially our domestic animals like our pet dogs?

The group:

They are so wonderful for us to watch. Your connection with them is even more wondrous, for here is a reflection of unconditional love and that is exactly where you are. Your dogs teach unconditional love. They teach it through their own actions. They teach it through who they are and, even if they have contracts with you, they will work with you on the areas of unconditional love. Unconditional love is a fifth-dimensional attribute you have been reaching toward, yet please understand, much of your own reality is still firmly rooted in the third dimension.

As many of you are still creating third-dimensional realities, the move from one reality to the next must be gradual and comfortable. For instance, please understand that even your marriage vows are a statement of conditional love. Yet even in that statement of conditional love, the more unconditional attributes you can pull into your relationships, the easier it is for those relationships to evolve to the next level … and the dogs are here to help you understand that. They will love you unconditionally, no matter what. That is part of the process each one of you can work with – some of your own friendliness towards them.

Now cats are a slightly different situation. Cats are fascinating to us, for we understand something you do not. They are creatures here to balance energy. For instance, we speak of you as a human being who breathes in oxygen and breathes out carbon dioxide. We speak of trees and the plant kingdom that breathe in carbon dioxide and breathe out oxygen, and the two kingdoms can live in harmony on the planet for they balance each other if you do not cut them all down. Now we speak of a human being who thrives on positive energy and loves to throw off negative energy. We speak of a cat that thrives on negative energy and loves to throw off positive energy. And there are times when you are reaching from your heart and are saying, "Oh come here, sweet kitty. I love you so much," and that kitty replies, "Get away from me," because they are wired in opposition to you and they work quite well. Instead, they will sometimes sneak up and sit at your feet, and slowly drink your energy and they say, "Oh, this feels so good." They are wonderful creatures.

We tell you also, in the plant and the animal kingdom are animals that have come in whose highest intent is to actually be part of your food chain. To you, that makes no sense for you see the suffering. You see what you imagine to be pain and think it is so difficult for them to do this. What you do not understand is, they are also in an evolutionary process and, as their evolution changes to the next level, someday they may actually evolve into a state that would be very similar to human form. If that were to happen, some of the best they can do in the interim is to offer parts of their own being and, in fact, become part of the food chain because, as you higher vibrational beings ingest the food, they actually become part of your higher being. In some way, it even lends to their own evolution. We love to include not only the plants here but the animals as well, for you have such a different understanding, as you love to segregate the two. We tell you, the plants are the same, for they have feelings just as the animals do. One of their greatest, highest purposes is to be here, to support you, and to be part of the food chain. You look out at a meadow of the most beautiful pristine green grass and you do not wish to step on it for you are afraid you will damage the grass. What you do not understand is, the grass may be there with the highest intent of cushioning your footfall as you step out there. For it honors you, too. Each vibrational level honors the next and makes it possible to move from one to the other, so you all work together in natural balance.

Enjoy the ride, dear ones. You will see miracles happen in your own lifetime. You will see things you never thought possible in your own lifetime. They are possible now because of the choices you have made, because of the energy you have endured and because of the love you hold for your life. Thank you for asking the question.

ASCENSION

Physical Changes

Lemurian Initiation #D0503 Reno, NV

Question:

I wonder about the coldness of my body and my hands. What is it and does it have anything to do with ringing in my ears?

The group:

There is a process going on of working towards a higher vibrational level within your own physical being. Much of what you have experienced as coldness in your hand is a process. Your physical being is the most dense part of you so, as you move to higher vibrational levels, you will experience ringing in the ears. You will experience vibration, awakening at three o'clock in the morning, heart palpitations, irregular heartbeat, and a wide variety of unexplained medical phenomena. It is simply the body's way of adjusting to the higher vibrational levels.

You are moving very, very rapidly and, much like your earthquakes, your physical body does not move that fast. So, all of a sudden, it feels the stress and it moves very quickly to catch up. In those times, you create strange phenomena within the body – aches and pains, odd things that happen and odd pains, many of which we have spoken of many times. The ringing in your ears is in direct connection to the new synaptic pathways being built for you to hold the higher energy matrix of your physical body. It is happening now and it will continue for some time, so do not be concerned by it.

The connection with your hands is a little bit different but is caused by the same vibrational rise. Again, you will experience it for a number of months and possibly years to follow, but it will go away. Enjoy the ride. Enjoy the ride.

Working with Gaia

Earth Changes #54 Kona, HI

Question:

Mahalo ("thank you" in Hawaiian). I thank you for the information about the energy that is valuable for us to work with. Can you please explain more to help us to assimilate the energy with Gaia?

The group:

The solid form of Gaia is an illusion. Please understand that. You humans have a problem with reality. You keep thinking it is real but it is not. If you understood your greatest density of material on a molecular level, you would see there is almost the same distance between atoms as there is between the planets in your universe. Matter is not dense; that is the illusion.

Now the adaptation you are experiencing now, that change of understanding the illusion of physical matter, is what is underway right now. You are here working with it, but we ask you to work with it first on the true level of energy, from the higher self through the heart instead of always through the mind, for the heart will shift it so much faster than the mind. Your sciences have been laboring very long and are only months away from the verge of uncovering great discoveries, but they are doing so because people like you are working with your hearts. That is what is unfolding, and we ask you to focus in that area first, for you will have connections with your parental races that are going to start making the rest of this whole process fairly easy. And many of the things that have perplexed you for so long will go away almost overnight. Open the doors. Make the connections. Stay grounded. Enjoy the ride.

Creating the 3rd Dimension Inside the 5th Dimension

Seven Stages of Life #004 Santa Fe, NM

Question:

I'd like to say that I really love your concept of already being fifth-dimensional and out of force of habit, choosing to continue to recreate a three-dimensional reality inside the fifth dimension. So, any recommendations for the easiest way to begin to picture, experience and work with 5-D and above?

The group:

We have many recommendations, of course, and many more will be coming in the form of our messages, Beacons re-minders from Home, and future books we will work with the Keeper on to bring a lot of this information through. Now let us offer you two specific examples that might help you to understand this.

One was brought up in the story of Leandra. Each life lesson provides the spirit opportunities to experience life with different filters. Leandra had a life lesson of Definition. Hers was simply about being able to define what was hers and what was not. She brought people and a contract into her field that moved her boundaries, forcefully sometimes, to let her know she had weak boundaries. She lived in that time where she always felt she had to put other people first. Does this sound familiar?

Many of you in this room, as healers, have taken this on. You have picked up other people's emotions because you do not know where your energy field ends and where another's begins. Some of you have brought master manipulators into your field and that does not always feel very pretty for you.

So let us offer you a tool for working in the higher vibrations of the New Planet Earth. We call it the Energy Inventory. There are times when you get so wrapped up in the day-to-day routine of putting one foot in front of the other that you do not understand you have choice. This is a tool for acclimating to the new energy. To use it, you must first understand that a "plus" is not good and a "minus" is not bad. Those who work with electricity can tell you that negative electrons have the same magic and power as electrons carrying a positive charge. Those old illusions came from the field of duality in which you have been living. Now every time you experience something, stop and take a quick energy inventory. Was that experience a plus or a minus? Ask, "Did that take away from my energy or add to it?" Imagine you get a phone call from your best friend, sharing the latest happening in her life. As you hang up the phone, take the inventory. "Did that add to me or take away from me?" There is really no need to even write it down; just making the honest determination within is enough. For a time, you reduce every experience in your life to a plus or a minus.

Know also you will not always make your decisions based on the inventory. That would be giving your power away and would also make you very lonely. For instance: Your teenaged son approaches you and asks if you can drive him to the mall. Stop and take the inventory before you speak. Since you already have plans that day, it is very clearly a minus. Even so, you may decide that being with his friends is good for him so you gladly change your plans to accommodate him. Now here is a big difference. The decision to drive him is yours and not his. He did not manipulate you. If you honestly take the inventory, it is not possible to be manipulated from the outside.

Taking the energy inventory puts the ball right back in your court and the power of choice back where it belongs. In every moment of every day, it allows you to very quickly assess where you are in the world and the Universe around you. That is clearly defining yourself, thus the life lesson of Definition. If you have a Life Lesson of Definition, defining your energy field is what you came in to master.

Many of you are working with this life lesson, as it is the mark of a healer. Many of you have come in with this very life lesson, not knowing where your boundaries are, because it affords you a tremendous sensitivity. That empathic ability is the mark of a healer.

Thank you for asking the question.

Ladder of Ascension

Q & A #013 *Edmonton, Alberta, Canada*

Question:

Yesterday you talked about us all being on a ladder of ascension, how everybody was on the ladder together and how we are all going to ascend as one. I am curious about how that really works because there's going to be all these different levels of vibrations on that ladder and if we can only ascend when we reach a certain vibration, how does everybody go at once?

The group:

Oh, we love the semantics you get wrapped up in as humans. Let us give you a broader perspective. Suppose one person is an E-note on your chromatic scale. Another is a C-note, another is a D-flat and a fourth is a beautiful G-note. Each one carries a slightly different vibration. Please understandm although the D may be higher than the E, the reality is, one is not better than the other. When you play them all together, there is a chord, a resonant vibration, of all of humanity and that is the trigger point. You feel this when you reach a trigger level that moves quickly to the next level , almost as if it were meant to be. That is where it is. When the entire ladder is filled with all of these most beautiful vibrational tones, then the entire ladder has a collective vibrational harmony and it all goes together.

You have had many lifetimes where you have gone forward to create the opening for others. The days of Lemuria were that exact thing, and from your hearts, your idea was to go ahead and partially ascend and open the door, and be there as a bridge to open the door for others. However, it did not work and Atlantis ended up sinking, mostly because of that. It was a horrible experience for most of you, and you still carry those cellular memories today. That is why you are afraid to step into your power. You carry these cellular memories with you and, when you start exploding into this energy and stepping into your work, you have this whole thing saying, "Oh no, I cannot do that." It is a cellular memory that goes way back to the Guardian you have put on the gate to keep you back, to stop you from making the same mistake again. We ask you to feel it, honor the Guardian, and then please step forward and do it, because that Guardian is an important part of you and now becomes part of your energy again.

We thank you for asking the question.

Physical Adjustments to Higher Vibration

The Age of E, #017 Mt Shasta, CA

Question:

I haven't had my period for seven months and I'm not pregnant and I'm feeling fine. I went to the doctor, I don't have anything and I trust it, but what's going on?

The group:

Your physical being is adjusting to a higher vibrational status. It is not easy. You will find many different forms of biological changes happening to you, such as irregular heartbeat that will happen to many, many people on your planet. The body skips a beat every so often to catch up to the higher vibration, and you will find yourself vibrating. It's not just women who will experience the signs of early menopause, but also men, and that will be rather interesting for them for they will come up with a different word for it. Many of the things you will find you are going through will have to do with the harmonic resonance of your own physical being. So at first, you begin the changes up here in your thought forms in the ethereal portions of yourself. Then they work their way down into the physical being. The physical body is the last piece to move, as if your higher self is pulling your physical body up and bringing it up into the higher vibrational ranges of the New Planet Earth and into the Age of E. As it does, it goes through some strange phenomena. We tell you, you will have your period visit you again.

Question:

Oh, but I like it this way (laughter).

The group:

That is why we told you that (laughter).

ATLANTIS AND LEMURIA

Tectonic Plates, Atlantis, Emerald City

Do You Know Who You Are? #D020903 Atlanta, GA

Question:

Would you take a moment and address the continent Atlantis?

The group:

As tectonic plate movement has happened over the eons, there have been break-ups and re-joining of places. It is no wonder that, in fact, you are on the edge of a tectonic plate. And not only are you on the edge of a tectonic plate but also, as the grids have adjusted to accommodate the movement of tectonic plates and continents, pieces of that magnetic grid carry that energy with them. So, it is not actually the land that is important at that point, but that segment of magnetic grid. That magnetic grid is you, which is why you came up with the word "Atlanta" in the first place. There is no joke about that. That is what you are experiencing. In fact, you will find that it will re-mind you directly, for you have a sacred spot not far from where you sit right now. It was a very sacred place in Atlantis. There is a power point that used to connect the power grids of some of the Atlantean structures, and the remnants of it are here.

On the west coast of this continent are pieces of Lemuria that are very similar to the ones here. The tectonic plates came together, formed the mountains and hid them well. Soon you will find pieces of those crystal structures that used to be important parts of Lemuria. We have not spoken of this before, but the Emerald City was a very real place in Atlantis and existed not far from this location. The Emerald City was the magical place that took the green heart energy and blended it with the power crystals so that it would be available to all through the power grids of Atlantis.

In those days, you were magical beings full of creativity. There was nothing you could not do. There was a strong fascination to blend human experience with nature, so you took the crystals and made them better. You even genetically engineered humans, and took different pieces of your structure and tried to figure out ways to blend your humanness with them. You even created a form of light that had never existed in nature before. Coherent light, or what you call laser light, had never existed prior to this time, which is why the Keeper is so fascinated with his little pens. It is a form of the coherent light that existed in the magical days of Atlantis. That is why he calls them Atlantean Light Pens, for it re-minds him of the perfect type of light that was created – a blend of nature and humanity, which is what Atlantis was all about.

That is the reason it was so magical, not because of doing anything wrong. You all re-member Atlantis for the mistakes that were made, but please re-member the magic as well, for you were very close to awakening as creators in physical form. God was singing Himself/Herself, and you were starting to do things in conjunction with your creative abilities. It was magical, indeed, and you are not only back there now but you have already surpassed it. There is no script in place, no grand plan in place, dear ones. You are waiting with a pen, and have already dipped it in the ink. You hold it above the parchment now and we cannot wait to see what you write.

There is nothing in place; you decide what is going to happen. You decide what is real and what is illusion. You decide which dimensional reality you will live in. It is a magical time indeed. Re-member the wondrous magic of those days. Re-member that part in your heart. It is very special, so dare to create. Fear it not. Are you going to make mistakes? Of course, you are. You have made mistakes all along. Are you going to get to the other side of it? Of course, you are.

We take the Keeper back to a very magical time when he was in junior high school, and he loved technology even back then. He showed up one day with a miniature calculator that actually fit in his shirt pocket. He thought it was so cool but he was sent to the principal's office, and that device was confiscated from him. There was great fear at that time and the teachers told him and his parents, "If these things are allowed to run rampant, no one will learn arithmetic. If you have something that can do it for you, you are not going to ever do this. This must never show up at school again."

His parents laughed and took it back. Of course, today's schools teach you how to run computers. But, please understand that you naturally resist taking your own creations and blending the human consciousness with the magic of the Gods you are. You feel a resistance about doing that, and you think, "Oh my goodness, God can create anything. This is nature. This beautiful tree here is all alone." But have you not learned how to prune the tree to make it better? Have you not learned how to thin your forests to make them grow healthier and stronger? That is the blend of humans and nature. Have you not learned how to give your children vitamins to make them stronger and even taller? Yes, of course, you have. You have already learned how to blend nature with humanity. But it is not human. It is the veil that makes you think you are less than god. And we honor the veil as a part of your Game. But we are also here to help you re-member who you are. That is our process, our purpose. Fear it not. Step out of the boundaries, make the mistakes, make wonderful mistakes, and watch yourselves grow. And re-member the days of Atlantis with joy, for they were magical times. And you are back.

We love to tell the story of the Atlanteans, for it happens so often. The day after it happened was a sad day, for it was the final days of Atlantis. It took several days for it all to get wiped out. You had chosen to send people off in the boats, in your travel machines. Your power grids were not working and your traveling machines were not working properly, so you had to resort to some of the lower technology of actually using boats. And you sent off some family members and hoped that some of them would reach this continent. It was a very sad time. That is the part you are all imprinted with that you re-member so clearly. You had shot down the moon. And it was sad, indeed. It was not intentional. It was a time when you had worked out of your hearts and had misdirected energy.

You got together as souls and said, "We are taking a time-out from this Game and we are going to get together and think about this." You came together as souls in spirit with time standing still – the only time it has ever happened. You made some commitments, and you said, "We are going to hide the crystal energy from ourselves. If we ever get a chance to come back, we are not going to touch that because it was too tempting and that may cause some problems here, today. We will have other forms of energy because we are very creative, but we will not let that one come back right away."

You set some other things up and each one of you individually decided you would set the big Guardian at the

Gate, and you said, "If I ever get close to stepping into my power again, I am going to have this big scary being stand in front of me and scare the living daylights out of me. That is another of your interesting human expressions. And the Guardian will scare me, and keep me from stepping into my power until I am checked and in balance, and am sure I am going forward."

This is what we have termed the seed fear. Many of you feel the seed fear and it keeps you from stepping into your work. We ask you to feel the seed fear, check yourself, understand that this is there for a reason. And then when you are ready and you are confident enough, you re-assign the role of the Guardian for he is actually a very strong part of your energy. And you put him behind you and allow him to be part of who you are, part of the great healer you are stepping in to be. And you re-assign his role, step forward and move into it.

The other thing that happened at that time is that you said, on the day that time stood still, "If ever humanity gets to a point where we can all jump in at once, we will all come in and try to do things differently. We will make sure we have got everything in check and we will all try to be back at that time. If there is ever a possibility of getting to that point, we will be there."

Well, that magical day happened. When Adolf Hitler left the planet, humanity took a turn and stepped into the possibility at that point that you would stop giving your power away and you started claiming a responsibility that had never before been taken upon Planet Earth. At that opportunity, many of the Atlanteans said, "Wait a minute. We may have a possibility here. This may actually work. We are going to get ready. We are going to try to set up life lessons first. We are going to try to set up circumstances to come in here if this works."

You watched carefully, and many of you quickly started jumping in. It was a wondrous time. At a certain point, you all started recognizing each other. You reached an age where you looked at each other and said, "Ah, I know you." And you had this wonderful party, which you called "The Sixties." Some of you even re-member it. Dear ones, you are back; you are here. Here with purpose. Re-member it with joy, with lust, with a passion of who you are, and fear not the mistakes. Step into your power as creators.

Know that there is no spiritual competition, for that is the second misdirection of energy you took in those days of Atlantis. You believed one vibration was better than another. You had learned how to genetically engineer humans. At the same time, you had a whole influx of immigrants coming in from Lemuria, for many chose to stay. Many chose to be in Atlantis rather than to move forward and ascend. So you had challenges at the time.

The other piece of the puzzle was that you did not take your power as creators, and you bought into "lack thinking." That is partly why the Keeper himself is so passionate about this. He is one who was very high up in the government that helped to make some of these decisions based upon lack. That is why he is now here, bringing in these messages. He is here to right it, to make it different this time. And you are, too.

As you step into that energy, you will see things happening. This is a magical time on planet Earth. You will now see advances in technology far beyond your wildest dreams. Fear it not. Your technology is a direct reflection of your spiritual evolution. If you do not evolve spiritually, your technology can only go so far. And even at the times on your planet when technology was dropped in way ahead of your spiritual evolution, it did not hold. And it would not take, for your spiritual evolution was not high enough to hold it. Fear it not. Step forward. Enjoy the times you have here. Many of you were here from both Lemuria and Atlantis. Re-member those wonderful times, dear ones, for you got so far, you got so close. Re-member it not as bittersweet, but with joy and the excitement of creating realities that you have. And we cannot wait to see what you do next. Thank you for the opportunity to speak that piece.

The Others of E-Vibration

The Smile of Spiritual Confidence, #013, Edmonton, Alberta, Canada.

Question:

Even if I don't know, it's the holding. Holding the energy is enough, even if I don't consciously?

The group:

Some of you will consciously put it on paper. Some of you will speak the words, write the books, teach the classes. Some of you will just hold the energy. Some of the greatest healing of all mankind was done by the Others of E-Vibration, and they did not speak a word. They came in, lifetime after lifetime after lifetime, holding the energies of the people who would not speak because they were the ones in Atlantis who were clones, who were taught to be less-than everyone else. And they found their true empowerment, which is why they are the Others of E-Vibration Beings activated in the Age of E.

We wish it was very simple for us to say, "Here is what is going to happen next, and here is what is going to happen after that, and here is where these teachers will come in, and here is where you will do your work." But it is all going to happen at once. You have been in preparation for this for eons, but many of you are tired of holding this energy. "Exhausted" is more the word. Well, now it is time to breathe, to take it and allow yourself to be seen. Put yourself in front and allow that to come through.

The Final Days

Hearts of Atlantis #D101802 Mt Shasta, Ca.

Question:

I have re-membered that in the final days of Atlantis when the boats were being dispatched, it was such a sad time. It really came very fast and even though we knew it was coming, we were unprepared.

The group:

You are correct in your assessment. You re-member much of that day, especially after being stamped and being tapped on the shoulder and having that downloaded on you. And we tell you, there was a special family, for then, all families were special and all carried their own emblems to help them re-member, and the insignias and special stamps you designed for yourselves as families. And even though some of those families were split apart and sent to different places on the continent, you found each other because of the symbols. Some of you did not even recognize the symbol but simply the fact that you saw it perhaps even on a billboard triggered things within your own biology and your own DNA to set you into motion to come back together as a family. But you may never even re-member the symbol. It has happened time and time again.

There was an inner circle of those, even in what you would call the Sanhedrin of Atlantis. Some of those were in the government and others were in what you would call spirituality, although you had a huge mix in those times, for it was not possible to be non-spiritual. You created a symbol that would help you re-member. It is the symbol the Keeper wears on his ring. It is what we have called the sign of the Human Angel. That is the Heart of Atlantis. We thank you for your re-membering.

Origins of Hawaii

Wings Over Mu, #D030303 Kona, HI.

Question (asked by a Hawaiian Kahuna guest speaker):

I have a passion to expand my knowledge of the origins of the Polynesian race, particularly the Hawaiian people. Monday night you said, "People believe that the Big Island is the youngest of the Hawaiian group, but you said that it is older than we think." In some of our Hawaiian tradition, it is said that the Big Island of Hawaii was the first born, the eldest of the island group and that all life sprang forth from here. I would like to have validation for this if it is possible. And is this what you are alluding to when you heard Hawaii was actually Mu?

The group:

Absolutely. The beauty that springs forth from the lava that comes from the center of the earth is the most fabulous being of all that exists. It is the mother to all things and all beings around it. And we tell you, in fact, that it was the origin, as Mu was the origin. The reason the Keeper held us to follow the belief that it was the youngest of the islands is because that is what he heard on the airplane coming over here. You are absolutely correct and, in fact, it is much, much older than people believe. Life springs forth from the center out. It is no coincidence that it is still springing forth right here. You have a dream, a pull. It began first as karma, and we think you know that. For there are things that must be righted in this lifetime that were important for you to deal with.

We tell you this not to embarrass you, but to tell you that you are on the right path. And, in fact, even though you think you have found somewhat of a block on the information you seek, you are right on the verge of uncovering something really deep. In fact, you are about ready to be another level of teacher. We ask you to find words to teach all of those of the beautiful essence of what this was built upon, because the original cave of creation was on Mu, and it's directly below us now.

Question:

I seek acknowledgment that the migration, which came from outside into the Polynesian Triangle and the Pacific, was a return Home.

The group:

It is continuing to this day. And it is not only continuing in beautiful brown bodies. It is continuing in all bodies. You may know the call Home, which is why you are here. That is what is happening at this time to allow that to happen. It is people like you who are holding the truth you know in your heart and who send out the call to the rest of us. It is a beautiful place but it is not necessary that each and every one of you come to this place and experience it.

What is really important is that the energy you hold in your heart be passed on well beyond these islands, for those are the peaceful giants, the powerful beings. You speak of power and of empowerment. You humans carry the power as creators while still in physical bubbles of biology. You must also learn to carry your own vulnerability, the true power, the essence of who you are, for when you carry that much power, there is never a need to use it. That is what the Polynesians, those of Mu, the Hawaiians and Native Americans have in common.

Building New Civilizations

Crystal Walk-Ins #D042102 San Diego, CA

Question:

I have more of a general question. I'm interested in helping people obtain harmonization of their thinking in bringing peace to earth. I was wondering if you could give a perspective on this in regards to building or rebuilding civilizations to facilitate this.

The group:

We tell you, it is not us who will do this; it is you who are doing it. It has already begun. We will point to some of the processes in your own reality here and now that will make a difference. For this, we do not take you back to the days of Atlantis but back to the days of MU. Please hear the reverence in our voice when we speak of that place. It was great beyond your understanding. You are not yet at a level where you can understand what happened but you will be soon.

Let us tell you that you will be emulating MU in your own businesses, in your own governments, in your own environments. MU was a wonderful place, founded on the opportunity to make space for empowered humans. It was founded on the principles of holding personal responsibility not only for your actions, not only for what you participated in, but also for creating your own happiness, for experiencing your own joy, being the best that you can be, and not for the people around you but for yourself.

MU evolved to such a wonderful energy that you did not have to have laws in those days. Instead you developed and honored customs. Those who wished to be a part of the energy had to add to the collective vibration by honoring the customs ... and they chose to do so willingly. They understood the Universal energy, for the Universal energy is nothing more than a sheet hanging. When you poke on this side, it produces a protrusion on the other side. Understanding the movement of Universal energy and the blending energy makes space for the empowered humans on planet earth.

You did well, far beyond what was expected of MU. It was a place of the heart, and you are starting to build that now. One of the ways you can build this very quickly has already begun. It is what we have termed the "Intentional Grid." It is a line of communication for you to know if you are connected to this person here or to that person over there. And even though this person and that person may have differences and consider themselves to be enemies, you actually have the same motivation. Most of the time, it is because you are so much alike even in your own motivation that causes you to be enemies. Then you understand the connection. And the more you can make the connection and educate all around you, the more you will understand that you all have the same primary motivation.

Understand that you are not just a piece of God; each and everyone of you are the whole of God. As you take that power, as you create that reality, and as you move that energy into your businesses and into your workplaces, churches, schools, environments, clubs, gatherings, and your own homes and your own Circles of Light, then you will find opportunities to work with other empowered humans. Find a way to take this person here and create first with yourself and then with them. Make space.

We think it absolutely amusing that you have found something that emulates so clearly the second dimension of polarity. That is something you call "competition." We tell you that is changing, for your competition will evolve into a different type of energy. It is not actually competition that has caused things to get better but the fact that you have focused energy in that direction. And if you had to do so through competition, so be it. The more energy, the more awareness you can make in each one of your areas, the more everyone will know they are all one and connected as one.

The Intentional Grid started by the simplest energy you call phone lines. Your telephones are a means whereby you can pick up your own conversations, talk to each other and know you are of the same essence. Your televisions have created the same thing, as have your radios. But it is not just about technology. Technology is only a facilitator of the energy. You see now that you are using these phone lines for what you call the Internet. The Internet has been a great connection point of light. Much light is spread across the Internet. As with the government of MU, the Internet works because no one is in charge. Each one of you holds your own power and your own responsibility for yourselves. Try as they might, no one has been able to completely harness the Internet. Isn't that wonderful? Where is it moving from here?

It is moving to an Intentional Grid, a grid of light. We tell you, it will not be long until you will not need the physical wires to transmit this energy. And even though it may remain much of what you call the Internet at this point, it will eventually move to a grid of light above your planet. Each and everyone of you, no matter where you are, no matter where the phone lines might be, will be able to tap into them. This is heading to where you will not need the light or even the Intentional Grid, for the Intentional Grid will be a grid of heart energy. You will not need computers, telephones or radios to tap into it. That is what Children of Crystal Vibration will help you facilitate. This is where you are moving. Act as if it were here now. Act as if everyone around you could know what is in your heart and fear not. Be open with them; tell them what it is, show them your heart, and encourage them to show their feelings to you.

We will create the Intentional Grid very quickly. As you do that, your own organizations, your businesses, your governments, will change and evolve very quickly. For, in the higher vibration of the New Planet Earth, we will change those organizations as clearly as you changed your own reality. And only those organizations will survive that are strong enough to make space for the empowered human. Only those that are strong enough will be able to emulate the government of MU.

Realize we have answered in general terms, for it is not quite time for specifics but we tell you, you are getting very close. You are the ones who will write the specifics, not us.

Thank you for asking that question.

Lemurian Government

Carrie and Sam #D042802 Fullerton, CA,

Question:

Last week you spoke of customs of the Lemurian government that made room for empowered humans. Would you please speak to that?

The group:

The government of Mu was not a government … and that was the beauty of it. It ran not with laws but with customs. Those who chose to play the Game and play it fairly and by the customs did well and were supported. But Mu is a much higher vibrational place than you live in now. We tell you, those who did not choose to do that or those who chose to violate and to rub against the Universal Energy felt the wrath of their own actions very quickly. So it was a different situation, but we tell you, you have much to learn from that.

Part of the reason the government of Mu worked quite so well was that it was formed on the basis that no one was in charge. There were certainly leaders, trusted servants responsible for certain things, but no one person or group was in charge, ever. They were the servants of Mu who simply pointed out when someone, something or some organization was going against the Universal Energy. It was up to that organization to decide whether it wished to change or not.

We tell you, you have something very similar to the government of Mu that is emerging very rapidly on your planet now. It is what you call the Internet. The interesting part is, try as they have, no one has been able to contain it. That is why it works. No one is in charge. No one rules your free speech. The Internet is an Intentional Grid created first through your phone lines. This grid is going because it is changing and, as your own technology and as your own spirituality rise, it moves to a grid of light in which coherent light patterns will carry this energy all over the planet. It will carry the communications, the love and the connections, and will eventually even power your homes. And it will not be long before you will not even need the physical grids of light, for they will become part of you, and that takes you back to the days of

Atlantis. That takes you back and it is all possible because you start taking responsibility for yourself, for your own happiness, and for your own abundance. It also means, if you are not happy with the reality you have chosen, then you have the courage to choose again.

There is much you will find from the days of Atlantis. There is much you will find from the heart energy and expressions of humankind you call Mu. Those days have returned, dear ones. You have an opportunity to begin. This time you are taking it from the heart energy. You are doing it well. Please know, even though your own guides seem to have taken a step back, you are never alone. We are right here. Always. We tell you, we have missed you since you left Home for, as much as you search for and experience the memories of Home, as much as you search to replace that part of you that you miss so much, it is not nearly as much as we miss you. For you are very definitely a part of us and we are a part of you. We hold the energy for you very closely as you go through difficult times on your planet. Dare to reach for that which feeds you. Dare to be the best. Dare to speak the words, There Before the Grace of You Go I. Dare to place yourself first in the energy flow, for that is your rightful position. We will be there, standing behind you, hugging you with the touch of an angel.

Before we leave this moment, we ask those who have been helping you to hold your energy to give you one last hug. Two on the sides and one behind you will now reach around and hold your energy for just a moment. In that time, you are giving more to them than you can possibly know – an opportunity, just for a moment, to experience the magnificence of being here.

Timeline for Atlantis and Lemuria

Earth Changes, Kona, HI, 05/05/05

Question:

The great philosopher Plato gives us a timeline and he spoke of Atlantis. We know the Lemurian timeline preceded Atlantis. So if you have some information on the Lemurian timeline and the ending, it would be appreciated.

The group:

You find it very difficult to bring the timeline of then into the timeline of now. If we can take you for a moment back Home and help you understand that at Home, you do not have linear time; you have Now time where past, present and future are congealed together. By coming down and pretending to be human and finite when, in fact, you are infinite, it is necessary to take on the attributes of linear time and pretend to have past, present and future, and to measure/mark time. It is a product of the left brain, for the left-brain really does nothing more than mark time of your experience and give you the illusion of that.

The challenge about the timelines and even though we are going to give you a number, we tell you that it is very difficult for people to agree on the same number, for time was kept differently. You were a different vibration, in a different experience at that time, and even your own linear time frame was kept at a different pace. Therefore, it was almost as if you lived in an alternate reality even now.

Lemuria existed nearly thirty-two thousand years before today. One piece of Lemuria has been uncovered in a cave in the Reno area, but there are a lot of challenges about that, for the carbon dating process you currently use has a tendency to destroy that which it measures. And the Native Americans have claimed the site as a burial place, therefore no further testing can happen, so your sciences are blocked at this moment. But it will only be a short time before you start uncovering pieces of Lemuria.

Human Cloning

The Color Clear, #D051902 St. Louis, MO

Question:

There has been a lot of controversy about the subject of cloning. Can you share some of your feelings about that?

The group:

Please understand there is no right or wrong in what we are about to tell you. It does not reflect judgment, for there are no right or wrong choices in what you are about to do. It is no coincidence that you have asked this question at this time, for we tell you the last time you had difficulties wrestling with this question was in the days of Atlantis. There were times you as Atlanteans had a problem, for we tell you, you are also people of the heart and are greatly spiritually advanced people. One of the mis-directions you made was in not trusting your own powers as creators. Mu had gone under and many of the people from Mu had migrated to Atlantis. Over a period of many years, the Atlantean infrastructure had suffered from the great influx of people. At the same time, you had learned how to genetically engineer humans to do some of the jobs you did not wish to do, but you made a great misdirection of energy. Because you believed you had had a hand in the creation process, you believed the clones were not divine souls, when, in fact, they were. They are the Others of

E-Vibration and you brought them in and created them from nothing, but you thought they were less than divine. You created a class system, with the Atlanteans on the top with the most rights. You had the immigrants next, and then you had the Others who had no rights. You literally made rules about how long they could live, rules against them procreating or having relationships, and rules about where they could go and not go. And, dear ones, that misdirection was so hard on the Others of E-Vibration.

We tell you, no fewer than fifteen of you here in this room have reincarnated time and time and time again, carrying the memories of the time when you were one of the Others of E-Vibration. You have carried that energy back over lifetimes, planted deep within your own cellular memories, to be here at a time when maybe the collective vibration would get high enough to where you could make a difference.

Is it "right" to clone humans? We would never take your power from you and answer that question, for right or wrong is an illusion of polarity. But we will tell you, you already have twelve cloned humans on Planet Earth and they are doing quite well. They do have souls, they have hearts, they feel, and they are just as human as each one of you is. And you have done well. Are you going to make mistakes in this process? Of course, you are. It is part of your own evolution and, in fact, it is part of the blending of technology and biology we have been speaking of since the first day we brought these messages through the Keeper. Do not fear your power, dear ones. If you are working from the heart, you have nothing to fear.

We also tell you, it is more than that for your dramas. You love to get wrapped up in your dramas, and we watch with such amusement. You love to scare yourselves, do you not? Now you will have all kinds of movies about the clones who take over the Earth. And your greatest fear is that you will be "less than" if you have a clone sitting right next to you who is exactly the same as you. And we tell you, simply look at identical twins and you will see clones, for that is exactly what they are. And they have the same DNA but different souls, different life purposes, and different personalities, and that is who they are. Do not fear them.

The other part of the misdirection of Atlantis was the spiritual competition, in which you thought one vibration was better than another. And that allowed you to create the class system that caused so much trouble. Watch those two areas. Fear not taking your power, and watch carefully for spiritual competition.

We have described the ladder of advancement to you. Humans think you must climb to the top of the ladder of human advancement for you to get to the very top and ascend, and we tell you, that is not the way it is. It is only when each one of you takes your place on the ladder, including the people at the bottom holding the legs, that the whole ladder ascends. That is who you are, and you are right at the stage where you have everything almost in place. Enjoy the times you have ahead, dear ones. Fear not your own creations, for you have nothing to fear. You are the creators. Understand that you have the creative abilities of God and you have a responsibility to use those powers of creation. Please understand also, even though we tell you that you are God, you are not the only God. Then all will be clear.

The times directly ahead of you are exciting. The energy will change and your own biology will shift. That which has been promised to you for eons about rejuvenation is right at your doorstep. Can you imagine the excitement as you take your power as creators? You have done well, dear ones; you have won the Game. That is why we are in such awe of you.

Here sits the Game that no one thought would take hold. No one thought it had a chance, for it had no direction. It was total free choice. Here you sit, not only changing your own Game, but also changing the paradigms of All That Is. Yes, we are a much higher vibration than you are, but we have not been able to do what you have done. And for that, dear ones, we thank you. In those moments when you lose yourself, in those moments when you cannot find your way, in those moments when you look in the mirror and you cannot see your reflection, reach out and let another reflect for you. Know that you are not alone. Find the color clear and you will find all those around you who are getting to you and want only the very best. You could not fall if you tried, yet some of you try so hard.

Spiritual Competition

Seven Stages of Life, # 004 Santa Fe NM.

Question:

It was explained to us earlier that, at the time of Atlantis, one of the mistakes we made was giving more importance to a higher level of vibration and setting up a sort of competition in that way. But what I wonder is, can we understand what each level of vibration means so we don't make the same mistake again by seeing one superior and one inferior? If we could understand what each one is for, then I feel this prejudice wouldn't exist, and we wouldn't have to go there.

The group:

Let us begin here by saying that the human need to categorize and label is only superseded by your need to complicate things. Allow us to offer you another vision. Responsibility accompanies power, for responsibility is the balance of power and it is not possible to walk into it without taking that responsibility. Yet one vibrational level is not better than the other; they are just different.

The purpose of all vibrational levels is to move through them and to advance. And, although you are in the process of moving into a higher vibration right at this moment, there was also a time when you first came to this Earth in ethereal form and the Earth began cooling. You began losing your connection with the Earth and your advancement at that point was actually to lower your vibration. You gained density to drag and change and evolve your physical beings to be an even more dense form so you could associate with the Mother. Now, of course, you are going the other way and you are looking to advance; you are looking to raise your vibrations.

Please pay attention also to what is happening to the Earth's temperature. She is heating up, is She not? For that is simply a part of the overall cycle happening at this time. It is right on target. As we say this, do not think you can continue to tread on the Earth the way you have been. You are rapidly approaching critical levels of irreversible damage. Yet it can all be seen from a larger perspective.

Now let us address another question, for you have brought up an interesting situation. You have mentioned the magical days of Atlantis. Dear ones, you were so close. We cannot tell you how close you came. It was the slightest of mis-directions that caused these problems and set things into motion. You had plenty of time to catch them but again, change is difficult for humans. You were working out of a belief system of lack rather than a belief system of abundance. It was very difficult for you to change that belief system.

We are talking about the "collective you" at this point, for there was much you had worked with here. We tell you, you came very close, and one of the most interesting impressions that was stamped on you forever during the days when you stood on the hill and watched the waters coming in and destroying everything you had worked so hard for. The water took everything and the lives of the humans who could not get on the top of the hills. You saw it come up to take even your own lives, and you were indelibly stamped. For those of you who experienced that, at least one incarnation has been stamped with that energy. Many of you experienced the seed fear for, as you start moving back into your healing, as you start awakening into the light and moving into this, you have this huge Guardian standing at the gate saying, "Wait a minute. You have a huge fear that is almost overwhelming." Please understand, it is the Guardian that you, yourself, placed there to make sure you do it differently this time. We tell you, you have already surpassed that time.

The day after Atlantis, there was a meeting. It was the only time in history that time stood still. As souls of the only Planet of Free Choice, you stopped the clock and said, "We will talk about this because we came so close. We must set things up for ourselves to not do this again."

You agreed that, if at any point, the collective vibration of humanity got high enough to deal with this, you would all jump back in. You agreed you would all try to be here at exactly the right time and help carry it out, and that you would move past your seed fear, take your power and blaze the way for others to work from the heart. Some choices were made, the evolution began, and the process started. There came a time when you were all triggered and said, "Okay, it is time to jump back in."

You jumped back in and began to awaken and take physical form. You all began to enjoy life and, as you began to move into the second, third and fourth stages of life, you all started to awaken. You looked around, saw each other, and recognized each other ... and you had a wonderful, great party called "the Sixties." Some of you re-member it and some of you do not. Oh what a joy you had, too, for you took your power, did you not? And here you are once again, moving into the next level of power, the next level of creation with your own process. You have no idea, for dream as we might on this side of the veil, all of heaven's highest dreams for humanity did not go as far as you have taken it even to this day. We are so incredibly proud of you. Can you feel the love? Look in each other's eyes before you leave this room, for you are making history on a cosmic scale. You should be very proud of yourselves. We hope that answered your question.

Thank you for asking.

Crystal Implants from Atlantis?

The Smile of Spiritual Confidence, #012 Edmonton, Alberta, Canada

Question:

Greetings. Are you aware of some people who may come forward from Lemuria or Atlantis with crystal implants? And if they do, is there a possibility that some of these crystals are of no use to them now?

The group:

We would like to clarify a little before we answer the question. Yes, there are many people who have traveled across inter-dimensional time to be here at a specific time to see if some of the challenges can be corrected. And we tell you, even though they are of great use, they will not be able to accomplish what they came to do because, much the way we tell you that all illness is not a sign of something wrong, the sinking of Atlantis was not a punishment for some wrong doing. It was a simple case of cause-and-effect.

You healers look to keep a level eye here, and anything that falls below that line, you call illness, disease, sickness, or catastrophe. Yet we ask you to see whatever falls below that line as opportunity instead. For the art of mastery is taking something that has fallen below that line and using it in its highest form. And that is the case of the times of Lemuria and Atlantis.

The Lemurians were simple beings. They were so far advanced that they were simple beings, the most loving beings who have ever experienced this planet. And they found it best to put themselves on an entire continent, running things entirely themselves, because the connection with lower vibrational beings was very difficult for them. And yet, here they are, trying to come back and make a difference. They will be very successful in planting seeds and helping us understand the rest of the energy around what happened at that point. However, they have also come back to correct something so that it will not happen. It was simply a lure to get them to come back ... and they are here.

Now, the crystal implants you talk about simply mean that they carry with them some of the crystal energy that was very prevalent in the days of Lemuria. Man was mostly of crystalline energy and they have brought that energy back. They needed to make adjustments to their own physiology in order to make the trip through the timeline from Lemuria to here, and those are known as crystal implants. Are they going to be effective? Yes, they will be, but not in the way you think. They have come back to fix something, to help change something, to help spread a crystal energy here.

It is already spreading, and is working well. They will see that what has happened here does not need correcting. You are already doing it. They will touch many hearts with their unconditional love and their beautiful crystal energy ... and that is beautiful beyond description. And you will see one if you have not already.

The Two Moons of Atlantis

Healer's Healer, #065 Las Vegas, NV

Question:

In the past two weeks, I've been dreaming of two moons. Walking outside at night, wishing for a second moon, and I just want to know why. Is it in the past, or in the future?

The group:

You had a second moon. That is what happened. Two big events have taken place on your planet, and we will very briefly speak of them, because you have memories of them that are intentionally well-hidden from you.

Humans carry guilt. It is the most useless human emotion in the higher vibrations of the new Planet Earth, but was actually very useful in the lower vibrations of who you used to be. As a result, you have carried some of these emotions of guilt, lifetime after lifetime after lifetime. Therefore, it was very important for you to put on the veil completely, having to do with some of these memories. That is why there is no written proof, and why it is considered to be a myth among scientists. Nor will they ever find proof, for you have intentionally hidden it completely from yourselves.

What we will tell you is, in the beginning, there were two main inhabited continents – Lemuria and Atlantis. Lemuria was so advanced that it was one of the most beautiful energies. It was simple, childlike. Many of your writings spoke of the children of Lemuria, who were really the adults. They were childlike, much like the sixth stage of life where you must become childlike in order to go through the acclimation process of the seventh stage of life. They lived in that energy all the time. Their lives were simplicity and, as that, they were very advanced. You were very advanced.

Keep in mind, both of these continents were around for over 20,000 years each. So, many of you had several incarnations on both. And, although some of you will resonate more with one than the other, it simply means you have moved very rapidly in your own evolutionary process or you had experiences that helped you greatly.

As you evolved as a soul, you gained wonderful memories, even of the pain. And that is what happens. So some of you have wonderful, beautiful memories, even of the ending of Atlantis. But Lemuria, the larger of the two continents, was very advanced, so it was decided that Lemuria would step into the next vibrational stage. It was at the stage that humanity is at right now, ready to shift into what you call ascension. We tell you something you already know: Lemuria did not sink; it ascended. It literally went before to open the doors. That set about a whole series of events that essentially shot down the second moon, and finally led to the sinking of Atlantis. It was very difficult, for it set about something you had not had on this planet before – separation. That separation, as much of the heart energy as it was, set about a whole chain of events that caused another imbalance. It began when you shot down the moon. The moment it was gone, it brought up the tears you are crying now. The moment it was gone, you all knew what had to happen to balance the energy ... and that was the difficult part. We tell you, the Keeper was there. That is why he is so passionate about being here now to try to make a difference. He has no conscious memories of it, for he would not be able to speak even now if he did.

There are those of you who helped make the decisions, who were in the governments of these times, who were the scientists, the healers, and even the metaphysicians who were actually working from the heart. That is why we talk so much these days about the universal energy, for that was the big mis-direction of energy. The universal energy is about blending together, not about segregation. Everything you do that blends together will be supported. Everything you do that separates will be resisted. This is why we ask you to stop thinking consistently about yourselves as beings of this race or that, or of this country or that. Look for the ways you are alike instead of the ways you are separate from one another. Focus that energy and you will return to one heart. And the second moon will return. That is the first time we have told that story in its entirety.

What Role Did You Play?

Hearts of Atlantis, #D101802 Mt Shasta, Ca.

Question:

Hello to the group on both sides of the veil. I do not have conscious recollections of Atlantis, but I've always been drawn to the crystals of Superman's caves and other crystals. However, I do not recall my connections to Atlantis or Lemuria. Can you help me with these things that maybe would be applicable to me now?

The group:

Who were you during the days of Atlantis? Many of you do not have direct recollection of those times. The Keeper himself has absolutely none. Yet there is this quiet draw. He has had little hints here and there that he feels almost a deep sadness or guilt. We have asked him to lose the Guilt, for it literally is the most useless human emotion you have. In the higher vibrations of the New Planet Earth, the G-word must go.

We tell you, those of you who do not have any recollections at all are sometimes holding that knowledge from yourself for this very reason. Not a single person in this room has not misdirected power or energy at some time. Twelve of you in this very room have been great spiritual leaders who have misused power for personal gain in some fashion during many lifetimes. That is part of your lesson, yet when you come back in, you will find a great resistance to moving into that power, but you will not re-member all the details. It will be an enigma to you because it was necessary to wipe the slate clean.

What did you do? Where were you? Four people in this room knew you directly and intimately, for you are a healer of great magnitude. You were outspoken. You stood right at the heart of the city, at the podium, and gave the news of the day, much like your newscasters, only you did not need televisions during those times. You used power in many different ways. You were a purveyor of information on a very grand scale, and you did so from the heart. There were times when you chose to proclaim what you were handed rather than what you felt. So today, you are a person who goes around very quietly behind the scenes, touching this person over here, and then that person over there, giving them the same information, but in a totally different way. That was one of the many lifetimes you had between Atlantis and Mu.

It is not imperative for any of you to re-member that directly. It is not important for you to decide, "Well, I think I was more in Lemuria than I was in Atlantis. I think I was more spiritual in Lemuria than I was playing with the electronic toys in Atlantis." You have all played the parts. The heart of Atlantis is all that we ask you to re-member. That is the part you kept in the crystals you planted all over your planet. That is what you have not fully discovered yet. And even some of the larger crystals that have placed the energy back into the grids have not yet been uncovered. You have seen some indication of some of them. We have spoken of the Bermuda Triangle, which is so confusing to your electronic and magnetic instruments because some of the large power crystals are down there. You thought it was a great place to hide them until you started losing aircraft through dimensional realities.

Do you understand what you are doing? You are beginning to. People such as yourself will start using that information in different ways. You will start re-membering little snippets here and there, and you will start putting it back together. And when you all come together, you will make sense of it all. In the meantime, you will go around quietly planting seeds. You do not even call yourself a teacher. We love the veil, for you have created it so thickly that it is amazing to us. We could go on and on, but it is not applicable to all those present, so we will entrust the Keeper with some information that he will impart to you personally. We thank you for the question.

CODES

Crop Circles

Wings Over Mu, #D032603 Kona, HI

Question:
Does the group acknowledge crop circles? Are they real?

The group:
Yes.

Question:
Is there some kind of message?

The group:
Yes. And there is not a book written yet that has deciphered what they are, for they are actually coming from all sorts of different dimensional realities that exist within your own time and space. We tell you, they are not written from spaceships. These are not beings who come down and move the crops. They are magnetic field energy impressions that originate in inter-dimensional space. The easiest way for us to describe this to you is to say they are coming from inside your Earth. No, that does not mean that there are big civilizations going on down below your feet. What that means is, there are other dimensional realities that exist within the same time and space that you do, but they are at a slightly different

vibration, all at ninety-degree angles to each other. And they are trying to help. They are giving you signals that you are trying so hard to interpret that you are saying, "Oh, there are the seven chakras, and this one is a planetary system, and here is the infinity sign, etc." Ultimately it makes no difference. Even if they are saying nothing more than, "We are here," that is enough to celebrate.

These are also triggers for your physical body. Your body needs signals that it is all right to advance and evolve. These signals often come with crop circles, but also come in other ways such as seeing master numbers like 11:11 and 12:12 on your clocks.

"Are they real?" you ask. First it will be helpful for you to define reality.

Note from Steve:

The group has talked at length about crop circles but generally says something very similar to what was in the above answer. You may also note that we did an experiment with reverse crop circles. This is when we stopped our broadcast one month and had everyone focus on the sign of the Human Angel. They helped us to focus that energy to some of the dimensions that are sending us crop circles. The beings in the other dimension are probably still asking; "Is it real?"

http://lightworker.com/beacons June 2006

A Cosmic Wink

Dolphin Flow, #D031702 Syracuse, New York

Question:

You left me two ribbons in my house for the second time. What were you trying to tell me?

The group:

You have forgotten the time when you were a child, for the ribbons used to mean something. You have forgotten the time of joy and carelessness. You have forgotten the time when you played, not only once, but twice. For you have shared that with another being and that is what the second ribbon was for. Re-member the joy of your childhood; re-member those pieces you have forgotten. Open the door to re-visit some of that, for it is the one piece that can move you the fastest. That is the one part of yourself you have moved through so effectively that you have somewhat left behind. It is a trigger, dear one.

You knew the moment you found it that it was not by accident, that it was a cosmic wink. It is not the only one. Pick up that piece of yourself that was with you as a child. Pick up that piece of yourself that was with you, that you shared with others and with a very close friend. For you have had one who traveled with you since a small child. You have had one who traveled with you on the other side of the veil and is so close. You have forgotten her only momentarily. It is easy. You get so busy with your everyday lives that you forget where you are. It is a cosmic wink, dear one.

We look at the direction you are heading and where you are going. We can see even what lies ahead to some degree. We have used the analogy of the double-decker bus. It is your bus, you are driving it, and you are in charge of it. Yet we sit on the top deck sometimes and can see a little further down the road than you can. And we may be able to tell you a little about what is down this street here, and that street there. But you are the one driving, the one in charge. At those times when we wish to help you re-member a little something about the direction you are going in and why you are heading that way, we touch you with the cosmic winks. You know that spirit is with you. You may not be able to figure it out completely, and we love to watch you as you interpret every little thing. Just use the energy, dear one. Just re-member the energy of the spirit, re-member the energy of the ribbons, re-member a time when those ribbons were in your life and you will have the secret of the cosmic winks. For it will not be long before you will be effecting those same cosmic winks yourselves, first among other humans, then among the Second Planet of Free Choice. You have quite a journey in front of you, dear ones. Enjoy it.

Synchronicities

The Third Vibration, #047 Sturbridge, MA

Question:

July 15 happened to be a day when I was thinking very strongly of Steve all day, and that evening, I received the Beacons, in which my name was mentioned twice. I wanted to know if there is a connection?

The group:

To use a very human expression: "Duuhhhh!" Of course there is, dear one. People think it is a grand mystery how this works, when it is so simple. Humans have to complicate things in order to understand them. We will complicate it just enough for you to understand (laughter). You are a part of Steve; Steve is a part of you. And the fact that the two of you have developed a relationship over a number of years and worked to fine-tune the third vibration means the relationship has evolved. It means the connection between you being a part of him and him being a part of you has evolved. And that connection is very strong.

When you have a thought, when you have an emotion, he has that emotion, too. And if he is in tune with it, if he is not too busy – his mind is quite busy – he feels that and connects with it. It stores somewhere in the back of your consciousness, for he has all these things coming in and puts them in compartments – he loves his compartments – and when he slows down enough to bring our energy through, when he slows down enough to really pull the things through, he pulls pieces from everywhere. Many times in channel, the topic of the message is triggered by people's thoughts in that very room. Sometimes they are spoken; sometimes they are not. This particular one was spoken this day at lunchtime. And that is what triggers the question in Steve's mind, which opens the door for us to give an answer.

Question:
So you were talking to me? Yes.

The group:
And you knew that.

Question:
Yes, I did (laughter).

The group:
You are all tuning to the same channel. Sorry, we could not resist that. The reason you are in each other's brain so often is because you share the same resonance pattern. Basically, you vibrate in harmony so when you connect, both vibrations are amplified. Now, here is the interesting part. Even though your name was mentioned multiple times, it was not just for you. We communicate with you on multi-dimensional levels where it reaches many, many people with different ears using the same words. There is actually a code we use to describe messages, to send and repeat messages. The editors and trans-

lators who are a part of this family and make these messages more palatable and readable get very frustrated with these codes at times, for it makes their job a little bit difficult. It is frustrating for them, they change something and we change it back when they are not looking if it is a needed code. Many of you are now taking out your pens and notepads to record this mysterious code but we tell you that at your stage of vibration, it is slightly too simple for you to grasp.

It is really very simple, for it is the vibrational purity that allows it to reach many different hearts with the same words and the same vibration. That is the reason there are very few contractions in our speech or in the written word which we use. The Keeper calls the English we use "formalized," but that is simply the way he translates. There are codes in the actual words themselves that help to reach many people. We are thrilled you got your message (laughter).

Question:

Thank you for supporting me.

The group:

Thank you for supporting Home. Espavo.

CONTRACTS

Twin Souls

Christopher Falls In Love, #D102002 Oostmalle, Belgium

Question:

I think I have just found my twin soul. Does the group know something about that?

The group:

As always, we ask you to take everything we say and run it through your own discernment filters, for some of this will resonate with you and some of it will not. Please do not judge yourself or us in this process of discernment. We only wish to show you a different perspective so you may have more choices. That is our sacred contract with you.

We will now take you back to the first dimension where you are Home, for in the height of Unity Consciousness, each one of you carries the same core personality you have carried throughout all that is. Suppose your father has gone to the other side of the veil and yet sometimes he drops in with the same silly jokes he used to do when he was alive. It is not that he is so bad at jokes but that he keeps the same core personality. To him, the funny part is still truly funny.

Those core personalities are not made up of male or female; they are core personalities that lend well to both. You have a full choice when you re-turn Home in the seventh stage of life, for it is you who decides which experiences will be incorporated into your core personality and then, every time you express yourself as a soul – whether through an incarnation here on Earth or any other Game you may play, for there are many possibilities – it is you who decides the process and what happens at that point.

Now, when you decide to come into an experience in the field of polarity or duality in which you have been playing, it is necessary to go through the second dimension. At that time, you define yourself as either male or female. Yes, there is another part of you that holds the energy while you have an expression as male or female. Most of the time, that energy is not held in human form at all. It is on the other side of the veil, holding a balance of your energy through your own higher self.

Many times, what you have been labeling "twin souls" is actually a reflection of the shadow side of you. There is another part of you, outside of yourself, that is accessible through your soul most of the time. There are extreme circumstances that could cause a soul to divide and bi-locate. But it is extremely rare and, in fact, in that case, if this were to happen, the two of you would come together with great magnetism and find each other no matter where you were in the world. This is usually followed by a short generally explosive relationship. In reality, you are so much alike that you lose your individuality and, after a short time, get very critical of each other. In short, you get on each other's nerves.

We are talking about something else, for many of you here have set up backup plans. You have no idea how imaginative you get when you are in the first stage of life. You have no idea of the complexity you set into motion as you lay your plans out. And you say, "You know, if we are not going to meet here, if for some reason this does not work out because we are going to a Planet of Free Choice, then we will meet over there. If that does not work, we will meet over there. And if that does not work, we will meet there." You set up unbelievable backup plans to make sure something happens when it is really important.

What some of you are experiencing are those backup plans. You have reached around someone you trust, usually someone you have had a relationship with in the past or have been very close to in a romantic setting. You say, "You know my energy. You know exactly who I am and who you are going to be there. Would you do me one great service? And if, if, if and if, if the planet goes to the next level and we do not explode it, and if it goes on and if I am still here, and if you are here and if all these things line up, will you come into my field? Will you re-mind me of who I am? Will you excite me to such a level that I will feel my power in some fashion? And if I am not the vibration I wish to be at this moment, will you fault me in my relationship? Will you fault me in my marriage, will you fault me in my own belief about myself so I can get on my vibrational path and either change the marriage or leave it, or even evolve to the next level?" Those are very difficult relationships, too.

Relationship Stretches

What Color is Love? #042 Tel Aviv, Israel

Question:

I am at a cross road at the moment including with my job. I'm about to finish working in a place where I've worked for many years. I'm grateful for the job that I had. While I was working with this job, I developed spiritually in the hours after work. I'm at the juncture also with my relationship with my partner and am very excited about what is coming up. But

I'm a bit confused and I would be grateful if you can give me some guidance or direction.

The group:

Some time ago, the Keeper used to call this a "spiritual awakening" but it no longer looks like that, for when people awaken, it happens so quickly that it looks more like a spiritual explosion. You have experienced such an explosion, and the possibilities are tremendous. Your passion is great and coming out of your eyes even as we speak to you. It is a wonderful connection, yet it confuses those around you. When one person moves from one vibrational level to another almost over night, the rapid change is very confusing. And we ask that you do not try to explain it, because words will never cover it. Even though in the beginning, other people worry about you because they are actually afraid for you, you have only to show them that light behind your eyes. When you talk about being in a relationship and you have that kind of passion, he'd better look out. Humans resist change at all costs. It is your normal structure to resist change of any kind but the change that has given you so much will also give to him. In fact, there will be a smile that will take many months to wipe off his face, but please understand, there is an assimilation period. And in those times when you want so much to tell him everything, just sit back and smile. And hug him.

We thank you for asking the question.

Mastering Communication

The Magic Wand, #022 Wageningen, Holland

Question:

Four years ago, I divorced from my wife. I have two lovely sons but I hardly see them. I see them only once every two weeks and that's not much. My ex-wife does everything to ensure that I see them as little as possible. I pray every day for her to be more open but don't know what to do because I know my children are suffering from this. Me also, but it's not that important. I do not know how to be a better father and to be there for them as much as possible. I'm very tired and frustrated because I want to help my ex-wife, because by helping her, I am also helping my two boys. But it doesn't work, so I don't know what to do.

The group:

There is something children like to play on called a tee-ter-totter. It is a board that spans a fulcrum in the middle. A child sits on either end and puts it out of balance so one side goes down and the other goes up. For every action, there is an equal and opposite re-action on your planet. Some have called this a Universal law but it is really just an attribute of the Universal Energy. The job of the Universal Energy is to balance. Like water always seeking inner balance of itself, the Universal Energy is always seeking to pull back together that which was separated for the illusion of the Gameboard. The challenge comes when you start to consider things good or bad. The good and bad thing is really a limited human obser-vation based on the field of duality you were living in. We know you miss your children, but your children in particular have an opportunity to gain insights in this experience that they could not have gained in any other way.

The oldest will be a powerful healer who heals with his words. More importantly, they will both work with relation-ships. That is the gift both of you parents have given them. That is the opportunity they have to work with because of your pain, because of your willingness to go through these difficulties. Understand that their energy is right next to yours, even though you cannot reach out and touch them, ask them how their day at school was, or what they are going to be when they grow up. You cannot share in their lives in that fashion.

However, you can share your energy with theirs. Blend it together. Pull them into your thoughts and your heart often, and send them unconditional love, not the sadness you feel because they are not with you. Let your thoughts of them bring light into your life, and you will put them in a space of empowerment. This will take them out of the energetic tug of war they have found themselves in.

At this point then, give them the best gift you have to give them. Dare to place yourself first. Please do not try to do so much for them that you end up shadowing their energy. Let them stand in their own energy and experience the creation for themselves. When you do have time with them, do not try to overcompensate for your lack of connection with them. They deserve to see the real you, with all of your perceived gifts and flaws. Hold the confidence that you have already touched them. A part of your heart will always be inside of them. For, you see, you have given them a gift of which you have no idea at this point.

You have come into this world working with an important life lesson called communication. It is very common amongst males. Many males choose this life lesson because their wiring allows for it. The life lesson is very simple. You come in to try to communicate. And, of course, on your world, you must communicate in all forms. But, when it comes to speaking from the heart, the challenge comes when the person working with the life lesson of communication has an extra thick veil.and you talk about all of the things you think, with everything up here. However, when it comes to telling someone what you feel, what you need, it is very difficult. Look what you just did. This is mastery of a life lesson. When you have the courage to speak your truth in front of a room full of people, you master a life lesson. And even if your children are not standing next to you, they win because you have set the energy for them.

All we ask you to do is to speak your feelings. Speak who you are. It does not have to be "right" or "wrong." It is just who you are. It is what you feel, what you need. And by speaking that and connecting with the energy of your own heart through your words, you set the energy for your children far beyond anything else you could do. And if it is necessary for you to go through a very difficult divorce and actually be separated from your children for a time to accomplish that, then you will find that it is worth the price.

Questioner:

Thank you. I will work on that and show my children! (audience cheers)

The group:

We are assured you will do exactly that. You may want to know that you have worked with this life lesson twenty six times thus far. (audience draws a breath)

Questioner:

Well that's OK. This one is the last! (audience cheers even louder) Thank you.

The group:

Espavo!

Note from Steve: It was interesting for me to experience the little energy play at the end of this question. When the group said the man had been working on the same issue for the last twenty six lifetimes, I cringed inside for I thought we might have embarrassed him. The audience's reaction was also slightly negative. What they were really doing was complimenting him that this life lesson took only 26 lifetimes.

Back-up Plans

The Small Step, #028 Atlanta, GA

Question:

I wanted to ask you about my brother because when we did the session, you said there was a brother who didn't come in, and my sister came in instead. I have always been looking for my brother so can you tell me anything about him, if I have met him, if he is here?

The group:

You have not met him, although you will. There will come a time in the near future when you will have an opportunity for your paths to cross. Whether you actually meet is up to free choice, for that is the only rule on the planet. The two of you have been inexorably linked because of a contract to fulfill between the two of you. That is why you have this vacancy where your brother should have been, why you have this place in your heart, and why you have always known you were going to have a brother and do not have.

He will be attracted to you at some stage of your life and his, probably in the near future, for you have a junction point coming up in the next two years, and we think he will seek you out and you will have to do nothing to enact this. But he will work his way in very close to you. This will not be a casual acquaintance, nor a client; it will not be anyone on the outside or one or two steps removed from you. He will be very close, so it will be a family member, very personal, who you will guide or work with, or he will come to guide you. It may even be a mentor of yours. But you will find him and the connection will be made, otherwise we would not have even seen the connection, for the contract is still valid. That is why we gave it to the Keeper.

Contracts with Space Brothers

The Small Step, #029, Atlanta, GA

Question:

(Asked at the close of a six day Spiritual Psychology facilitator training.) I want to thank you for providing the opening for the healing that has started this week. And when I complete this healing, and I will, all the way down the timelines, I believe that is part of the contract I accepted when I rewrote my contract. I would like to know if that is going to generate the space I've needed for my space brothers to come in.

The group:

Yes, your heart holds the space for them to come in, and they are already coming in. The biggest challenge is that your memories have been shaded from you by your own doing, for it would simply overwhelm your heart at this point to do that. But you know what is there, you know what your role is, you know what you are here to do. You know, with authority, when you see a person carrying that energy, you can help them awaken and understand what they are feeling. And all that is left is this little tiny, little step, but you have already stepped. You just have not quite shifted the rest of your weight into it, but the momentum is moving, it is in motion. And you should be very happy with yourself for, as painful as it has been, you have set it into motion and the healing will go forward and backwards in the timeline; it can do no other thing. And it will create for you an opportunity for you to step fully into your passion and to set that into motion. For it will move, and it will move now.

Personal Choice

Seven Stages of Life, #004 Santa Fe NM

Question:

My question has a personal microcosm level, and a global macrocosm level. First of all, microcosm.

The group:

As do all questions.

Questioner:

First of all, the microcosm. When I was young, my father became disabled and I've spent my life at home being the caretaker because I felt that was what was needed, and that was what I was supposed to do. Now I'm forty-three and I don't have a mate and I don't have children, and I realize how much I've wanted that love. It seems like I've wasted my life and missed the opportunity.

The macrocosm is you mentioned the Sixties earlier and the grand party. I was a child in San Francisco in the Sixties and saw the wondrous opening flower of energy and I thought, even at the time, that people were just not focusing and bringing it all through. It's like there was a party and there was a hangover and now here we are. To those who had the opportunity, was there a window there? It felt like there was this window. Is that as irrevocably wasted as my youth?

The group:

Firstly, a life is never wasted, dear one. When you hold the mirror in front of your nose, is there evidence that you are breathing? That is the "acid test" that will tell you if your contracts are complete. Your life could never be wasted, for you are here now to step into your own work and your sacred contract. The truth of the matter is, had you not gone through the difficulties you did, had you not experienced some of the challenges and thinking the way you did for so many years, you would not be able to help all the people who you are just about to help. You have put yourself through some very difficult situations. Those experiences gave you the credentials you sought as a soul. That gave you a confidence that can be had no other way. And now you are wondering if you have wasted your life.

Questioner:

Well, yes. All lessons are valuable but I feel like I missed the boat, like I blew my contract somehow.

The group:

What we are saying is that the boat has not left the dock. We tell you, there is lots of time to get into motion. We tell you that you have resentments about putting other people first all your life, which is part of your life lesson, part of what you have come in to do. Let us speak for just a moment about primary life lessons, for you wondrous humans think you are so bright and we tell you, you are, but you have to understand, there are times when you have come in between twenty and one hundred lives and looked the other way and never worked on your life lessons.

Can you see the joy we experience as we see you even having the courage to stand up and ask a question like the one you are asking, because it illustrates that you are at a point where you are ready to put yourself first? Ah, that is what the life lesson was. If it took you until you were ninety-eight and one half years old and you were going to leave at ninety-nine, and you only had six months of putting yourself first, your life would have been a grand success. We tell you, you have much more than six months. Step out of the past, move into the future, and lose the guilt. It has no place in the new vibrations of the New Planet Earth. The most useless human emotion that you carry forward from the third dimension is guilt. The Indigos will show you just how useless it is.

You have a contract to have a daughter that you have known about for some time and even though you may choose to not have children, your daughter will come to your life. And if you choose to have children, she will be the first in. We only tell you that because it helps you to understand you have purpose way ahead of you but you do not see it.

Drawn to the Land

Cosmic Winks, #059 Mt. Charleston, NV

Question:

I have a question about my land that is prairie. I feel that I was drawn there to be the keeper of that area and I guess I am asking, is that complete?

The group:

The answer to all of those questions is yes. And it does not mean you need to leave the land. What it means is, the contract that originally drew you there is now complete. If you choose to leave, you will find another contract that will excite you and a place that will support you.

The Keeper was a contractor up until not long ago and he helped people fix up their homes and sometimes remodel their homes. He found a very interesting situation, for when a person would buy a fixer-upper, he would be called in. They would have all these grand ideas of all the things they were going to do. And when they were talking of these grand ideas, they were in a heightened state of creation. They beamed and showed passion. Then the projects would get under way and sometimes years would go by while they fixed this plot of land to house their energy perfectly. They would say, "Okay, I no longer need to remodel my house. I am getting tired of the dust. It is time to let all the workers go home. I am going to just sit and enjoy my home from now on." Within six months, they would usually sell their home and move on. For it is not about the destination; it is about the journey. It is about finding that creation. It is about having the dream of what you can do and the possibilities. Stir your soul with the new challenges of creation and your energy will be supported wherever you land.

CRYSTALS

Pink and Green Crystals

The Small Step, #029 Atlanta, GA

Question:

(From a six day Spiritual Psychology training, Our day out was to Stone Mountain, a high power spot on the outskirts of Atlanta.)

From the bottom of my heart, I feel I am representing my family from Home. They are very grateful for your unconditional love, and we are grateful for you taking ours. I had an experience in Stone Mountain that I wanted to share and ask about. I went to the top of the mountain, and I saw the mountain almost splitting in half. Then I saw a white, powerful beam of energy come from the middle. I also saw millions of figure eights coming out and one of the angels told me it was infinity signs. It was powerful, and it was suddenly all over.

I knew that I had to go up there and get my crystals, a pink one and a green one. I didn't hesitate, I knew I was going to find them. I got up there and was guided. I found them and took them home with me. When my son saw them, he said, "Mom, the pink one is pure love, and the green one is giving."

Today as we went to Stone Mountain again, I saw those stones split in four. As we were on our walk, instead of going up, I saw myself going down into the Earth.

The group:

When you came upon the mountain in the first place, did you not see there was a white line dividing the mountain in half, on the very top?

Questioner: Yes, OK

The group:

It is because, energetically, it does divide apart; energetically the portal does break up into the different pieces and allow travel in at different times. We used to tell you, since it has been brought up, there is more to this, for it is no coincidence that the word "Atlantis" was brought up at this point. For Atlantis was run by great power crystals, and different people were in charge of the grid. There was a great man by the name of Tyberron who ran the power grids at that point. And there was a special, unique spot in all of Atlantis that was very isolated, all by itself and well-guarded, for it was the place called The Emerald City. It was the place where the green crystals were to bring the heart energy of the power grid onto the grid. It was not just about lighting your lights or heating your walls; it was about living in the energy of love. The green crystals from The Emerald City were here to distribute the heart energy out onto the power grid. That is the reason the Keeper wears a green stone. Some of those sacred stones are in that mountain, which is part of what you saw. And you will see much more of that as time goes forward.

There are other stones in other places throughout your reality and your world. One of them in particular that was a very important power grid was in what you call the Bermuda Triangle, and it confuses your navigational systems even to this day. The airplanes that flew directly over it were almost in another timeframe.

Now that those crystals have found you, take them to a space that is sacred for you, but not in the same space. Take each one to a different space and plant it on its own. They will find their way back to each other opening the portal in the process.

Talking to Crystals

Breath of Spiritual Confidence, #074, Genk, Belgium

Question:

I would like to ask something on crystals. I brought one with me, because I feel I have a connection with it. And not in the last Beacons but the Beacons before, you talked about contacting crystals and you can ask them questions. I would like to know how I can increase my contact with crystals and how we can work more with it.

The group:

Such an excellent question. When we speak about multiple dimensions, you immediately go to space beings. Well, that happens, so we have actually been giving you messages about some of the space beings you are contacting, but you have no idea how broad a spectrum this really is. For when you become multidimensional beings, you can contact all levels of dimension very quickly. This includes the mineral, plant, animal and all other levels.

So, therefore, to have a different perspective with your crystals is a very exciting idea. Crystals are record keepers for the most part. They hold energy imprints so they can hold energy imprints of history, of love and of a person. Many of you have decided to very mysteriously sneak a crystal into these channels, because every time you come to one of these channels, it fills with a little bit of our energy. We tell you that is absolutely true, it does. And when you take that part of the Earth with you, which is a living breathing sentient being and part of the top of the mineral kingdom is the crystal level, it brings energy to you and it shares energy with you.

We tell you, women in your societies have a tendency to live longer then men and you have always equated it to the fact that men go off to war and therefore get killed. Therefore, women's longevity has a tendency to be longer than men's. It has nothing to do with that; it has to do with the fact that women typically feel more comfortable wearing crystals on or close to their bodies. They receive energy from the crystals that men generally do not. The moment we spoke of this, the Keeper went out and got a crystal. Not because he actually wishes to live longer, but because he is one of the people who is there at all of the channels. So it is a collection and that is what happens with you. When you look at anything that is living and breathing and you breathe your magic into it, it reflects magic back to you.

Can you ask your crystals questions? Of course you can. Talking to crystals is easy; the more difficult part is listening to them. We jest. We have even given the Keeper an exercise where everybody carries a crystal with them for two days and then they come into a room and exchange crystals and read each other's crystals. Play with it, try it, and enjoy it. For what will happen is you will see that those imprints go into the crystals very clearly. Then you do not need to do the exercises. You may take someone's crystal right now that they have had with them for any time and feel energy from it, and if you ask that crystal a question, it will be very similar to asking that person's higher self the same question. So it is one way to bridge the gap between heaven and your biology through your higher self. You have so many of these, it is absolutely magical and yet, when you look at the ones you love, you will find magic. We thank you for asking the question.

Man-made Crystals

The Small Step #029 Atlanta, GA

Question:

I just wonder if we can once again manufacture crystals as we did on Atlantis.

The group:

Let us explain the reason we used the word crystal so much, for we really are on a crystal kick. Crystal is the form that is taken as you move from Unity Consciousness. All of humanity is becoming crystalline. The first step into what you call your reality is the essence of the Central Sun. The moment you step into the Central Sun, the center of your Universe, it is the first step of becoming infinite or becoming finite. As you take a step from the infinite to the finite, the first stop along that path is the Central Sun. The Central Sun is crystal, because you are taking the crystal energy from the infinite Unity Consciousness and expressing it through the Central Sun as you are becoming different rays of the rainbow as reflected through the crystal that you all are. In this reality, the ray you are is gold. You are of the gold ray. You are among the ambers, yellows and golds. That is why the second book of the Keeper has that particular sunset on it. It, too, runs between the yellows, ambers and golds. Your entire ray of the Gameboard here is gold. It is the most beautiful color you can imagine from our perspective, for it glistens in the light.

It is also the same thing that allows you to try to complete yourself in relationships. As you pull yourself into a relationship with another, quite often you celebrate that with what you call a wedding band, which is the most beautiful gold. And the celebration of what you call "engagement" is the combination of a most beautiful crystal on a gold band. It is the expression of the Universe and the Unity Consciousness coming from the infinite, through a lens of pure crystal, which we call the Central Sun, into a finite expression.

So can you make crystals? Without a doubt. This is also one of the things you have hidden from yourself, as you have hidden crystal power. That is one of the challenges of why you have not yet done it. You have been able to take crystalline form and create it in the laboratories, yet you have not been able to bring that into physical crystals yet. Yes, you will. Yes, you will also re-member the crystal energy that will be returned to you very soon. You will find ways of doing that. In the meantime, you will play with transmuting some of the natural crystals you already have – even your leaded crystal is one of these – of being able to take forms of silica and turn them into a crystalline form themselves, for that is as close to being a man-made crystal as you have achieved at this point. And you will find ways of creating a crystalline structure that can actually not only generate the crystal power itself – we will call them generators even though they are actually transmuters – but also those that can power the lines of the crystalline grid, which you will use as distribution crystals.

You will find these very soon. Shortly after that, you will find remnants of the Atlantean crystals you used to love. Some of you already know where they are. You just do not understand what you are seeing. You will see them. You will understand them after you make this discovery yourself. But in those times, you will be able to find crystals very easily. You have an energy here that you re-member well, for you have a very clear re-membrance of the days when you used to do that. And you will bring it back in, and find the others, too, for there are many like you who have very similar re-membrances. Connect with them. The magic will begin very quickly.

Activating Crystals

Portals of Lemuria, #D032403 Kona, HI

Question:

I've been told by two different sources that there is a giant crystal under the ocean floor that I will help facilitate in rotating. However, I would not excavate them, but they would come back up, and then I would be part of the activation team. Do you have any comments about that?

The group:

Take a deep breath right where you stand. Do you feel it? Do you feel the energy of the crystals you have felt before? They are grand, indeed. There are many places upon the Earth, some you know yourself. You are not far from them, and when the time is right, you will know, for that feeling in your own being, the essence of who you are when you breathe, will lead you to that. These are the same crystals that have posed challenges to humans before.

Questioner:

We were told that we buried them because we needed to put them away for that time.

The group:

It was a collective decision you made. Since that time, you have not had what you call crystal energy upon the planet. As you look upon the crystals you wear and carry in your pockets, you know they are alive. You know they have an essence, an energy, but you do not quite know where it is. And, of course, your science misses that entirely for they are not able to find anything. Gee, you have done a great job. But when the time is right, it will be important to re-introduce that energy into the planet in a safe, comfortable and responsible way. You are one of the guardians of Mu, and yes, you will play a part, for you have used an energy similar to that. As close as you have been able to come to that particular energy, only it does not transmit in the same way, it is what you use to light your light bulbs, heat your homes, and dry your hair. It is called alternating current. This is as close as you have been able to come to replicating the crystal energy. For the crystal energy can be shot across the room with no problem. If there was free energy transmission, you would be very excited about the possibilities. You read about it every day. You know it is true in your heart, for you hold the key to some of the greatest transmitters and energy transformers.

Sea Crystals

Amor—The Emerald City, #D041402 Bemidji, MN

Question:

Will you tell me of the sea crystals?

The group:

Many crystals on the planet have been placed in perfect order to plant the seeds of light. There are no less than twelve thousand sea crystals on your planet at this moment. That may seem like a lot to you but it is very, very few. They will be uncovered as time goes forward. You have uncovered some already, and you personally know where one is. Twelve of these have been in the form of what you call the crystal skulls, for they were holding the markings of the energetic grid until the collective vibration of humanity was high enough to hold it on its own. And those have been disseminated upon the Earth and moved to different locations for it is no longer necessary for them to hold it. They were the first of the sea crystals. Sea crystals are usually found in salt water as salt is a soluble crystal itself that activates other crystals.

There is a grand crystal, green in nature, at the very heart of what you call the Bermuda Triangle. There is another very close to that, and the interaction of those two crystals is what causes confusion among your navigation systems in that area. Many pieces of the sea crystal have been moved to different places to distribute the energy and for you to make sure you have it available to you when you are ready for it. It is you yourselves, dear ones, who have done this. It is you yourselves who have even hidden the crystal properties of power within crystals from yourselves because, in Atlantis, part of the agreement you made with yourselves when you came back was that this time, you would do it differently and you would block the properties of crystals completely from yourself. You would not allow that to be seen. So, even though crystals have tremendous properties of power transmission, you cannot see it happening; therefore, you cannot collect it. The closest we can tell you that you have emulated this is electricity, for electricity is a source of energy very close to the crystalline energy. The cosmic joke here is that alternating current was developed by a crystal child – Nikola Tesla. It will not be long now before you start seeing the rest of it, for there is much energy there and sea crystals hold much of that energy and information.

Question:

I do know where some of the other sea crystals are, but as I realized today, there's a crystal of emerald energy. Will that be raised by your presence here? Are you allowing that veil to open right now and draw the people who will raise that sea crystal? Will it be bringing the healing needed?

The group:

Yes, yes and yes. If the power is not harnessed and used, it may cause a great energy vortex that could result in the formation of hurricanes in a repeating pattern. Yes, it is part of the reason we are here. You are creating the healing vortex within yourselves now. Please understand it will now move very quickly. You are the ones who will open the vortex. The energy of Atlantis has been activated. That which you hid from yourselves is now returning.

Many of these lakes you see scattered all across your land are actually liquid portals that will be used for much, and the sea crystal that lies in the lake you mentioned happens to be the key to them all. They will help not only in the healing of the Mother Herself, but they will also help in the healing of Atlantis.

You will see many opportunities for this because there are many of these crystals around. Look for them, search them out, reach for them with your intent if not your eyes, and they will be known to you. You will know exactly where they are, and if you send your own energy and open your own heart chakras to send those crystals energy, they will turn green in a moment and connect to the rest of the grid. Only now, the grid is down below; it is in another reality very close to your own, an inter-dimensional reality that will be accessed through portals. This is becoming important now in these days, dear ones, because you are no longer the only Planet of Free Choice. There is another and it also exists within the same time and space as does yours, but it is on a different timeframe. For it was important that you open and heal your own planet to make space for all that is to come.

Crystals in Your Bed

OverLight, #010 Oostmalle, Belgium

Question:

I would like to ask you a question concerning the subject of tools you were talking about. You said tools are there and in form here on Earth but that we don't really need them. But where I live, we have crystals in our bed, but now you are saying that tools are not souls and we don't need them, because maybe I would like to use them to help other people.

The group:

We would re-mind you that your highest hope was to come in and be confused, and you are successful. Let us help clarify. This is part of the reason we ask you to use discernment in everything you do, because it is important that you do not hang on every word we say. Please do not do that. Take only the pieces, the ideas and the concepts that resonate in your own heart and do not try to figure everything out that you work with. We only offer a piece here and a piece there, and we offer it in many different opportunities for you to see. In fact, quite often, we talk on many different levels simultaneously, so someone in the back of the room is hearing one thing and someone over here actually hears something else. That is why we speak through the Keeper the way we do. And it translates quite well. So please, understand the powers within you.

And now let us speak about the tools. The tools are wonderful and tremendous. They give you the ability to re-member Home by looking into a beautiful crystal, for the crystals are the highest vibration of the mineral kingdom. That is why you wear them. They are wonderful tools, so enjoy them. Play with them. You are not unspiritual because you use tools. Enjoy what you have. Teach it to others. Share your tools with others, for they may awaken them. Just understand that the tools are not necessary. There is a Game that you cannot use them. That means you have it all within you. When you have the choice of talking to yourself or talking to a crystal, sometimes it is actually more fun to talk to a crystal. Use it often. In fact, the cosmic joke on you is that when you look in the mirror and talk to yourself, you are actually talking to a crystal. Think about it.

Story Tellers

The Age of E., #017 Mt Shasta, CA

Question:

I just received into my care a special crystal that is a Master Weaver crystal. Can you give me any information about that and how I can be of highest service?

The group:

A crystal is part of the highest vibration of the mineral kingdom, and we tell you that crystals interact with biology more than you know. You look at that crystal and you see an unbelievable incredible beauty and a story. So, rather than ask us to tell you the story, you tell the rest the story, for that is where the power is. This is the Age of Empowerment. We will not go there with you, for you are the one who knows the story. So, although you are looking for validation, we tell you, when you look into that crystal, it reflects the most magnificent part of you and the story both of you have to tell. You have been recently re-united with this dear old friend. And we are glad you did. Thank you for listening.

Crystals to Celebrate Love

The Age of E., #017 Mt Shasta, CA

Question:

My partner and I each have a crystal that we gave each other and recently the chains have been entwining and the crystals have been moving together. Now they are actually making shapes and patterns, so I'm curious about the meaning of this and the energy behind it.

The group:

The energy behind it is your own, for you have infused the love of each other and the love of yourselves in those crystals. As you have exchanged those crystals, they blend together and become one and vibrate together as two strings of the guitar vibrate together. Although they are separate, they lend their harmonic vibration to each other. That is what is happening in your own relationship. You can see it in your eyes. It is beautiful, so what makes you think those crystals would not emulate that? As beautiful as the things you will see with those crystals, they are not as beautiful as looking in your eyes. Flash that smile. Hold that truth, and be the crystals.

Messages from Home?

Grace, Tiendeveen, Holland, 10/12/02

Question:

Fourteen years ago, I got a crystal from a good friend of mine who passed away this year. When I got this crystal, my life at that time was upside down. The crystal was crying and I thought I had to do something but I didn't know what. So, I put the crystal in a bowl of water and put some candles in the bath itself. I think I did a kind of healing at that time.

When I looked in the mirror, I was not in front of the mirror but sideways. I met a beautiful man, I think about forty to forty-five years of age, gray blue hair and beautiful eyes. He told me he was the Crystal Keeper. He said there are more of them in this world and when it is time, they will come out. Last week, I was triggered from the crystal in my computer and all these remembrances came back. Can the group tell me something about the huge crystal formations that are not only for pleasure?

The group:

And you took our challenge and made it a good one. We speak of crystal this and crystal that. We use the word "crystal" as we speak through the Keeper and we tell you, you are in the crystal energy. There have been many connections with the word crystal. It is not unusual that you would all be attracted to crystals. You are attracted to the diamonds you wear and the different stones in your rings. Even the Keeper has a green stone that is a crystal. It is the green of his own heart. He calls it his channeling ring. We tell you, many of you are attracted to these things. It is because it is the highest vibrational energy of the Mother Herself in what you call the mineral kingdom. For the crystalline energy is the return of the Christed Energy as everyone moves to the next level.

The crystals you received in your own ceremony are what we have termed your "Michael Crystal." The story of the Michael Crystal is simple. Within the Family of Michael, we have a tradition. When there is one who moves your heart dearly, who makes a difference with you in some fashion, who reflects you in such a wonderful way that you love looking at yourself, you give them a crystal. It is a crystal of your own heart. And when you receive a Michael Crystal, it is a gift and the responsibility for it is not just for you. When you receive it, you feel the weight of a burden of something you must do, for it is an activation.

Before you try to figure out all the things you must do, we ask you to simply take the crystal and do some sort of ceremony with it, where you share the energy in that crystal with other crystals – at least two more. When those other crystals are vibrating at the same rate as the original one, give those away … and those become your gift of the Michael Crystal. The one you were given then becomes yours to keep forever. In that way, you have touched another angel and the Family of Michael is drawn together as one, for it is the crystalline energy that connects all of the Family of Michael.

Each one of you will receive one soon. When it is given to you, take the challenge. Create ceremony with it in some fashion. Float a candle in your tub. Give it a bath. Soak it in salt water, whatever; it makes no difference to us. Create ceremony, for you are the magicians. Lend that vibration to two more crystals and then give those away to very important people in your life. In that fashion, the energy of Michael will come back together. In that fashion, there will be a unity consciousness experience all the way around, for the crystal vibrates on many levels.

Grandfather Rock

Hearts of Atlantis, #D 101802 Mt Shasta, Ca.

Question:

I'm Grandfather Rock and I'm grateful for every chance to dance with the group. I feel that when I was torn away from my loved ones in Atlantis, a huge amount of information was stored in my crystal structure, in the rock structure I carry with me, and I feel it is still there. I have no idea what it is or how to release or use it. Could you help me?

The group:

You are in a massive state of evolution as we speak. Many of you have discovered there are many, many more strands of your DNA, and you know this in your heart, even though you may not know it in your microscopes. And yet, we tell you, as this evolution continues, as this begins happening, you will see changes in many dimensional realities of your existence. One of those changes is in the mineral kingdom, of which you are very much a part. You have stamped yourself with the energy of the minerals. You have started out as the Grandfather Rock, proud in much the way you went to the mountain the other day and there was a guardian that overlooked the entire valley. That is who you are – the guardian. You have done well to carry that energy, and yet you are in a state of evolution, much the same way all the mineral kingdom is evolving, for Grandfather Rock is now emanating light and that is only possible in crystalline form. Grandfather Rock is becoming the most beautiful crystal you can imagine.

In that state of evolution, you will hold the energy of knowledge of the stone and the mineral kingdom. You hold the surety that allows humans to actually place their feet upon the ground and feel supported, to feel like the Earth will not move beneath their feet. As many of you here in the room do, in all of your work and the souls you touch, you provide the place for stability on planet Earth. How is your work evolving? How are you evolving? You are shining the light. You are becoming the crystals. You are becoming the grandfather crystal. Enjoy the ride.

DNA * PHYSICAL

New Chakra

Dolphin Flow, #D031702 Syracuse, NY

Question:
 Could you speak about the chakra at the base of the skull that we read about in your book? Is it opening?

The group:
 You have several chakras that are opening on your new energetic structure as you move from a physical structure of only two strands of the DNA to being connected to twelve strands of the DNA, the other ten being magnetic. You will find evidence of this as you will evolve to the next level. You have spent much time in what you would call ethereal bodies or Lightbodies. Without the dense, physical bubble of biology you now carry, you would have had difficulties keeping your connection. The cycle of evolution you are now seeing is preempted by a 10% decrease in magnetism on your planet over the last 100 years that is playing a part in the thinning of the veil.

 Your connection was very important so, as the Earth cooled, you began to transform your vehicles to a denser model. This was the beginning of the bubbles of biology you now have. You had help from the six parental races, but we will tell the story at a later time. Once in the physical, you needed to be of the Earth to stay there and this was when you developed digestive tracts. You began with the tips of the leaves and pristine growth full of life force energy that you began to ingest. You began to assimilate things of the Earth into your being to gain density to keep the connection with the cooling Gaia. Soon you moved on to eating the nuts and the most delicate of the fruits. This grounded your new biology enough to allow the spirit to temporarily inhabit these bodies. Today, you eat things such as meat and chocolate, especially when emotional. You ground very easily with these things. We tell you, dear ones, the Earth treat you call chocolate now can be found on the other side. That is why we tell you with all honesty that chocolate is ascension food.

We offer you a brief history here so you may clearly understand the path ahead. The biological form of our bodies has gone through incredible change and adjustments through your many experiences as a soul. The reality is, humanity is now facing another opportunity to go through such a drastic evolution. It is a choice most of you are making.

The new chakra on the back of the neck is a power center and one of the new chakras opening at this time. This one is a single-sided chakra as are five of your current chakras. This will also lead to physical symptoms such as a runny nose that hangs on for a long time, and ear and throat problems, as well. The activation of the new physical parts you will develop will begin soon.

We stop for a moment and ask you to feel the energy in the room, for even a fifth portal has opened to make more space. Since we opened the portal when we began, it attracted a lot of attention on this side. Four more have since opened and we are having somewhat of a parking problem right now. No problem we will resolve it.

As you continue to evolve, you will find many new modalities popping up on the Earth, as you will need to find new ways of working with people. Seven of you here in this room are holding modalities that were waiting to activate at the right time. As this process continues, you will see much more of what is ahead, for the connections will become very quick and your soul will be able to have a lighter connection to the physical body. Instead of wrapping you up in snow survival gear, we will be giving you a light jacket for your soul to wear. For the new Game is at hand. You are making it up as you go, dear ones. There is no grand plan in place and we cannot wait to see what you do next.

Enjoy the ride.

Magnetic DNA

Magic Hugs, #D031002 Baltimore, MD

Question:

It's been said in a number of places that the human DNA was at one point altered and that the existing strands we are aware of are fairly obvious. The part that has been altered is magnetic in nature and that it may be a very long time before we understand our DNA. Is that, in fact, a correct approach to this? And as Human Angels, are we upon the path?

The group:

In your language, yes. Yes, yes, yes. First, you have played the Game of Free Choice. You were brave enough to put these veils on, and when you first did, how many things did you walk into? It was quite humorous for us to watch. We picked you up whenever we could, yet you had the courage to play the Game of forgetfulness as to your own essence and who you were. And yes, you were taken over and yes, it was part of the overall collective Game of vibration. We thank you for playing the Game. And yes, part of what happened was they altered your DNA. Yes, they disconnected ten magnetic strands, they have always been magnetic. Again, we tell you, you have yet to learn to measure the subtle fields that will reveal these to you.

Currently you are trying to bounce electrons off these things to see the electrons pass right through, for they are magnetic in nature. But there are actually twelve strands of your DNA, all intertwined in the most beautiful spiral within a spiral. They are incredible to see and you will really see this in the years directly ahead, for it will be uncovered. And you will find much more about the DNA, for you believe it at this point to never change, but we tell you it does.

Every thought you have goes out, very much like a radio signal. It is collected by the outer sheath of the DNA itself and transmitted first into the magnetic strands of the DNA, which ever so slightly alters the DNA. In that process, every cell you have that replaces itself or grows within your body checks first with the DNA which are the blueprints, and decides exactly the attributes it is going to have. This is much the way you do in the first stage of life. That is the mind over matter process that puts you in control of your physiology. For the thoughts you think become part of your DNA and, therefore, become part of every cell in your body.

It used to be that every seven years, all the cells within your body would be replaced, with the exception of very few. That process is happening much faster, and you will uncover much of this. What do you need to do to reconnect the DNA strands? Exactly what you are doing. Yes, there are many courses you can take and activations. As in all modalities on your planet, the good news is that they all work. The bad news is, now you have to find out which ones work for you.

The more important answer to your unspoken question is: Why do they all work? Because you are the creators. If you believe in it, it works. Your field can temporarily intermingle with another and offer sympathetic vibrations. That is how one can help others heal. We tell you to bring the power within you. It is fine to believe in anything you want. There are no rules short of free choice. If you wish to call the door-knob there a higher power, and you believe it ... it will heal you. This does not mean you must always heal yourself. That is the reason so many healers are being called back in at his time. It is easier and more efficient to utilize each other.

Do not discount what we have said about the doorknob, dear ones. We have seen your Universe and we tell you, there are some very powerful doorknobs out there. When you see creations unfold or miracles happen, it is always a reflection of the person creating it. It is reflecting the same energy that you send. This was what was referred to in the Bible where it says, "Man was created in the image of God." Interesting to think they may be one and the same.

The DNA is activating and re-activating the strands. It was a very simple process at that time in your evolution to hide and disconnect the electrical signals from those portions of the DNA. That is now changing. Please understand that, from your perspective, it seems to be taking forever. You sit around and wonder, "When is something going to happen?"

From our perspective, this entire evolution is happening in the blink of an eye. You are evolving as human beings and as physical beings. Your own scientists will bear that out very soon. They are starting to see the beginnings of that evidence now. You see, in your energetic structures, things do not work the same. You are seeing it in your emotional structures; these are the connection between your ethereal being and your physical body, so you will feel things through emotion first. If it starts on the spiritual side and change is happening over there, you will feel the emotion of it. If it starts on the physical side from the other direction, you will feel the emotion of it. It is the connecting part.

Your DNA is now in the process of re-connecting. Although we cannot make a blanket statement and say 2.5 of those strands are already connected – which is what you would love to hear – we will tell you the process is well underway. And that, in fact, the next sixty years on your planet will complete the process as it stands now. Please understand that when we speak, we cannot tell the future. We can only tell where you are heading at the moment. To you, sixty years may seem like a very long time, but you have to understand, if you only live another ten years, the average life span will shoot to one hundred and twenty years. If you are sixty years old, you are only half way there.

Much is happening in the areas of physiology. The magic will be the blending of the physical and the metaphysical sciences. That is happening now in the area of physics, and some other areas you are starting to understand, such as the connection between the spirit and the body. You do, and as you honor that connection, the magic will start unfolding. Things that have been very elusive to you will become very clear. That is already in process and for that, we are so pleased.

We say thank you. Thank you for the work you are doing. Thank you for the courage to sound like you are "out there," because, if you did not have that courage, this would not be taking place. Many of you have been here planting seeds very deeply long before these words were popular. You are known as the Aboriginal Healers. This has enabled humans to awaken. Even the Keeper has only recently awakened because of the seeds you have planted.

For that, we all say thank you.

New Children & DNA

Wings Over Mu, #D032603 Kona, HI

Question:

The new children coming in have the DNA connected that was disconnected eons ago. Has that DNA been reconnected in these kids today?

The group:

The intent to reconnect is held within each and every one of you. There is not one of you here in the room who is working on only the original two strands. Not one of you here is working on less than eight strands of the twelve. Only a year ago, we told you in channel this was not possible, so you can see our excitement. You are moving at the speed of love. And it is faster than the speed of light. The children are being born with all twelve in place. Since they do not have anyone to model the usage of the other strands for them, most are not aware of the full uses they have awaiting. Watch the children.

Spiritual DNA

A Day of Rain, #057 Oostmalle, Belgium

Question:

Some months ago, there was an article in Time magazine about DNA and how some medical people were doing research concerning DNA. Apparently, they found that spiritual people have different DNA, like spiritually oriented people feeling unity with the cosmos. Did we get this DNA at birth or has it been modified during our lifetime?

The group:

It is actually both; your soul has evolved into this over many lifetimes, yet it was not actually given to you until birth. To the other question: "Or has it been modified during our lifetime?" the answer is yes. It is the natural evolution for all humans in all dimensions to evolve into spiritual beings. You are returning home. You are spirit pretending to be a human wearing a bubble of biology. Everything else is the illusion. It is the DNA itself that holds the illusion. DNA can change by thought, for your thought is what originally connects you with your Higher Self. That is the biggest challenge, for you have asked for spiritual communication and connection. You have asked to channel and to hear your own guides. As soon as the flow begins, you say, "Oh, I must be making that up," and you push it aside. We have said many times, in the days ahead, everyone will learn to connect in the way you call channeling.

DNA is a very magical part between your thought process and the physical being, the dense part of your being. Let us give you an analogy. There is a sheath around the DNA, almost like a sack. That sheath is magical. We believe it will not be long until your medical scientists start rewriting medical science. There is a tremendous amount of research currently in DNA, and they are beginning to understand and change their beliefs about it. Currently, some of the greatest identification on your planet is happening through DNA research. You are discovering that each person's DNA is always different, and therefore much greater than fingerprints. You are able to connect people with their DNA and identify them through their own DNA.

Your belief systems tell you that the DNA never changes, but we tell you, that is not true. DNA evolves, and you will find that to be true as you grow. The sheath around the DNA itself is like a radio receiver. It picks up signals, and integrates those signals into the DNA strand itself. What you know to be DNA - RNA stores the plans for all of your biology. It holds the imprints of the cellular memories. It holds the ideas of what each part of your body is going to be. It tells you how your feet are going to develop, how your brain is going to develop, how the different physical structures of your being are going to be. Now, the interesting part about it is, the trans-mitter of those waves is in the brain. That is why we tell you, if you can hold a pure thought for seven seconds, it is yours.

Now, previously, your DNA had to go through the entire process. If you scraped the back of your hand, you would literally uncover and kill cells on the outer layer of skin, and new cells would literally come up beneath and replace those cells you scraped off. In fact, other than some brain cells, the truth is, all the cells in your body up until recently have replaced themselves every seven years. So you literally were becoming what you have been thinking every seven years.

How long do you think it took for you to hold a thought to change your body? Seven years, for you changed the DNA, but the DNA had to get into the outer cells that actually make the difference. So it took up to seven years, but no more, for you are evolving. You are changing your own abilities to com-municate with your own being. Your Higher Self is actually connected more to your physical body than it has ever been. It no longer takes seven years. Currently, it takes about three and a half years for you to effect change. And, although it still takes about seven years to replace all the cells in your body, the truth is, those cells can now impregnate and change the other cells around it. So a sympathetic vibration is sent out by the new cells that realigns and reprograms the old cells. And they, too, begin changing.

The excitement is that, when you are Home, you can create everything in a split second. You can create anything you hold in your mind. It is not possible for humans to have that ability at this point, because you have not yet become masters of your thoughts. You do not know how to hold only the highest thoughts. You play with the negative, and you are attracted to drama. You love it. That is not wrong; it is just your human attribute. Therefore, it is necessary to have a time lag so you are basically protected from your own creative ability.

This is what makes you think you are not creators – basically that you do not see your own creations, you do not know you create the path beneath your feet before your foot hits it. But you do. And that is part of the fun of the veil. You are going to get Home and laugh hysterically about the veil. And you are going to say, "That was wonderful. I couldn't re-member anything. I could not even re-member that you and I had been brother and sister before. And I could not re-member any of the things I'd set up for myself."

It is happening at a much faster pace now than ever before. And that will be a joy. Not only for you, but for us to watch. We thank you for asking the question. Before we leave, there is one more thing you must know. Dear soul, on a personal level, you are a grand scientist and that goes back many, many, many lifetimes. You are here to watch some of the creations you personally have set into motion in the evolution of humanity. And we thank you for being here.

DREAMS

Creating the Healing Center

The Third Vibration, #047 Sturbridge, MA.

Question:

I thought I was following my dream and I hit a brick wall. I was doing everything to make things happen and I hit a brick wall. And now, I have been taking little steps and I'm just wondering if you see that it's building momentum somewhere I don't see yet?

The group:

It is not the dream that hit the brick wall; it is the interpretation of how you believe the dream was going to manifest that hit the brick wall. What happened was, you ran across a very strong resistance of energy. That is the easiest way we can put it. It is much easier to hit that brick wall and stop right there than it is to go on for several years misdirecting energy and finding yourself slowly drained and pinned into a corner through your own belief system.

Questioner:

Hmm. That makes sense.

The group:

So, first, bless the guidance of the brick wall for you know which direction not to go, do you not? Look for the passion.

Go back to the passion of the dream, not the interpretation of the dream. Go back to the feeling, to the spirit of the dream and what it would bring into your life.

There is a common dream we wish to speak of here as many Lightworkers have a very similar dream. Most find great resistance when they attempt to manifest the dream. You all have the dream at the center. You all have a dream of creating a place where people can go to find Home. Most interpret it to be an actual, physical building you are going to create your life from. It is a shared vision, Dear Ones, but it does not always translate into a physical place or an opportunity to create a physical center. That is an illustration for you. But yet, you all have the opportunities to interpret these differently, for you are not talking about your healing centers, per se, but about the center of your energy as someone who can create a space of Home for other people to experience. That is the dream, but your interpretation of it was what got you off-track. The dream was that you would create space for others to heal. Go back to the original dream of where that passion is and what was going to be given to you by creating that dream. Do not get discouraged or discard the dream; instead look for ways to interpret the feeling of the dream differently.

We know it is very difficult, for we do not live in the field of duality, so we do not have discouragement. We still do not understand it completely. The Keeper loves to laugh at us and say that someday, he is going to sit up here and laugh, while we are going to come down there and play the Game. We are sorry to disappoint him but that is not going to happen (laughter).

The reality is, you see similar visions because of a common interpretation, even as your dream lets you see people walking into your center. Find the feeling of what you get from that, and not the actual interpretation. Go back to the center of the feeling, and start the manifestation process from there. Yes, of course, some people will build centers successfully, and many of you are now thinking that is you. But keep in mind, a place for people of like mind to gather rarely brings that result because those of like mind all wish to create centers of their own. Let the essence of the dream fill your spirit, and look for other ways to manifest that same feeling and you will find the side doors opening. You think you are going down this hall here but, as you get toward the end of it, you are going to see another door that goes off to the side that you could not even see unless you went down there. You just went a little ways too far. No problem. Go back to the origin of it. Go back to the original idea. Find that unique piece you wanted to accomplish and to spread, and you will find a way to do this.

The White Robe

Lemurian Initiation, #D050503 Reno, NV.

Question:

Last night, I had a dream of you being cloaked in a white cloak. Then when Ronna channeled, she spoke of everybody having a light white cloak on. I just wondered if you could expound on that because it was such a very big part of my dream. (The questioner was attending a joint seminar we held with Ronna Herman who had channeled Archangel Michael just prior to this channel from the group.)

The group:

We think it quite interesting that so many are on the same channel. There was one time where the Keeper actually thought he would do a television show and he was going to call it "The Channel Channel." *(Note: this was prior to the VirtualLight Broadcast)* The interesting part is everybody could have been on the same channel.

The whiteness shows the purity of heart, the release of guilt in place of forgiveness. Dear one, you are the only one who can purify your own heart through forgiveness of yourself. That is the beauty. For only those who allow themselves to walk with full forgiveness of themselves can walk with the white robe and the purity of heart. That is necessary to walk to the next step. That is a critical part of releasing your limiting belief systems about yourselves.

You have been playing the Game with a veil on. You could not re-member who you were. Your greatest desire was to come in here, jump into this beautiful, physical body of yours, make mistakes and be confused. We tell you, you have been wildly successful! On the other side of the veil, those things you call mistakes are an opportunity for us to see God. Please, make good mistakes, and make lots of them. Allow yourselves to forgive yourselves. That is really where the purity of heart comes from. Then you are donned with the white robes.

EMPOWERMENT TOOLS

Balancing Male and Female

The Smile of Spiritual Confidence, #013, Edmonton, Alberta, Canada

Question:

Can you talk about balancing male and female energy?

The group:

We will simply say that the Keeper is very excited to hear the answer to this one as well, for the Keeper happens to think that women are very special. Women have held the energy imprint of creation, for they are the creators in the first place. Your biblical stories about Adam being the first man are not quite the way we see it. Taking the rib from Adam and creating Eve was a beautiful story and we are not quite sure that Adam ever got over that. But we will tell you, the first creation was woman. It was necessary to divide. You went through the second dimension. Each one of you has the opportunity to split off into one gender or the other for each lifetime. You choose that during the setup of your own life lessons. Yet the woman was the first creation and so she carried the creative energy into her own body which is what enables her to give birth – the greatest of creations.

The woman is the first creator, and man has been trying to catch up ever since. [laughter] We know you are in a male-dominated society. There have been very few women leaders in your world, but that is about to change. More importantly, however, is that you have been balancing the male and the feminine energy. The feminine energy will allow you to create even more than ever before. And the blend of the two is where the real magic is held.

One of the most exciting parts of pretending to be a human is when you combine and you come together in the act of what you call making love – what a special connection. For, in that moment, it allows your souls to blend together and re-unites the essence of who you are as a whole being. And it is a beautiful connection you make. That connection carries the vibrations from Home and holds the greatest creation energy a human can hold. There will come a time soon when you find new ways of expressing this energy and ways of focusing it as a tool of creation. It is easier than you now think but let us just say, even masturbation is a powerful tool of manifestation.

We tell you, as time goes forward, you will find the differences between male and female quite different. There were times on your Earth you do not re-member, but now the women are saying, "Yes, we are going to come back into power. We are going to awaken the goddess energy."

If you think back far enough, you know that women were once in the dominance also, and they made as much of a mess as the men did [laughter] but here you are. You will find the balance to be much more in accord than which gender is the dominant one, for dominance is what creates the problems and what you call war on your planet. The feminine creator energy is within each one of you, especially the males in rooms like these. Dear ones, you can change your world very quickly. When the Keeper and the Keeper's Keeper first began these seminars, they had less than ten percent males showing up at these seminars. Now they get close to forty. They are very excited about that. And we applaud you for balancing your energy.

Stretches in Marriage

The Third Vibration, #047 Sturbridge, MA.

Question:

One of my passions is taking care of children and I've started to do that. It's definitely not my husband's. He doesn't like it and resents it, which takes away from it a little bit.

The group:

You will have difficulties with him at this point because he is very intolerant. Because of his own mis-direction of energy, it is very difficult for him to have any extra tolerances at that point. All of his energy goes into dealing with his own mis-direction of energy. To have any strains on his energy from the outside is difficult and you will probably see an overreaction.

Question:

But I can still keep doing it?

The group:

We will not give you a simple yes or no, because that would take your power from you. That is a human challenge. We are simply here to reflect both sides for you to make your own decisions. All of it is okay. Find your happiness and stay with it. Share it with him; build it with him. Help him build on his successes. Empower him in every way you can to find the unique things he is good at and re-mind him of those things. Re-mind him of the things that light up his eyes and watch the spirit return. That is where the magic is.

Empowering Views from the Spirit

The Third Vibration, #047 Sturbridge, MA.

Question:

Thank you for helping me to re-member my passion. When I came down from the stage, I felt a bolt of electro-magnetic energy run through my body and it's here now. I feel I'm made of electricity. I'm just so full of this current, so powerful and it feels really good. I almost don't know what to make of it, but it feels tremendous.

The group:

You need not make anything of it. You have earned it, enjoy it.

Question:

I am. I have had a great healing here today. A very deep healing. I need to live in my passion all the time, which I haven't been doing. And I've had a pattern over this lifetime of holding back, a reluctance, even here, and I wonder how can I let go of that and stand fully in the light for myself.

The group:

We would love to give you a simple answer. The Keeper has a little magic wand that someone gave him, and he would love to tap you on the shoulder and just have you shine that light for the rest of your life, but he put it in a drawer some-where and has not been able to find it for several months (laughter). But, let us reflect a different view. You typically see yourself from the inside out. Those in this room see you from the outside in. so let us show you what that looks like. All day yesterday, you were tentative. You were doing everything you could, wondering if you fit in. You were enjoying yourself, giving of yourself. You were doing everything you could to nurture those around you but to actually receive all the energy for yourself and let it shine fully through you was very difficult for you. But somewhere in the late afternoon, evening time, it completely overwhelmed you and it beamed right through you. You allowed your own energy to manifest in the room. Then this morning, when you came into this room, those here will tell you, you were beaming a smile that was lighting and warming the entire room. Had you done this yesterday, everyone would have been a little more comfortable, for we understand that it was cold in here (laughter, as there had been a problem with the heat the previous day). And yet you felt as if the beam was somehow an intrusion into their world. You are so sensitive about others feelings that you often hold back your true gifts. You are afraid to beam too much energy out because you know it affects other people. But what you do not know is that it fed everyone in this room. You assume others have the same sensitivity and boundary issues you do. When you let that pure full energy of love come through you without attachment, thought or understanding, or having to understand any of it, you are beautiful beyond description. And everyone who gazes on you from the outside in is fed and becomes more, from having seen that smile of yours. Just let it go.

Are there going to be times when you cannot do it? Of course there are, for you are human. Are there times when you are going to feel pain? Of course there are; we guarantee it. But the more you can beam that energy, the more you become on purpose in everything you do. There are healers who heal in many different ways, some with their hands, some with their words, some with their music and their vibration. There are healers who heal with herbs, with drugs, with any number of different energy forms. Then there are the healers who heal with their smile. Give your gift. Let it flow through you. There you go. (as the tears came.)

Question:

It feels so good.

The group:

Thank you for manifesting Home on Earth.

Chocolate = Ascension Food

Magic Hugs, #D031302, Baltimore MD.

Question:

You explained about sex on the other side. You explained about always being with us, so the next important – or maybe frivolous – question is, is there chocolate or its equivalent on the other side?

The group:

You expect a humorous answer, but we have a very serious one for you. Yes, there is. Actually, we had to say that for the Keeper, for it opens the synaptic pathways of the brain and releases what you call endorphins. Your scientists love to label things so we go along with that temporarily.

There is a blending of the metaphysical and physical sciences that leads to an understanding of bringing the magic back to all of it. But, in the meantime, what you experience in those times is very similar to the vibrations of Home. That is why so many Lightworkers seem to love chocolate. No, it is not a prerequisite to being a Lightworker, but it is one of the fun parts.

You have learned to do this with your own energy. The ingredients in chocolate trigger a chemical reaction within your body that sets about your own personal brand of euphoria. It actually opens the heart chakra for most. That is why you give chocolate for Valentine's Day; it is the closest to the love feeling that can be replicated outside of the love experience. So, in a way, yes there is chocolate here at Home, and we live in it all the time.

Enjoy the ride, dear ones. We tell you, you have such experiences, for so many of you have experienced what you have called struggles. What you do not re-member is, when you get Home, we are going to ask you, "Did you play your passion? Did you dance among the dance? Did you play life?" And some of the grandest, most wonderful experiences you will re-member about the human condition are the pain and struggles. For even though it may be bittersweet, quite distressing and what you may call "negative," it is very human. And when you come Home, you will re-member that it was such a joy, so fear it not. When you take a bite of the "Home in a box," think of us with a smile, for we will validate what you have always known – chocolate is Ascension food. We thank you for asking the question.

Feels Like a Rock

Clan of the Bright Eyes, #037, Baltimore Md.

Question:

Whenever we do this work, other people say they see things. I see nothing. Why?

The group:

The Keeper had a very similar question, as many times he has been told there were entities behind him and different colored lights and all the changes he has in his auric field. He would love to see them, and he always says, "Yes, I hear that a lot. That is wonderful. Thank you for that." And people come up to him and say, "Do you see those entities on her shoulder over there?" and he nods his head and says, "Yes that's very nice." But he doesn't really see them. People bring him their favorite crystals that have been with them to Machu Picchu, Sedona, the Great Wall of China, and all the sacred spots of the Earth, and they ask, "What do you feel?" He says, "It feels very, very nice," but to him, it feels like a rock.

Yet he is a very high vibration. Those are simply not his gifts. Everyone has unique vibrational resonance, so there are certain things you will resonate with and certain things you will not. So please understand, many of the things many people typically feel, some of you will not feel any of them. It does not mean you are not moving vibrationally; it means you have a unique resonance that will become more valuable elsewhere when you discover it. It also means you have a unique gift waiting somewhere. Enjoy the journey.

Carrying More Light in the Body

Reflectors of the Light, #051 St. Louis, MO.

Question:

As we reflect light and love back to other beings, and at times receive fear and anger reflecting back to ourselves, what's the best way for us to stand in that level of energy in integrity and love and continue to do the work that is so much needed at this time?

The group:

There is no best way we can offer. There is only one key we can offer with all of this, and we have offered it over and over again – find your passion. Find that place where you vibrate the highest and allow yourself to be in it as often as possible without judgment.

You have been studying the angels. There are those of you who talk to the angels and have learned how to do processes, therapies and healing modalities around angels. Your fascination with that ethereal form is because you are moving back in that direction.

In the meantime, you will have this wonderful push/pull love/hate relationship with the physical body. That is part of why it is very difficult for some to release or to move forward and yet, as a whole, all of humanity is already carrying more light and beginning to adjust the physical body as a result.

You will find evolutionary changes on a grand scale that are even recorded in your medical sciences over the next few years. They are underway now, but it takes time for you to record them, assimilate them and finally publish them in your medical journals. But it is underway now and you will see evolutionary changes like never before. It will, at first, be attributed to consciousness. You will find that people began losing weight on your planet because weight loss becomes popular. That is what your scientists will say and yet there will be the push/pull. There will be the times when people will start moving in that direction and then jump way back because grounding is beautiful and the body resists a loss of connection with the Earth.

So, as you move into ethereal form, there will be resistances from the body. But as a whole, you are already carrying more light energy than you ever have before and that will have definite long-term evolutionary changes on the physical body.

The long term, the large picture of that is that it will not be very long before you are in ethereal form. How long is that? We are not able to say. We would love to say it would easily be within your lifetimes. At current rates, that is not the case, but you have taken many lifetimes.

Grounding

Reflectors of the Light, #051, St. Louis, MO.

Question:

In the work I do, I have come to understand it is very important to be grounded in order to function well on the Earth. In metaphysical circles, a lot of people like to leave their body and really aren't fully present. Could you explain to me the benefits of being grounded versus not being grounded? Are there benefits to not being grounded?

The group:

You are asking us to reflect something to you that is not possible for us to reflect because there are benefits of both. You will have a tendency in a field of duality of seeing one thing being better than the other. Is one good or is one bad? That is simply not the case, so it is not possible for us to say this is necessary or that is necessary. Having said that, let us speak to you specifically about the Clan of Reflectors of Light we have just mentioned. They must be grounded because it is not possible to reflect light unless you are grounded. That has been your calling, and we thank you for holding that space and energy, not only for other people but for us.

Missing My Inner Child

Earth Changes, #054 Kona, Hi.

Question:

My question is, I'm one of those many souls who stifled my inner child to take care of younger souls, and now I'm having a difficult time remembering that inner child. I believe now that the inner child will help my ascension, so what can I do to access my inner child that doesn't seem so painful on a daily basis?

The group:

Dear one, there is no growth without pain. It is misery that is optional. Staying in the pain is what humans have a tendency to do, so we ask you to simply experience it. If you understand that, when you were in your first stage of life, the planning stage, you asked this person to be mom and this person to be your first lover in high school, and this person over here to break your heart for the first time. The difficulties you have had, you set up originally so you would have the knowledge you hold right now. Now please understand also, a truth unshared is not yet a truth so hold that energy and knowledge of what it takes for you to understand the truth of the beauty of the inner child, and how that will heal you. The moment you step into that, you are the teacher. That is the way you think.

If we were to give you a little box right now, you would look at that box. Your first thought would be to wonder what you could use it for. Once you found a use, you would close it and set it on a table. Your second thought would be, "How am I going to teach somebody else?" That is the way you are wired. You are a teacher. You simply have not allowed yourself to step into the role as of yet, but you are right on the verge and we are right behind you. Along with eight million or so other angels on this planet now awakening. [This channel was presented on the beach in Kona, Hawaii and at that moment, a very brisk wind blew through, cooled everyone and stopped.] The wind you feel now is not coming off the ocean; it is the flapping of our wings in applause. Espavo.

Reverse Eyes and Emotion

Earth Changes, #054 Kona, Hi.

Question:

I have a question about emotions. I have quite a lot. Sometimes I know it is for releasing tension. Most of the time, I actually have a knowing of why it is, but can you tell me something more about it? Why am I this emotional?

The group:

In the beginning, the Keeper had the same problem. As we began coming through him, we overwhelmed him with emotion. It is important to know the flow of spiritual energy through the body. The Higher Self is connected directly to your imagination. That is the reason why most of you do not think you channel. It always feels like you are making it up. Because of this natural mistrust of your own creative flow, it is necessary to activate the flow of spiritual energy to make sure it gets through. That activation can only take place in the heart. The imagination can only be activated by emotion. Many people have told the Keeper they cried when they read one of the books. That is normal and we also share with you that he was crying when he wrote them. Then he began to speak our messages out loud. The challenge with that was, many times, he was in the process of using his vocal cords and the first thing that happens was that he would shut off his breathing tube and close up as he felt our love, so instead of speaking beautifully as he does now, all he could do in the beginning was to squeak his way through. Very few people really understood the words at first. He wondered if he would ever be able to do his work in a public forum.

One day, he learned from someone how he could still have those emotions and breathe through his mouth instead of his nose. It has helped him greatly to still be able to feel the love in a very personal way and still keep him in balance enough to get the message through. To this day, you will often see him crying while talking. We tell you this story because he had to learn human tools to openly work with spirit. There are many human tools for enjoying emotions while not being controlled by them. At one point, the Keeper asked when the tears would stop and not hamper him any more. We told him we hoped never. For you see, the new humanity has something we call reverse eyes. You do not cry when you feel pain. You do not cry when you are hurt. You cry when you experience something beautiful. You cry when your heart opens, and it does not mean that it needs to be open more or that you are crying because it is rusty, like old hinges have to be worked out. That is not the case. You cry because you feel Home. That is your own Higher Self connecting and flowing love through you. Own the tears. Know they are a blessing. They are a beauty from your own Higher Self that you will not lose. And we promise we will not let him lose them either.

Lifting the Veil

Human Angel Tools, #034 Elspleet, Holland.

Question:

Hello. I have been through a rough period before I came here and it is not the first time. I sometimes find it very hard to live and to see myself. Now I feel so good this week. I feel empowered and I am very happy, and I am going home and I am scared. I hope you can lift the veil a little bit for me and show me a little bit about myself and the gift I have to give to myself and also to others.

The group:

How about taking Home home with you? The greatest of all illusions on the Gameboard is the veil. It is what allows the Game to take place and to accomplish the task of defining god. It is what makes you think you are a human. Dear one, you are a spirit pretending to be a human, and the veil has been quite successful. Yes, the courses we design are all aimed at creating Home and helping you to re-member your true nature. We wish to tell you, even though it is a fear of yours, you are forever changed. Your life is in motion and things will now be different.

You came here wondering if you were going to stay. [tears] You are wondering if you are able to do the contracts you have set out for yourself. Believe us when we tell you there is no right or wrong about what you choose. You are loved beyond your understanding. But also know, you already have exceeded your highest hope for this incarnation. You have done very well, dear one, and if you return Home, you will be celebrated as a hero. And if you decide to stay, all of humanity will benefit from your passion. If you stay, you must reactivate your spirit within the bubble of biology. You have done that this week. Now that your spirit has been activated, there is only to change the habits you have developed.

Because you came in with such special gifts, you also have special wiring. We tell you, when you are not in control of your own life, your own wiring puts on a pair of dark glasses. From that point, you see everything through a filter that keeps you from seeing yourself. Whatever you look at, the hope is hard to see. Yet, when you do find those little rays of hope, when you do find that one piece of it, you can bring it inside and amplify it out in areas you have never seen before.

You have spent much of your life in self-defense mode, trying to protect yourself from all the things that are coming in. As difficult as that sounds, we will offer you a suggestion. Open up and let it all in. Is it going to hurt? Yes, probably. Are there going to be tears? We can pretty much guarantee that. Instead of trying to protect yourself, just let it in. Allow yourself to be totally open and vulnerable, for you will find a new strength that you are unaccustomed to using. What will happen is, there will always be the tears, for that is how you process things, yet the tears will be used for different things now. Tears are now nothing more than "life lubricant."

Many of you cry when you are lonely or sad. Many of you cry because you cannot re-member Home and yet we tell you, there is another wiring that can also be done in the physical body. The Keeper has reverse eyes. He does not cry when he is sad but when he sees something beautiful, and he is crying right now. Can you accept that beauty? The beauty he is see-ing is yours. You are a unique spark, and your light will bridge the gap for many people. Many people will touch the heart that touches yours. And when you do decide to come Home, you will be welcomed Home with a hero's welcome beyond description. Enjoy your choice. Espavo.

Feel the Fear

Angela's Broken Wing, #D6301 San Diego, CA.

Question:

I have known for some time that my passion is to teach. What I have not known is when, how or where. Now I have come up with a plan within the last year or so, and the more I think of it, the more clearly it comes to me. I have even gone so far as to give it a name. And this plan entails starting a crusade nationwide starting with the high schools in our country and taking it across the nation. But I'm afraid. I get so far and then I just get petrified. I have all these excuses why I shouldn't step forth and do it, not knowing whether it's my ego or something else I should be doing. I would like to have your input if I may please.

The group:

You stood at the edge of the valley. You looked out at the city below. You knew this was one of four cities in the immediate area and you saw the people running up the hill. Everyone was trying to reach higher ground as the waters came in. You looked to the sky and said, "Why? What have we done that was so horrible?" And that energy was permanently stamped in your psyche. You asked to carry it, for you made a commitment that day. And it was easy to carry that commitment in lifetimes after lifetimes – to know you had some higher purpose that was to come. But the day it started to come about set off the fear: "What if I do it wrong? What if I am not up to it? What if I do not step when I am supposed to step?"

Feel the fear, dear one, for the fear is your friend. The fear is the illusion of the vacuum you have purposely carried within yourself. Wear it proudly as a badge. Use it to check your own energy, to check your ego, and then step forward. Feel the fear and then take confident action. You have come to help others. Make your crusade a quiet one or it will not take place. You will be the quiet teacher, the gentle healer who speaks when the opportunity arises. Fear it not. You will reach many hearts.

You have a specific contract in the next two years to make contact with six individuals on the planet who have the same dream. No, you will not form a partnership with these six people; you will simply come into contact with them. That is part of what you felt is your purpose. That is part of why you are here, part of what you have chosen to do. Even though you may never know who these people are, by the time you have reached the sixth person, you will have your answers. Your dream is becoming clear because you are being led down a path. Your own higher self is opening the doors and creating the circumstances that open this for you.

Thank you for having the courage to walk it. You are doing well. Trust your own guidance. Yet please, do not be so attached to this path that you do not see the side doors. For we tell you, you have many of those on the road ahead. There are many opportunities when you see what is inside a room and you choose the path that gets you to that room exactly. You come upon the door to that room, you see the engraving upon the door and you say, "That is where I want to go."

So you go to school to earn a diploma to get in there, or you buy the key, or you pick the lock, and you walk in the door boldly and say, "I am finally here." Then you look around and say, "That is not what I wanted." All we ask you to do is to be patient, for if you look closely, you will see, leading off the room, there are doors you would not have seen had you not gone into the room. Those are the magic doors. Those are the doors that will open to your dream.

Teach when asked to. Speak when the moment arises for you to be heard, because there have been many crusades on planet Earth and most have not ended very well. All were meant in the highest intent from a heart space. Do not be evangelical and you will see your teaching abilities, for you will reach many. Millions of hearts will be touched by a single touch of an angel. Thank you for feeling the fear. Thank you for walking past it far enough to be here. For in looking around the room, there are many of your original spiritual family who will now give you the courage to walk past that. Take that with you as you leave here. You will see the doors open.

Human Angel

In the Beginning, #003 Cortez, CO.

Question:

I want to know about us being teachers. How do we recognize the people who will come to us and need our help? And is it possible that we could fail and not be able to be the angel and help the people we want to help?

The group:

Such a beautiful question. Thank you for asking it. Yes, of course it is possible that you would fail. Is that not wonderful? Yet it is not your responsibility to judge yourself as failure or success. Your responsibility is not whether your gift as a Human Angel is accepted or utilized; it is only the opportunity to give it that you are looking for. Give your gifts and you will be fulfilled as a human. To do that, you must release all attachment to the outcome. So how do you tell whether the beggar on the street is asking you for a dollar to use for alcohol, or whether he is going to use it to feed his family? We say it makes no difference, as the gift belongs to the giver.

Are you actually enabling him and making things worse by giving it to him. We tell you, there is an easy way to answer that: Does it add to your energy or does it take from you? The only thing we ask you to do is to search your heart, for there will be many times when you will say, "No, thank you." And you will not always know why.

You will know in your heart if this is an opportunity to be a Human Angel. The expression of love in any form, the gift belongs to the giver, not the recipient. So, allow yourself to be placed at the perfect juncture of time and space where you can make a difference in another's life. Once the gift has been given, release your attachment. Oh, can you imagine the mess we would all be in if we angels took responsibility for all of your human actions? Oh, boy. Fortunately the G-word does not exist on our side of the veil and we hope it will soon not exist on yours. The G-word, for those of you who do not know, is "guilt" – the most useless human emotion you have in the higher vibrations of the New Planet Earth. We simply say, to release it, either deal with the situation or forgive yourself and let it go. If there is something you can do about it, do it. If there is not, lose the guilt. As an angel, it is not possible to carry guilt, for it will bring you down very quickly. Take the actions and have fun. Play at it and enjoy yourself.

Why Now?

Cosmic Winks, #059, Mt. Charleston, NV.

Question:

I've been on a spiritual path for about thirty years after an awakening experience, and I study just about everything there is. About a year ago, I discovered you, the group. I discovered a new world I didn't know existed. Why so late? Why are you keeping me so dumb all these years when I was searching diligently. Why now? Can you give me some insight into that?

The group:

That is such an excellent question. Yes, we can, for it is important that you understand that timing is very important. We worked with the Keeper before. He believes he was a contractor until we came into his life but the reality is, we have worked with him twelve lifetimes in a similar way. This is the twelfth, and during those eleven other lifetimes, he actually carried our message in different ways. Like most of you hearing these words, you have all planted seed-thoughts that you believed never sprouted. In fact, even when we began bringing the messages through him, it was still not ready to be heard. Only in very recent times are these seed-thoughts finding fertile ground.

A collective vibration of humanity had to be reached. If you can imagine trying to teach Reiki to people one hundred years ago, you can understand that the collective vibration of humanity back then would not have supported it. The seed-thoughts could not sprout in the collective. And you probably would have been locked up in a straight jacket. At that time, people feared things they did not understand, more so than they do today for the collective vibration of humanity is rapidly rising. Since time is an illusion that does not exist at Home, the timing of the rise of humanity was like attempting to hit a moving target, That is why the Keeper has, as many of you have, been here as a teacher before.

However, it is not coming out just through the Keeper. It is coming out through others, for there is a new level of empowerment he calls spirituality spreading through all humanity, one heart at a time. It is an awakening process, a quickening. Many things had to be in order for that to happen. Many people had to take their contracts. Many people had to walk into their fears in order to plant seeds that would open the door for this, so the collective vibration of humanity could reach this level.

One of those things was called an "aboriginal healer," which you are. An aboriginal healer means an original healer. And you came in with information, with ideas, with concepts you were searching for. You became a professional seeker about thirty years ago. You looked everywhere, took every course, read every book you could, trying to find that validation for what you knew in your heart, for you carried it yourself. And even in that seeking, you were teaching people and planting those seeds, dear one. It would not be possible for us to be here had you not done your job. And now you look around and see a whole new level you resonate with, and you think it is new and wonderful, and you cannot wait to find out more and to play in this area. You do not even know you helped start it all. And we thank you, Grand Master of Time. And we tell you your grandmother is very proud of you, for she held the energy before you did. And she is right over your shoulder. [His smile filled the room.]

Original Spiritual Family

Dragonfly, #69 Las Vegas, NV.

Question:

I want to know my relationship to the Keeper and why my work and teaching, especially with group dynamics, has paralleled his when I never met him before.

The group:

Very interesting question. We will tell you a little bit about it. There are certain families that the Keeper is still very unclear about, so when he is asked the question, he does not always have the answers for this. When we talk about original spiritual family, his thoughts immediately go back to the Original Five Hundred souls that began physical life on Earth, and that is not always the case. We tell you, in Heaven, what you perceive as archangels are actually Angelic Purpose. In other words, each one of those beings you call archangels, each label you have given, each personality you have imposed on us in Heaven, allows us to bring through that one personality, an Angelic Purpose. Michael is about Truth, for instance. So, it is about finding and grasping a higher truth. There are different archangels for different purposes, and all those souls in Heaven who want to work in this specific purpose become part of that Family. It does not also mean they may not also become part of another family at the same time. Your humanness would have you believe you can only be of one family much like you believe you can only love one person. Your family of purpose for several lifetimes has been the same family as the Keeper. That, plus the time you were best friends, brings memories back to you of times when you both taught together. In those times, you attempted to create a space to teach true empowerment. And we tell you, that is and was not an easy concept to teach. With true empowerment comes a level of responsibility that most humans are not accustomed to taking. Humans are looking for the shortcut. It is part of your nature as energy beings, for energy always follows the path of least resistance. Now, we are not telling you that you need to find the most difficult road. That is not the case. But we tell you, you have come in with a specific purpose and to work with a higher level of true empowerment means taking responsibility for your reality, every step of every day. That is what you have worked with together with the Keeper.

Now, if you wish, we can go back in and tell you there was a time when you and the Keeper were cousins and you had a strong connection. You fought as children and got to be friends as adults. And were very supportive of each other. There was another time when the Keeper and you had played the Game of business together and you did not do really well but you learned a lot from each other and it was wonderful (laughter). And you had a good time but you did not call it a success because the business ended up failing. But the reality is, the Game was in motion and none of the outcomes made a difference. What makes a difference is that you resonate with the concepts of true empowerment and stepped into your role as a teacher very much like the Keeper. The Game of Human Angel is simple. Tag, you are it. Pass it on.

Mastering Life

Dragonfly, #60 Las Vegas, NV.

Question:

My main issue is trying to overcome my childhood with my mother. I've been dealing with that my whole life. I want to be a Lightworker and wonder what you see as my future.

The group:

Your future is wondrous for it is where you wish to go. It is what you allow yourself to have. That is where it is. Please understand, you are in complete charge at every moment of your reality. Your happiness, your future, your every step of every day is determined by what you will allow yourself to have and what energy you allow to flow through you. It sounds very simple and it is, but it is not easy. If it were easy, everyone would want to be a human.

If you can imagine you have energy flowing through you every day, you would say, "Oh, I will just open myself up completely and let all the energy flow through me." But that is not possible, for that would wash all of you away at some point. So it is about holding the essence of who you are, while allowing as much as possible of that to come through you.

Therefore, people choose different levels of what you term "status in the community." They choose different levels of abundance where they feel comfortable. All levels of economics have challenges and none is better than the others. As you know, a higher economic status is not better than a lower one. Just understand, your own belief systems and those energy stamps you carry are what determine what level you will choose to live your life.

We tell you, we have worked very, very hard to get you here (audience laughter), but as much as we would like to take credit for it, you are the one who heard the call and responded. You are the one who said, "I do not know why I am going but I know I am just supposed to be there."

And had you not done that, nothing would be changed in your life path as it now is. But as it is, everything is up in the air right now. You are the juggler who managed to get all five balls in the air at once. You are waiting for the first ball to drop, having no idea what you will do with it. You are not returning the same person you were, and that is why you had to be here. All change leads to something better. Part of you has always wondered what it is, for you have looked around the room and have seen the people who deal with the cards. You have seen the people who deal with the stars and all these other modalities of tuning forks and Reiki. But you just have not felt you are a part of that. You have felt it is great that all of those modalities are available, yet there is more. You are the teachers who dare to bring in the other pieces and just being who you are is going to turn you into a tremendous teacher in the near future.

The short answer to your question is, once you begin reaching levels of mastery of your own life lesson, you will begin to teach. The students will just show up. Now, since the life lesson was catalyzed and activated by your mother, it would make sense to know the role she played in your life. You are closer than you think, as you are frustrated with the pattern in your life. That is reason enough to master it now, and that process has already begun.

Now, we tell you this. Your mother's energy is all around you, and there will come a time when you will thank her for the role she played, for it will allow you to be more of the teacher than you ever imagined. In fact, those difficulties you had in childhood are not to be erased. Those are your credentials for being the teacher and the healer you are. And it will not completely fit into the modalities of those around you. It will be your modality. And you will find a way to spread those seed-thoughts of light, even if it is doing nothing more than offering people hope. When you give hope to another, you give permission for them to create. And that is what you are here to do, to work with, and that is why you came.

We tell you now, when you leave here, it will be confusing, for you will return to your daily life a different person and you will ask, "Okay, how can I assimilate any of this? Was that just a dream?" You will try to push it away at one point, for that is just the normal process of how you assimilate things. But it won't go away. It is who you are and the cosmic joke is that you think you are new at this (audience laughter). You are not new. You have been the grand wizard so many times with the powers of Merlin that it is very difficult to keep that veil in place, but we have been trying very hard and, so far, have been successful. For, if you pulled the veil aside and saw the opportunities of what you have already brought to these beings here called humans and the planet itself, it would not allow you to play the Game of being humble and having the challenges in your childhood you have had. That is what gives you your credentials to be the healer and the teacher you are. We thank you for listening.

Being the Bridge

The Age of E., #017 Mt Shasta CA.

Question:

I understand that as I go forward from here, one of my primary tasks is to help in the bridge-building between the illusion and the reality of living in the bubble of biology. Is there any specific tool or phrase you can give me that will help me to be clearer in communicating that to others?

The group:

Three words: from the heart. It is the way we asked the Keeper to speak in the very beginning, for he came from a whole field where he thought things through and lived in his head quite often. He was concerned, much as you are, that he was being tapped on the shoulder and given some very important information which he wanted to be sure got out there, but he did not know how to go about it. And, of course, he believed he needed credentials. He was surprised when we told him he had credentials. We told him to speak from the heart. For in speaking from the heart, you can tell no lies. You cannot misdirect the energy and more importantly, when you speak from the heart, everyone sees the real you when they see their heart in yours. Yes, the key is to allow yourself to be vulnerable enough to allow your heart to be seen.

You will be the bridge dear, one. You know it in your own heart and we can only validate that knowing. The phrase you seek has already been given to you. Enjoy the ride.

Placing Yourself First

The Age of E., #017 Mt Shasta CA.

Question:

I've been moved to start writing down the things I know work to help direct parents with their children and it seems to be flowing pretty well. I was just wondering if you have any extra direction for me with that.

The group:

What we ask to do at this point is to reflect on something you learned last night. When you take time for you, you give the greatest gift to those around you. If you teach children that, they will be way ahead of the Game. Since all children learn much more from example than from teachings, it is easy to see that the best teachers are those going through growth experiences themselves and being honest about it. Sharing your life with your children can be the powerful tool you can use to teach them. Often parents try to hide their life challenges as to not upset the children. For instance, the paradigm used to be that two people who fell out of love would stay together for the sake of the children. What that will produce now is a lot of children who had no idea of what a relationship was really about. Since they had grown up in an environment of neutrality and lack of sexual energy, they will quickly grow into adults who have difficulty with commitment and physical intimacy. If you simply pretend that all children are what you call psychic and can see everything, the more you can share with them about who you really are, and the more they will learn and respect you.

We thank you. You have been moved many times to do exactly what you are now doing. We thank you for taking pen in hand and beginning the process. Espavo.

Multidimensional

The Age of E., #017 Mt Shasta CA.

Question:

(*Note from Steve:* The day before, all of us at the ESPAVO conference had a multidimensional experience during a channel in a valley on Mt Shasta.)

I know I am a multidimensional being. I had certain experiences and yesterday, I was amazed at the fact that I am multidimensional. With quite a lot of people around, I noticed I'm connected with them. Do you have any information for me that will give me a bit more insight for it?

The group:

We will do our best to describe a phenomenon that may frustrate many of you, so we would like to tell you about it before it does. As these portals are beginning to open on your planet, people will begin to have mystical experiences. They will tell you about all these wonderful things and you will be the wide-eyed child who will just sparkle when you hear these things, and yet you may not experience them yourself.

Question:

That's frustrating

The group:

Yesterday on the mountain, when they all walked into the valley and disappeared into another dimension of time and space, you were the one who watched it all from the top of the mountain. You bi-located without being consciously aware of it. You saw them in the valley when they disappeared to everyone else because you are the multidimensional being who works on both sides with no difficulty. You have carried this gift, dear one, for a long time. Keeping track of what dimension you are in at any moment has been your greatest difficulty. Fortunately you found your partner who has the ability to balance your energy and ground you. When you were seven years old, you shut it off entirely. Someone went into fear around that gift and asked you to quiet it down, so you hid it from yourself, but it did not go away.

As more people are experiencing phenomena such as time holes, where someone loses their keys in a time hole, you are the one who can reach in and get them. Please understand, you are leading the way for the Crystal Children, for that is a crystalline attribute you carry, for you are a Crystal Child. And although you do not have all the attributes of a Crystal Child, you will open the door and make it safe for those children coming in. There could be tremendous fear as they come in, but people like you will make the planet safe for the Crystal Children.

So, we ask you to please, be an inter-dimensional being and be the best one you can be, for you are gifted beyond your knowledge.

Joy

Masters of the Gameboard, #D101302 Oostmalle, Belgium

Question:

How do I get to enjoy the Game?

The group:

You have no idea who you are, do you? You have no idea
as to the magnitude of the implications of the question you
just asked or the effect it has on humanity. We see you in a
different light than you see yourselves, and what you have just
uttered are words of a master, someone who is a "last timer."
Not only is this a last timer who did all the mastery lessons
and did not have to come back, but chose to come back one
more time just in case she could make a difference.

You have come to place seeds of light in very difficult
places and you have already done everything you set out to
do. Do you see the honor we have for you as you stand here
asking, "What can I now do? What can I do next?"

You have no idea what that feels like to us, for you can
come Home any time you want. You have been close and any
time you choose to come Home, you will be greeted with a
hero's welcome. And here you sit here asking, "What can I do
now?" You can smile. Amidst the greatest of difficulties or
the most difficult negotiations, you can smile. You can find
an inner peace at a time of most difficult misunderstandings
and you can just smile for, in that moment, you will send the
light of Home straight from your heart.

It is not about the looks of your smile, for you can do it in
a dark room because you carry the energy of Home. You have
already planted very deep seeds in very important places and
you find yourself in situations where you are wondering what
to do next. If you are wondering whether to stay here and
make a difference, or if you are going to be able to be heard
as you slip in some of your pieces of your truth, all you need
to do is smile for it is contagious. When you smile into one
another, as Human Angels, you have the gift of this. When
you just smile, you emit the energy of the love of Home, for

you carry it in your own cellular memories. And if you touch any person on the planet with that love, they will re-member it, and even if they walk off grumbling and huffing, stuck in their own dramas, you will have planted important seeds that will sprout later on, even in the most difficult times.

We thank you for the work you have done, for having the courage to ask, "What can I do now?" You can hold the love of Home in your heart and you can smile. Whether you are in the Parliament or the grocery store, you will make a difference with that smile. Carry it well. You have been entrusted with an important job, so do not forget to smile.

Passion

Grace, #D101202, Tiendeveen, Holland

Question:

Yes, I am thankful to be here and it is great to meet you. For many years, I thought my passion was guitar playing, but I still can't play that well so I don't think it's the thing for me. The question is, how does one know what their passion is?

The group:

Such a wonderful question, for you are not the only one who has had that question. In fact, you have just asked for six more. So let us address that, because once again, your first thoughts were, if I enjoy the guitar, it must be my passion, yet I don't play well so how can that be? Dear ones, it is not important for you make a living at your passion. For when you move fully into your passion, you will find yourself supported from many different areas. Once you begin to move in the direction of your passion, you create a force behind you that helps you steer into it. You may find you have raised your vibration to a point where you have to lower it every day to go to work. And you may say, "If only I can move into my passion; if only I was good enough to play my guitar, then I could quit my job and go around the world playing guitar, and I would be in my passion then." We tell you, you would only break strings, for that would not be your true passion. That is thinking of your passion, not being immersed in it.

First of all, we ask you to pull the camera back for the larger picture, take your vision off of only the guitar, and simply call it music for now. And if you dare to pull the camera back even more, we tell you, dear one, that you are a vibrational healer. You have an understanding of vibration that you equate to the form of music. There is more than one way to use that, but none of them are necessary to make a living at. Even if all you do is to play the guitar once a week and it brings you joy, then you are in your passion and it changes the energy of everything around it. When you experience only five minutes of that passion, it changes your entire day. So, if all you are able to do is experience your passion for five minutes each week, you will shift your entire life.

If we can help you remove this from the timeline, you can see it is not about moving into your passion as much as moving in the direction of your passion. To move ahead in the new energy, it will be really helpful to move from destination consciousness to journey consciousness. It is not about what you achieve, but about the experience of achieving it.

All we ask you to do is experience that which brings you joy. You are not accustomed to doing that. In your grandparents' day, the work paradigm was only two words – work hard. Then in your parents' day, they dared to changed it to work smart. Today on the New Earth, the work paradigm is once again only two words: work passionately. Are you still using the old paradigms? Has it worked for you? It did for your parents and your grandparents, but you are not living in the same vibrational range as they were. On this level, you must rethink all paradigms, including your work paradigm. Your success on the New Planet Earth will be directly proportionate to the amount of passion and joy you can experience on a daily basis. More importantly, experience passion on any level you can. It sounds so simplistic and we tell you the truth is always simple. We will complicate it just enough for you to understand if you like, but it is simple. Play the guitar. That is all there is to it. Experience the music and if later, you find another door opening that brings you joy, then follow it. Share it with those around you, even if you think you cannot make a living at it. Even if you think no one will listen, just the fact that you are doing it yourself will raise your own vibration. Then, when you walk out into the grocery store, you will touch another. When you call one of your friends on the phone, you will touch another. Pretty soon there is a whole lot of touching going on. When you touch each other with your passion, it activates passion in them. They see the light in your eyes and they want it for themselves. Such a gift you have to give.

There may even come a time in the near future when you discover you have properties to heal vibrationally. Then we tell you, you will be in your joy full time. In the meantime, play with it. Enjoy yourself. Most importantly, enjoy the ride. Thank you for asking the question.

Self First – Selfish

Stitching the Hearts, #D102002 Leeuwarden, Holland.

Question:

I'm so focused on myself. How can I change that?

The group:

What you have just heard in this room is a very coura-geous question. There are those of you who come in with wiring to help you facilitate life lessons. A lesson of Charity is perhaps what faces many of you. We will explain this in the opposite to begin with, so you can see it. Many of you here on the Earth at this moment are learning to place yourself first in the energy flow, for you have been taught thoroughly by your parents not to be selfish, to put everyone else before you. "A successful relationship is when you put your husband or wife first." Or, "You must be a good mother or father; therefore, put your children first."

Please re-member the call of the Human Angel is: There Before the Grace of You Go I. You must come first. There is a difference between what you call selfish and self-first, although they look very similar at first glance, for both of them place you first in the energy flow. As you come into the energy flow, a person who is self-first puts self first in the energy flow so that they have more to give other people, whereas a person who is selfish puts self first in the energy flow and cuts other people off.

Please keep in mind that none of this is done consciously. There are no bad people. Oh yes, some of your world leaders will tell you opposite to control you with your own fear. We think it is so humorous when one points to others and calls them evil. The games you play are very humorous to us. Yet we tell you, you are all in the same boat. You are all trying to awaken from the same dream and when you do, you will find you are all a part of each other. You are all trying to re-member who you are. You all know there is something out there, but you just do not re-member what it is. We tell you that you have already won the Game. We tell you as you hold this within yourselves, a difference can be made within each heart. To hold the energy firmly within yourself is the most important part at first.

Now we will answer your question, for some of you have come in to work with different life lessons. We have just described seemingly the opposite of what you perceive as your challenge. Some of you have come in to work with a life lesson of what we call Charity. Charity is the connection to other people for, in a Unity Consciousness, you understand that your connection is through the hearts of all other people everywhere, not only in this dimensional reality, but even with us through all the timelines and all the dimensional realities. You are one. What you do over here affects everything you experience, and what you do over there and your choices affects this one back here. You do not see that, so you have not acted accordingly.

Those of you who come in with a life lesson of Charity are especially blind to that connection. So you would think it is all within and no connections are without. We tell you, it is most important to have both connections, to know the connection you have with each and every one around you. And you also have the courage to place yourself first in the energy flow so you can have that connection. To answer your question specifically, we ask you to dare to place yourself in the heart of each person you talk to. Have the courage to feel empathy with that part of you within them. Focus on the connections and do not look for the disconnections.

You have the connections; it is a given. As you come in, you all have the same connections. Some of you choose to develop them further; some of you choose to shut them off. That is your choice, for there is only one rule: free choice. Even though it is difficult for you because of the way you are wired, we ask you to not see the heart, to not see the reactions of other people sometimes, to constantly place first yourself and then the people you are talking with. Then, with the people you are connecting with, dare to go all the way into the heart ... which means making yourself vulnerable. It is not easy. Explore your vulnerability. You will find the answer to your own question. Explore your connection all around you, and you will move very quickly to be the healer and teacher you are. Thank you for having the courage to voice that question.

Opening to Channel

What Color is Love? #042 Tel Aviv, Israel.

Question:

My passion is to channel and heal, and I wonder why it is not happening. What is keeping me from doing that?

The group:

Let us tell you a little about the channeling process. As humanity evolves, more and more people will open to channel. Each one of you has a strong connection to spirit. It is a direct connection to your own Higher Self. That connection goes to your imagination where it first enters your physical being. All channeling, creativity, inspiration and spirit connection must enter through that space in your imagination. It is part of your internal makeup to not trust your imagination.

But especially when it comes to spirit connection you have the feeling that you are making it up and suddenly the flow stops. We tell you, it will always feel like you are making it up. Get over it, get used to it and get on with it. You humans have such mistrust for yourselves it is amazing. If you receive a message from the highest of high, you will bring it through and share it, but if you think you made it up, you will discard it and let the opportunity to share it pass. What if you and the highest of high were one and the same?

Another important part here is for you to find your first form of channeling, for there are many different forms. There are people who play the piano; there are others who paint; and others who heal. There are people who speak. It is not possible for one to teach you to be left-handed if you are right-handed. It is possible to show what it is like to use your left hand but it is not possible to teach you to be left-handed. So knowing that, before you start the channeling process, it is first important to identify your first form of channeling and the flow of least resistance. Once you know the space in which all the energy comes through the quickest, it is easier for you to try some of the other avenues. And; although you definitely have contracts to channel with your words, there is another form of channeling waiting for you to discover. Once that door is open, you are going to be very busy. Your life will change very drastically. Are you ready?

Question:

I am ready but it is not happening (laughter).

The group:

We will ask you to add only one word to that sentence. "Yet." For you may wake up tomorrow and find things moving very quickly.

Question:

Is there anything I need to do, or any suggestions?

The group:

Only to change your perception slightly. Your reality is always determined by the point of perception from which you view it. If you humans ever understand how magical you are, you will never stop laughing. All you need to do is to look at something in a different way in order for you to shift your reality. So let us offer you another vision. Every day that you feel restricted or stuck will add to your ultimate channel and strength when it does come through. Most of this is now timing. So on those days when you try to write and nothing comes through, bless it and go to the beach. We thank you.

Espavo.

Channeling

What Color is Love? #042 Tel Aviv, Israel.

Question:

What I want to ask you is: I feel paralyzed inside me and not able to communicate this creativity inside me and it frustrates me a lot. I don't know what my way is and if we talk about channeling my own personal way, I don't know what that is.

The group:

It is wonderful that you would ask this for there are no less than 72 of you here in the room who have a similar experience. There is a sensitivity that is necessary for healers to have. Many times a healer will come in with a life lesson of Definition specifically so that they have that sensitivity. But, on top of a life lesson of Definition, you also carry crystal energy and are extremely sensitive to begin with. You are the perfect example to show this to other people.

In a normal conversation, two people, two souls, talk and yet when someone is as sensitive as she is, this soul here, the sensitive one, before she speaks, she places herself on this shoulder over here so she will know exactly what that feels like. In situations where there are many people around them, there are many of those people who are sitting on other people's shoulders, waiting to see what reaction that is going to have.

Much of your life has felt to you as if you have been walking on egg shells. We are going to ask you to get out your stomping boots and start breaking some egg shells. For the reality is, you will never lose that sensitivity. It is so wired into you that you will learn to draw from it, for it is not a bad thing you need to overcome. It is something you simply need to learn to channel.

With great sensitivity also comes great power. For she is one who can sit in front of another person if she were being a healer like the Keeper does, and she would immediately know where the problems are and what the challenges are.

Questioner:

It's true.

The group:

And if she were a massage therapist with a body lying there on the table, she would know exactly which muscles to work on. And in working with empowering people, you know exactly what to say.

There is another situation we wish to identify for you, so you will understand. As a crystal elder, it is very difficult for you to feel a part of things, even in rooms like these. In some ways, you have always felt like you were on the wallpaper, observing, and more of an observer than a participant. But you have opened the door for all that is to come. We are very proud of you. And we thank you.

Four Lines of Integrity

Lemurian Initiation, #D050503 Reno, NV.

Question:

I think I can speak for all of us when I say, thank you for the activations, especially the one yesterday. It was a six-hour sleeping one. I want to know what we or I can do to help others see what I am seeing when I see the cities of lights scattered throughout the Earth. When is it going to be apparent or how can I help them see that which is reality?

The group:

First of all, in your regard to thanking us for the activation, we had little to do with it. You did it yourself eons ago. You had the courage to step forward into the space for activation. The space was created for you, you had the courage to step into it, and for that, we thank you.

As far as the activation and how you activate your dreams, and how you bring them into reality so you can help others to see that, there are many ways, but first, we must talk of trust. Trust that it is already underway within yourselves. Trust that your heart is vibrating in such a fashion that things are moving out into the ethers right in front of you.

There are four vibrational lines of integrity that we ask you to pay attention to: one is what you speak; one is what you think; one is what you act; and one is what you believe. Typically people walk around with two or three of these in accord with each other, in vibrational harmonics with each other, and the other two are canceling everything out, so you end up sending out a very fuzzy signal into the Universe. When you put all four of those in integrity with each other, you send out a very clear signal. This is the spiritual confidence we are beginning to see in your own smiles and everything you carry. When you have that, you can find the most challenging situation and simply smile, and create all of it. We ask you to hold it first within your own heart and do not worry about how to measure your success on the outside. Create your vision here, for you will send it out in your own vibrations. The integrity of who you are is already surpassed and that is no longer a concern of yours. We thank you for holding the dream.

Trust

The Spark of God, #041 Ankara, Turkey.

Question:

Where do I stand in my process of development? And what can I do to develop myself further? Do I have any obstacles to overcome?

The group:

Would you believe all of those questions are answered in two words? Trust yourself. All the answers you have ever received that have made a difference in your life, you have known somewhere in your heart. Yet trusting yourself is the most difficult part. With a life lesson of Trust, the greatest manifestation of that is the spirit does not actually trust the human body to support it. But one thing you must know, for it will answer your first question, is that you have already done a tremendous amount. You have been through many, many difficulties that have placed you here. And those challenges have helped all, for you have learned from each one. That then comes out into the universe and shares with everyone. Learning further to trust yourself can further advance your soul.

Where are you on the scale? We hate to disappoint you, but there is no scale. You are about here [at this point, Steve moved his arm all over the place]. Enjoy the ride.

ENERGY AND HEALING

Why Illness?

The Color Clear, #D51902 St. Louis, MO.

Question:

I want to know what physical illness is about. What role does it serve?

The group:

Illness in different forms always serves a purpose. You are here as spiritual beings trying to cope with a physical bubble of biology. Some of you do it quite well; others of you have more difficulty. Please understand, how you deal with the physical body is not a reflection of your spirituality. Many times, you have come in with contracts that lead you in a certain area. Other times, the physical body becomes the catch-all, for every time you misdirect energy, it lands in the physical body. We have recently explained a turmoil around many of you who have outgrown the vibrations of what you call work. When you are in a situation where you physically have to lower your vibrations to go to work every day, it is only a matter of time before it shows up in your physical being. When that happens, you have choices. It can be the barometer or you can continue hitting your head against the wall saying, "I know this was successful in the past so I will just try harder." And you fall further into physical illness. We tell you also, there are many healers. Please understand that all illness is not a sign of something wrong. In many cases, it is simply a process that is underway. In many cases, there are simply pieces of the puzzle that are coming together to facilitate your experience in different areas.

Largely due to "manmade illnesses," you are right on the verge of uncovering some huge discoveries of your own sciences that will be wonderful for your evolution. The blending of biology and technology, the blending of your sciences and your metaphysics are really where the magic is. We tell you, you are right on the verge of starting a process. Make space in your own life for the empowered human. Make space in your own life for you to change, and you will see a different relationship to your own physical body and to that which you call illnesses. Please understand, sometimes there really is nothing wrong. Thank you for asking the question.

Boundaries in Healing

A Theory of Reality, #D020202, Toronto, Canada.

Question:

September 11 had a great impact on a lot of Lightworkers, including me. I became very ill. I have been struggling for over four months. My problem is, I know I am a healer of children. And I have continued to do so but the more I heal, the more I become sick. I seem to have lost the balance, and no matter how hard I try, I've lost the focus. I've lost the balance. Can you suggest what I, and possibly other Lightworkers who are in the same circumstance as mine, can do?

The group:

Oh, dear one, you would not be a powerful healer if you were not an empathic sensitive. You pick up on other people's emotional energy so clearly. It is so beautiful to us to see, yet it has caused you much difficulty in your life, particularly in high school. It made you feel separate; it made you feel confused. As a young child, you did not even know you were different; you thought everyone had these feelings. You are the person who can sit down in a restaurant and find yourself getting angry and not know why. You may find out that, in fact, there was an argument at that table before you got there.

The difficulties you have experienced as being an emotional empath also allow you to be a great healer. Someone comes in and sits before you, and you tap right into their energy ... and it is beautiful. Ah, but what if one comes in to you who has a headache and you put your hands on his head and he walks out feeling fine, but now you have a headache? Yes, it happens to you more than you could possibly know, for in the lower vibrations of the third dimension from which you came, it was possible to have this sensitivity and not be bothered by it. Simply by increasing your grounding techniques, you were able to pull the energy through you and rid yourself of it. But it is no longer possible at the higher vibrations to the degree to which you used to do it. There is only one way now and that is to develop good energetic boundaries. This is not a wall that cuts you off from feeling your clients; it is an imaginary line in the sand that defines your energy field. When you do this, you can clearly state where your field is and what you are picking up from others. You can then say to others: "My energy field is here and yours is over there. While we are together, I will feel and support your energy and if you let me, I will love you, but I will never take responsibility for your energy or your healing."

In the higher vibrations of the New Earth, it becomes important to not take responsibility for anyone else's healing.

When that happens, it is possible to 'back feed' the energy from your clients. If you find yourself drained of energy from those around you, it is largely because you are taking responsibility for them in some way. You know, dear one, you do it out of a heart space, as do so many. But it is also important to protect and nurture the healers on Planet Earth, for you have gotten the place this far, dear ones. Enjoy. Celebrate life.

Do not take the responsibility for the planet either, for there is much more going on here than you can possibly see. Yes, September eleven was difficult for many of you to see. We tell you, in those darkest hours, it allowed you to shine your light, but do not take responsibility for illuminating the planet. Only take responsibility for shining your light; that is all that is necessary. Feel the pain and let it move through you. Do not deny yourself the joy. For, without the joy, without the passion, you have nothing to give to anyone else.

We ask that you declare your boundaries, for your boundaries have been weak. We will offer you a simple suggestion – take a very simple energy inventory. Everything that comes into your field – whether it be a phone call, a piece of mail that is opened, your children asking you something – at the end of that interaction, ask yourself, "Did that add to me or did that take away from me?" This is not being selfish; it is being self-first, for it helps you to define your boundaries of where your energy field ends and theirs begins. That has been the blurry part for you.

When you can clearly define where your energy fields are, you become more in control of your life, and other people's energies no longer bleed into yours without your knowledge. We are not telling you that you are only going to do things that feed you. Many times, you will choose to do things for others that take away from you, but this time, it will be your choice. That is a very simple key to help you define your energy field, because by defining your energy field, your own field can strengthen within. That is an important part of your process, for you need the healers here who are awakening on your planet.

You are a powerful healer and have planted many seeds. You have taught many people. Now watch as those seeds sprout and go to the next level. So much is happening on your planet, dear ones. Understand that the energy is blending. Trust yourselves, for there is so much that has happened. You have experienced a little bit of the celebration of joy this day and we tell you, you have no idea how much joy and passion is here at Home. Oh, dear ones, if you only re-membered even the smallest bit, you would pull aside the veil and you would leave and you would come Home immediately.

E-volution, E-vibration, E-mpowerment

Magic Hugs, #D031002, Baltimore, MD.

Question:

I'd like to ask a question of the group, It's rather personal and has to do with the E-vibration and E-volution.

The group:

You are way ahead of us, dear one. It is no coincidence that you have never asked a question before. It is no coincidence that you feel so close. The joke is, you are on the same channel in the same information. That is the E-vibration of the Others. There is much that will go forward as you follow that path, for the E-volution of Planet Earth is now in progress and will be activated by those of E-Vibration. That is why you came. You have an important part to play. The last time, you were denied the right to play your part but this time, it will be different. You, and the others like you, have made that change by being here and daring to reenter a very harsh world for you. You have known this in many areas you have prophesied in for many years; it has even shown up in your Bible. "The meek shall inherit the Earth." It does not mean the quiet or shy; it means those of great power who have no need to constantly blaze a trail for themselves. The E-mpowerment is also a part of it, for that is leading the way of your E-volution. You have asked these questions knowing full well the answers you hold inside. This is your validation, dear one. You are right on time for the work you came to do. Write the book, dear one. Do it now, we challenge you.

Questioner:

I accept.

The group:

The fluttering you just heard was our wings clapping. There is much applause here in heaven much as there is laughter.

Chronic Reversed Polarity

Magic Hugs, #D031002, Baltimore MD.

Question:

You mentioned reverse polarity, and I wonder if you would speak more of the causes and corrections of the condition.

The group:

The magnetics of the physical body have been very misunderstood. There are parts of the physical physiology that are magnetic in nature and you have much more control over magnetics than you know. You have not yet learned how to measure the subtle energy fields that your own physiology creates.

When you look to magnetics, you look to people who have done the magnetic research, such as your MRIs and the other areas where you have used magnetics under test conditions. But, you are not yet able to measure the own subtle energy fields of your physical body, so you have not yet found the effect that magnetics really has on you. There will come a time soon when you will understand more of this but in the meantime, it will probably be held in the alternative field because that is where you put things you do not understand.

So, your field has magnetic properties and, even though each one of the organs and sections of your physical body has its own field of polarity, the overall physiology has a field much like you would have a north and south pole within your own physical body. When you experience stress for which you have no outlet, the magnetics of the body take and store this stress for you. If the stress is not released over time, it has effects on the overall magnetic field, causing the magnetic poles to reverse. If you were to take a bar magnet and beat it on the ground, representing stress, it would not be long before the bar magnet would only be a piece of metal. You have scattered the molecules in such a way that it loses its magnetic properties. If you continue beating it on the ground even further at the same rate, with the same force and at the same angle, those molecules will soon turn all the way around and you will actually magnetize the bar. However, what used to be north will now become south, so you will be in field of reverse polarity.

In the physical body, this does not feel like an illness. If you do this to yourselves through stress in different forms, you simply feel like things just do not quite work right. You just miss. Even things you have been successful at before are just not the same. When you fall into reverse polarity, most of you have difficulty sleeping or you sleep a lot and wake up tired. This is the basis of most of your energy disturbances.

All of you go into reverse polarity from time to time. The physical body is a wondrous, energetic being and it can rectify things very quickly, for a physical being can heal itself. However, if you do not relieve the stress that put you in this condition long enough for the body to heal itself, over a long period of time, it becomes chronic and the body believes this is now the normal condition. Ah, you have fooled your bodies once again. When that happens, even though you do things to bring your body into the rightful position, it wants to pull you back to the new way. And it does everything it can to hold you until its survival instincts kick in and hold you into this reverse polarity situation. And that state becomes chronic. Once you fall into a chronic reverse polarity situation, you then pull in what ever is waiting in your energetic line. [The group uses this phrase to describe the genetic line.] Now, how do you get out of that? Good question.

Number one: We will break the physiology of all ailments into two very basic parts to begin with. If you have a cold, you know perfectly well that a cold is a repressed emotion. If you walk around with anger or frustration, and someone with a cold germ sneezes, you are going to catch a cold. Now, you have the cold and you go back and speak words of anger at that person to relieve your frustration, but you still have the cold. So we will break it into the ethereal and the physical.

We will show you the physical aspects of reverse polarity but we must have you understand first that only you can relieve the ethereal part, which is the stress that put you into the situation in the first place. Learning how to deal with the stress is most often about your belief system. You have belief systems that you must be this way or that way. You live in a field of polarity and see things as "up and down, " "good and bad, " "right and wrong, " "black and white, " "love and fear." But they are not. They are all part of the whole. It is not about good and bad. It is not about right and wrong. It is about, "Where am I at this moment?"

Those are the questions you should be asking yourself. And we have spoken of this before and we will re-iterate it here. You have an emotion that has served you well in the third dimension but which is absolutely useless in the fifth dimension – guilt. Do something about it or let it go. If there is something you can do about a situation, then get up and do it. But, if you cannot do anything, lose the guilt because it will hold you back drastically in the fifth dimension. Release it, let it go and move forward. Most of the time, that will relieve the stress that put you into reverse polarity in the second place.

Now we also tell you there are many here on the verge. Many energetic techniques can change your reversed polarity in a split second. However, please keep in mind, if the body believes that is the normal position, in about twenty to thirty minutes, you will be right back. So there are times when you need to reverse the polarities of your body on a repetitive basis. We also tell you, we will not give you those answers, for there are healers in the world who will be working on them and bringing them into your dimension. It is not up to us to drop these answers in your lap. We will simply show you some of the problems as viewed from our perspective so that you, the masters of the Gameboard, can work on them. Many techniques are here that will work with this. We also give you a hint to watch in the area of pH balance within your own physical body, for when you are in a chronic reversed polarity situation, you will find the blood very acidic.

There are many techniques, including the ones from the master alchemist Keith Smith. The Keeper will share these with you after the channel if you wish. There are many, many more and we tell you that you will discover much about the magnetics of the overall physiology in the days ahead, for much is coming. This is only a small part of the puzzle, however. Are you really up to the whole thing? You hold the answers in here. And we thank you for asking the question.

Malevolent Energies

Six Precepts of Holding Power, #D032202, United Nations, NY.

Question:

Last week I felt very intense, malevolent energy, the kind of malevolent energy I haven't been able to feel before. I knew it was not my own, it lasted at least three days and I wanted you to comment on it, please.

The group:

We will be happy to comment on it, for there are several things going on here. First, please be aware that as you move into higher vibrations of the New Planet Earth, you become aware that there are inter-dimensional realities within your own time and space. You have created portals through the intentional vortexes you have placed on your planet, and other portals that have been there for a very long time are now starting to become activated. It is entirely possible for you to make connections to other dimensional realities you have not seen before. Some of them are higher vibrational realities; some of them are lower.

Please do not judge them as good or bad, for in that time, you have created a judgment that will be difficult for you to release. If you simply feel that it is an energy that is taking from you more than it is adding to you, then you adopt the flow energy of the dolphin and move through it more quickly. For in that flow, nothing can attach itself to you. You simply feel this and say, "Oh, is this not interesting?" and move right through it. Then it has nothing to attach itself to. For you see, even though this is what you would call "malevolent energy," even though this would be a lower vibration, in reality, it is attaching itself to you. From their perspective, they are reaching for the light. They are not intentionally out to cause harm; they are simply reaching for the light. There will be times when you will be able to do that effectively and help them reach the light, and times when you are not, and there are no right or wrong times for that. It is simply where you are in your space.

Become aware of your own energy field, dear ones, and take responsibility for it. Know that no one or no thing can take your energy from you without at least some of your permission. There are times that, by contract, you have set up to help other beings or other entities in alternate realities. And if it does not feed you at the time, know you still have choice, for all contracts must be chosen.

Allow yourself to pass through it and bless it, for a part of you that it is, and simply choose that it not be that part of you at this time. Breathe deeply, ground yourself and allow it to flow through, much as you would be the dolphin swimming through very sticky waters where nothing sticks to you. We tell you, there is more in store, for as you have moved to higher vibrational energies, in the next two months, you will see many more of these portals opening. They are as they should be, and there are many waiting to activate them, and then there are some that are totally unattended, which is what happened to you. Do not fear it, or that fear will be amplified. Recognize it as a part of the energy you are moving through, and allow yourself to move comfortably through it.

And reach out and take the hand of those around you, for they are there to help pull you through, much as the dolphins swim in families of pods. We thank you for asking the question.

Awakening Healers

Six Precepts of Holding Power, #D032202, United Nations, NY.

Question:

I've been working as a crystal healer for the past fifteen years. Is there anything I can do to enhance my work for the future for peace on the Planet Earth?

The group:

The most important thing you can do is to follow your heart. For each and every one of you holds a special key to healing in some form. You would not be here sitting in the front of the class had you not been one of the master healers who are awakening on Planet Earth. The time is right for you to activate, dear ones, for you to be here. The healers will now awaken and they will come from all walks of life. There are many of you who have been holding this energy and planting these seeds long before they were popular, and there are some of you, like the Keeper, who have recently awakened. Bless you, dear ones, for holding those seed-thoughts.

The question you asked indicates that you are connected and will have more information coming through. "What can I do?" you ask. You can dare to place yourself first. For as a healer, you are so wrapped up in wanting to help other people that sometimes you forget to put yourself first. And yet it is your rightful place in the Universe. There is such resistance to becoming selfish, so let us tell you that to place yourself first in the energy flow and cut other people off is what you have termed "selfish." But to place healers first in the energy flow so that they may fill their own cup only allows you to give more.

You are holding a modality that is not quite there yet, for it is important that the collective vibration of humanity be high enough to support the modalities that are here. There are no less than seven of you here in this room who are holding higher vibrational modalities that will activate as the collective vibration of humanity gets high enough to support them. For some of you, it is difficult, for you know it is there, you know in your heart where your passion is, and you feel frustrated. Breathe, dear ones, for you are making more of a difference than you know. Hold that energy in your heart, hold that passion of who you are, hold that knowingness and when the information comes in, even though it feels like you are making it up, we ask you to trust it. Measure it against your own heart. Trust your flow of energy, for the veil and the spot on your forehead will keep you from seeing who you are.

We think it is absolutely amazing that you call this the "third eye." It has been closed for a very long time as part of the Game you are playing, but you are getting to the point now where you are starting to open it ever so slightly. As a collective vibration of humanity, each one of you can make a difference. Trust yourselves. Hold that knowingness in your heart, hold that love. For at this stage in your evolution, dear ones, you are now becoming Human Angels to each other. If you see an Angel falling, help them up. Work with each one around you. Use the empowerment factor. Offer them the love of Home, for as each one of you creates your version of

Heaven on Earth, the collective gets a little higher.

You have been so blind to yourselves. You have your name stamped on your forehead, but if you look in the mirror, it is backwards and you cannot read it. The only way you can see it is reflected through each other's hearts. Do that first. Hold your hands out, dear ones, and connect to each other, and help each one of you know who you are. In those moments, you will create Home very quickly on the planet. The higher vibrations of the New Planet Earth are at hand. They are very difficult for many to acclimate to. You will be holding the door open to the fifth dimension and, as they step out, as they are scared, as they cling to the old ways, as they charge forth, you will be the ones who hold in your heart the truth of the love of Home. You are right on target, and we are honored to be in your presence this day.

Crystal Activation

Portals of Lemuria, #D032403, Kona, HI.

Question:

About a week ago, I experienced three times during the night an energy coming in through my crown and it woke me up. It was so strong I had to hold my ears. I was wondering about that. Three separate times. And the second part is that my friend Crystal and I were swimming in the salt water lagoon and we were both floating and experiencing crackling sounds in the water that sounded more like electrical energy. We're both curious about that.

The group:

We will address the latter question first. The crackling was literally new synaptic pathways forming that have been facilitated by the salt water itself. It is a cosmic joke that her

name is Crystal, for, in fact, it is a crystal energy that is causing this to happen. She knows who she is, for she holds the
energy well. What you were doing was sitting in salt water
crystalline essence, a crystalline-enhanced water that allowed
the synaptic pathways to start vibrating. It is very unusual that
it would produce a sound you could actually hear, but that is
exactly what was happening that day. And we tell you, no less
than five of you have experienced similar phenomena in the
room, but only two of you are now making the connection
of what that is. We cannot wait to see the expression on your
face when you re-member the rest of it.

Kundalini

Lemurian Initiation, #D050503 Reno, NV.

Question:
    On the way here, I was told I was being taken down for
integration, and the images that appeared were energies that
were snake-like, white, undulating upward, a diamond heart
superimposed on my heart area, followed by a sapphire heart
superimposed in the heart area. My question is: Does this
apply to the group here? Will you shed more light on this?

The group:
    What you were seeing is part of the energy matrix you
have always called Kundalini energy. There is a new energy
matrix which you yourselves are developing within your own
physical being of energy. And the connection between the
physical body and the energetic body is integrating into one.
Because of that, a new energy matrix must form. It has been
in process for some time. It puts a marker right there so you
never can fall back, for it is possible to raise and lower your

vibrations. What you have done here this day is to allow the acclimation of the new energy and to start forming the new connection of your energetic body in connection with your physical body. What you saw was the Kundalini structure, and it does apply to all.

Magnetics and Absorption

The Smile of Spiritual Confidence, #013, Edmonton, Alberta, Canada.

Question:

Greetings. I am actually interested in what they call barometric pressure. When it is cold, a lot of people here can feel the weather in their bones, their joints, and then if it gets another way, it goes away. Is there anything you can do for that healing or to help people in that area?

The group:

Yes, actually what we will tell you about that is, you are chemical/electrical beings and therefore, any time you have an electrical field, you have a magnetic field. You do not understand this at this point with your science because science has gone in the other direction. Science has looked for connections between the physical bodies and the magnetic field, and science has created such strong, incredible magnetic fields that they believe do not have an influence on the body. The body is a magnificent creature. You have devised it very well. Generally, large magnetic fields will have little effect on the human body. Yet when you learn to measure and harmonize with the individual subtle energy fields found in each body, you will find many answers to the questions you hold. The physical bubble of biology has incredible protection mechanisms in place so when you bombard it with a barrage of energy, such as a huge magnetic field, it protects itself. You have not found this out yet. In the meantime, it is affected incredibly by subtle energy fields, which is what you do when you send healing energy to another, or even when you heal with your thoughts and intent over a long distance.

Those harmonics are synergies – very simple and subtle energy fields that work with you and the body. They combine the spirit and the body together, which is why we are talking about the spirit body now. Barometric pressure is one factor that can change the way you work with these subtle fields. Shift the barometric pressure and you shift the harmonic on which you can work with the magnetic field. This is one reason why some people feel better in one location than in another. Many people are living in an area where they have many harmonics to their unique energy fields.

Those who have lower resistance and lower walls in those areas will find they can forecast the weather by an ache in their toe. That is the difference between how they process their own magnetic fields and how they absorb energy around you. We also wish to add that you have another sense you are not aware of. Actually the Keeper has called it your sixth sense, but in truth, it is about your eighth, but we will try not to confuse you with that for now.

The other sense you have is called "absorption" and it is the way in which you absorb energy. Many of you have a wide variety in your field of absorption. Some of you are very dense and some of you absorb everything. We are not talking about emotional energies here but about the subtle energy fields. That is the reason science has not been able to quantify many of your energy healing techniques at this point. If you do your double-blind study where you do 100 clients, perhaps only 25 or 30 of them will be able to feel and show results of what you have been doing. So that is changing. As your eighth sense develops, you will see that more people will become resonant with those types of subtle energy techniques.

Physical Changes

Healer's Healer, #065, Las Vegas, NV.

Question:

Some of the challenges I've been having are not sleeping very many hours, staying up most of the night, having physical symptoms such as heart palpitations, temperature changes. What can you tell me about them?

The group:

Human beings must go through many changes as the physical bubble of biology adapts to house the higher energy of the new humanity. It is not easy for you to make this transition. As the children are being born into your new world, they are being born with a higher vibration in a higher density of matrix that allows them to carry this energy in different ways. But you must make physical adjustments to do this.

Originally, we have spoken of a process you can go through that will help you attain the same vibrational level the Crystal Children are born with. This is the OverLight process, where more of your own soul can fit into the bubble of biology. It is your desire to move forward that sets everything into motion through your own Higher Self. Yes, there are modalities that can help you make those transitions. The first and probably most important is that you have knowledge that this is not uncommon. For as creators in the higher vibrations of the new planet Earth, your creations now have a very short time lag. So the biggest challenge is the moment you wake up at 3:00 in the morning four days in a row and wonder if something is wrong, so you actually create something "wrong" when nothing was there. So the time lag is gone, and the safeguard that protected you from your own thoughts is gone. This can put you into a cycle that can turn out to be full of dramas, difficulties and challenges.

Getting comfortable with change is the hard part. Now you are also balancing a physical bubble of biology, which has its own needs. These are also health and illness issues. So you are still looking in those fields, and are wondering where the line is between health and illness, what you should be concerned about and what is "normal." No one can answer those questions for you, and there are no tests that can be taken. But when you go inside and speak to your own physical body, it will tell you what it is concerned about and what it is not.

Many modalities can help you communicate with your own physical being. Letting the spirit communicate with the physical is the challenge, for it has not been in place up to this point, but now that area of the veil is starting to thin. So you have new communication techniques, new modalities, different things that will help you to thin the veil in those areas. Use them, play with them. Find the one that works for you.

Many of you have noticed that, all of a sudden, all these modalities are popping up out of nowhere. We have good news and we have bad news. The good news is, all of them work. The bad news is, you have to find out which ones work for you. So it is important for you to find one that resonates with you, then put your power behind that one, create it for yourself, and learn to speak to your inner knowingness.

Please understand, as souls, you placed yourself here at this exact junction of time and space with the highest hope that you would go through these difficulties. So your perception can be one of two things. "Oh, my God, what is going on? What is wrong with me?" Or, "Is it not grand that we are all waking up in the middle of the night?" Some of them are painful, and we understand that. We understand your perception of pain, for we have not been to Earth and experienced that which you call pain. You have intentionally put what you call pain on your side of the veil alone. It does not exist elsewhere in other Games in the same way it exists in your reality.

Much of your energy is based around what you call pain. Your lives are based around it, and you do everything you can to teach yourself through pain, to experience it in different ways, for it is a uniquely human experience. Of course, you do everything you can to relieve pain. But keep in mind, when you get Home, you will slap each other on the back and say, "Wasn't that a great time we had when we were in pain together? Wasn't that a wonderful, beautiful human experience where we cried and we actually felt physicality?"

Healing Mother Earth

The Smile of Spiritual Confidence, #013, Edmonton, Alberta, Canada.

Question:

We've been talking about healing people. What about Mother Earth? Some of us have come together from, oh, about a couple hundred years ago and we are a great disaster. And we've been asked to help with the energies of healing Mother Earth. Has this been going on all over? Are there people in various places, holding the energies to help heal Mother Earth?

The group:

Absolutely, there are many people and that does not make your plight any less. There are many people who come together with focused intent to bring together the healing and to create a safe, sacred space for her to heal and reset her energy. The truth of the matter is, you are part of her and she is part of you. We have talked about how each one of you is part of the other but you are also a part of the asphalt that makes up the parking lot outside, for she is a part of Mother Earth, too. You talk about the chairs you sit on being man-made but they are a part of the Earth, too. So is the carpet. And the reality is, when you create the space for her to reset her energy comfortably, she does it. The reality is just simply honoring her in that process. Thinking in those terms has created a great shift, which is now going throughout all of mankind. For the first time in your history, you are working with the Earth. No other people have ever done that previously except the early natives who prided themselves on working in conjunction with the Earth. And that is happening on a global scale now. You are becoming ecologically conscious, which is working in conjunction with the Earth. When you learn to tread comfortably on the planet without damaging her, you will have magic.

Allergies

The Smile of Spiritual Confidence, #013, Edmonton, Alberta, Canada.

Question:

Greetings. My question is rather simple.

The group:

It is okay. We have a simple answer.

Question:

You were talking about the energy of the rocks, the animals, their impact, and how they're blending with our needs.

How then do we look at all the allergic reactions of people to animals, to trees, to grass, seeds and flowers? There is something there that doesn't seem right in the context of where we are going. Could you explain?

The group:

Yes, of course. As you shift your body, you are actually going to see much more in the way of what you call allergies on your planet. Most allergies, not all, but the vast majority, are caused by environmental pollutants within the last three generations. Most allergies are caused and even handed down through the energetic line [the phrase they use to describe genetic line]. Now, because the human body has had to adjust to some of the environmental pollutants it has to put up with, these are not natural allergies, where one is allergic to hay, for instance, or what you call hay fever. This genetic structure has changed down the line to where they have these allergies to cats, dogs and other things of that nature.

Add to that the fact that all of humanity is raising vibrational levels at an astounding rate. When you change your vibrational level, you change your relationship to everything around you. This is also when it is possible to become allergic to something you have never been before. In this case, your bubble of biology has simply hit an inharmonious chord with the vibration you are allergic to. In this case, you have only to keep your vibration moving and this too shall pass.

When the body is balanced, it has a perfect mechanism. As you come in contact with another human, a part of this human becomes a part of you in some way, through your nasal cavities, and even through your sense of absorption. Part of that energy enters yours. The same is true with a cat. You absorb part of that into you. If you are not balanced as the whole being from the inside out, you develop allergies, and there are things you like and dislike. There are things your biology will tolerate and others it will not tolerate, and that is what you are calling allergies. This will increase before it gets better. That is a normal process, so please do not worry about it. It will bring to light those balances you are looking for.

Increasing My Powers.

The Smile of Spiritual Confidence, #013, Edmonton, Alberta, Canada.

Question:

Greetings. This being recognizes Home and I say, "Welcome." My question is, I have done work in the contemporary field known as medical intuitive and it has been very helpful and very powerful for many people. I'd like to know, is there some way I can enhance this talent and bring more skill to it to be of more use?

The group:

Yes. Two things. Use it and trust it.

Question:

That's very easy.

The group:

Sounds simple, does it not? We will complicate it if you like.

Question:

Go right ahead.

The group:

It is much like a muscle. If you use a muscle, if you lean against the muscle, if you allow your legs to support you and to run, your legs become stronger. The running becomes easier. You become smoother at it. Your physical bubble of biology is a master at adaptation. Your lungs adjust to take in more air and your body adapts.

In the same way, your energy body will adapt to you using your energy. You have a gift. Many people in this room are looking for their passion, for their own connections they can learn to trust. You have seen yours, you know it is true, and the hardest part here is to take that first step. We honor you. We understand what a difficult challenge it is. We led the Keeper right up to the edge of the cliff but he had to take that jump off there. We know what that is like, for we have worked with many of you here to help you take that step.

Chronic Cough

The Smile of Spiritual Confidence, #013, Edmonton, Alberta, Canada.

Question:

I have had a chronic cough for about ten years. It is still with me and I feel it is about needing to bring forth something or speak some truth. Can you give me more clarity on this?

The group:

Yes. The physical manifestation of things that happen to the physical body where the doctors cannot find out anything wrong is typically some little thing you have off to the side that is a stuck emotion or a re-activated emotion from a past-life experience that keeps coming back. Many of you have died of the dagger stuck in your side, only to have chronic heartburn. Many of you have had difficulty catching your breath because you died as it was taken from you. Some of you have been told not to speak and therefore have difficulties expressing yourself or have pain in the throat or nose.

Additionally, there is a new chakra rooting itself in the nasal cavity. For practical purposes, you can imagine it to be a single-sided chakra that opens at the base of the skull. This new chakra will be activated in humanity in the days directly ahead. To prepare this area for the new chakra, the nose and surrounding areas often go through prolonged changes. A prolonged runny nose or cough often results in the nasal cavity stretching to receive the higher energy. That is not related to your case directly but it was necessary to speak as it will help many here.

Much of what you have done here relates to your father. If you will go back there and re-work that energy and that connection, you may lose the problems you have had in the lungs and the throat. It began very early with your father. His struggle for creating his belief system caused you to be the vent of his frustration and anger. He was harsh and quick with you, and he taught you not to speak from the heart. We know this will not make sense to you but the funny part is, he did it out of love. He wanted more for you than he had himself.

Increasing My Powers

The Smile of Spiritual Confidence, #013, Edmonton, Alberta, Canada.

Question:

I have been trying diet and exercise to reduce the size of my bubble of biology and unfortunately it hasn't been working well. Is there something else you might suggest that I try?

The group:

In the very near future, as the Earth reaches the level of all humanity and you are a collective vibration, more of you will have success at what you call dieting. From our perspective, this is quite humorous because the bubble of biology is a perfect bubble. It is your concepts of it that causes all the problems. Nothing more. For if you have a concept of a super-slim body, your body will actually create the opposite when it tries to ground itself so, many times when you get in that situation where you are visualizing very clearly a skinny body, your body is saying, "Oh, my God, she is going to put me through pain." It does everything it can to put on weight. You can stop eating and gain weight. Is that not fun? Actually, we have not been in physical bodies so we have a limit about that, but we see the Keeper and his challenges, and there were times when he tried to make his bubble very large to handle his energy. And he is doing better at it.

There will come a time when each of you will reach a plateau in the energy field, where you will have more of a relationship with your physical body and are able to gain back the energy necessary to bring it down to a more comfortable level. It is no longer there for survival. That is the difference.

The moment you try to change the body, the body resists. In a primary motivation of survival, if you cut down the amount of food it gives you, the first thing it does is to take all the rest of that food and convert it into fat. So it has more of a challenge of reacting to that.

You will find it does not really make that much difference. You will find new things will work for you that you tried only a short time ago. The funny part about it is, as you become smaller, it will become less important. You will find that is really the definition of who you are anyway. Some of you will choose to remain large, for it helps your energy to hold itself and, even though your doctors tell you it is going to affect your heart, or you are shortening your life, you may actually choose to have that condition so you may be the jovial self of the big energy. There is no judgment about what you do; there is no right or wrong. You are here to be happy, to find your passion and your joy. That is all that matters for, when you find your passion and your joy, no matter what it is, you become the highest use to the Universe you can be. Work on your spirit, first. Make it happy. Your body will follow.

Circles of Light

Grace, #D101202, Tiendeveen, Holland

Question:

I have a question on light circles. I am a member of a group of nine Lightworkers and we have worked together since September 1999 and things have progressed immensely. We have experienced the vortexes, we have seen some crystalline connections between other groups, which we were very pleased about. The last four weeks, we experienced a kind of waiting area, a kind of hall where we are waiting for something. Everything turned out so quickly last year and, all of a sudden, these last four weeks have seemed a time of waiting. Is there anything the group can say about it?

The group:

Don't you hate that? [laughter] You see, we love to play with your human expressions. You have such imaginative phrases. Yes, we can tell you quite a bit about it. You have set things into motion here which are changing not just your own reality, but All That Is. You have felt the energy shift in this room even as we began to speak, for many times over now, the energies have filtered into this room to watch what you are doing. When you sit in peace, with intent to open your heart and mind to listen to the other side, it is not just us who comes through; it is All That Is. We tell you, it is quite crowded in here right now. For that reason, you will feel shifts in the energy and even in the temperature. We love the fact that you have chosen a group of nine. We, in fact, ourselves are a group of nine. It took a long time for the Keeper to get that information out of us, for he wanted to simply know way too much. There are eight of us and one of him making up what he calls "the group." We take pride in that union. We make a difference on this planet and so do you. Although you may not see it all the time, you are being divinely guided beyond your understanding, and that which you see as a holding cell, as a hallway of waiting, is very real. You are waiting for the collective vibration of humanity to make decisions for you to move.

You will not be waiting long. At the very outside, March 3 will mark a day when everything will jump to the next level. Ready or not, here you go, for you have set your intent as humans to move forward as healers. But, in order for you to release some of the modalities you have, and to use the information of higher learning, it was also important that the collective vibration of humanity reach a level where it could be accepted. It is right on the edge at this moment. It is only a matter if the collective vibration takes a step back before it continues to move forward. At the very most, you will do so on the date we have given.

We tell you that the Keeper is noting it is very unusual that we would give such a specific date. It is not unusual at all, for it is simply a day of celebration. It is no secret that the 01/01/01 was a very big day. It was no secret that we asked you to celebrate the 02/02/02, then 03/03/03. Can you see where it is going? 12/12/12 is going to be a very exciting day. Is that a prediction? Absolutely.

Are you all going to go up to the hillside, stand on the mountain and ascend to the next level? We hope not, but you will sure have fun. That is the most important part.

Dear ones, we do not wish to take away from the magic you will create on 12/12/12, yet we must inform you that you have already brought forward every part of the magic that was to begin that day. You have already ascended. You have already stepped into the fifth dimension. You have already moved into a heightened state of creation as creators living behind a veil of forgetfulness in a bubble of biology. What you do not understand is that you wake up every morning in the fifth dimension in a hugely heightened state of creation. You get up in the morning and brush your teeth, and you expect a three-dimensional reality, therefore you create it inside the fifth dimension. We never would have thought of that one. You are so imaginative. As you begin to learn and use fifth dimensional tools, you will begin to use the magic of the fifth dimension. Little by little, you will bring the fifth dimension right to you, right now, but you have already stepped into it so no longer look for the road ahead to bring it to you. It is here now.

We shared recently with the Keeper something we wish to share with you, for many of you are here from the days of Atlantis. You are here from a time when you almost made it. You came very, very close. And there was even a time when you stopped time altogether and said, "If ever we get the opportunity to come back and bring humanity back to that level, we will do it differently this time."

We recently shared with the Keeper that you have now passed that vibrational level. You are beyond the greatest days of Atlantis as we speak. This is why we love to tell you that you sit firmly with the quill in your hand, the ink has already been dipped and the parchment is ready and waiting. And we cannot wait to see what you are going to write next. Neither can the 8,522 entities in this room watching for it. There is a thunderous round of laughter going on right now.

Intentional Vortex

Hearts of Atlantis, #D101802, Mt Shasta, Ca.

Question:

My question is, when we went up on the mountain as a group, I know we all did our own individual work, but I'd like for the group to talk about any information we all should know about what happened up there and what we created.

The group:

We tell you, it is only possible to come together and amplify your own energy so much. As you do, you come together and amplify that energy so clearly that everything in all dimensional realities comes together and, as you do that in your pure heart of intent, you connect that energy with the Earth Herself, for you live within a field of polarity. That is the way you have devised the Game and, although that field is now changing to the fifth dimension, it still exists to some degree, for it is necessary to create the veil of illusion. "Ah, but the veil is getting thinner," you say. Yes, of course it is. And yet if we lifted it, you would all go Home in that instant. So, in order for you to stay, part of that veil must remain.

In that field of polarity, it is you who sees yourself on different vibrational levels as the Earth. You may not even know she is a living sentient being, and that Earth Herself – we call her 'she' when, in fact, she has no gender – is complete and whole within herself. But the reality is, she is a being with feelings, with love, with energy. She breathes in and breathes out. She does all of these things in her daily life in a direct harmonic to your own vibration. Her greatest desire is to sprout the most beautiful tree that would open up its leaves and reach into the heaven and grab the sun, which will bring a part of Heaven to Earth. Her greatest desire is to provide a soft cushion for humans to walk upon, that would evolve into the greatest conduit of light energy in a different form to come into Her. You are all connected. You are a part of each other and when you stop and acknowledge that, She smiles in a way only She can smile, and when you stop and do that in groups, particularly when you create double vortices like you did, then it is magical beyond belief.

That day you were up on the top of the mountain, and were in a very large clearing, you could see for hundreds of miles around you in all directions. Yet with all the visitors you had, there was somewhat of a parking problem, for the excitement you created within all dimensional realities called all these beings to come and watch what you were doing. You were connecting all the hearts with the heart of the Mother. That honoring process is something that has been held by only a select few, but now will become common knowledge.

Any time you create an intentional vortex, it is a cosmic event. Yes, we love it when you go to your "hot spots," as you call them. We love it when you go to Sedona and breathe the energy of an awakening portal. Many of you feel drawn to the energy and move there, only to find that it is like standing in front of the refrigerator on a very hot day. Yes, it feels wonderful but you cannot live there for long. And we love it when you go to the wonderful places and honor the great energy of the Mother and the beauty of the Grand Canyon, the Catskills, the Isle of Iona [Scotland] or this magical place called Mt Shasta. Yet you do not understand the excitement as you sit privately even by yourself in your own room and create an intentional vortex of energy to connect your heart with others. That is beyond belief, dear ones. That is what creates a cosmic event for us. And now, you are taking your power as creators.

Please go visit these places. Go visit those places so you can feel what that energy is like, and then come back and create where you sit this very moment. That is where the magic is. And that imprint will never leave any of you, for you have seen magic upon the mountain reflected in the Hearts of Atlantis.

Low Energy Field

The Spark of God, #041, Ankara, Turkey.

Question:

People who deal with energy tell me that my energy level is very low and it's somehow disappearing. I also feel this and that's the reason why I'm here. What can I do to go back to my original energy level?

The group:

People have low energy for many different reasons. One of them is a simple case of reversed polarity, which simply means you have not been dealing well with stress over a very long period of time. More than anything else, the rejuvenation that will help you more than anything else will be to be taken care of, to be nurtured. That is not easy for you sometimes because, in reality, you are a very strong person. So allowing yourself to be nurtured by those around you can help you change that energy pattern. We also tell you that energy dissipating in this fashion is exactly what happens as the spirit begins to leave the physical body.

However, you have been on this down energy cycle for some time, and it is about to change anyway, for you have just been through what is called the Phantom Death in which you had an opportunity to leave. In that opportunity, you changed the purpose and the reason you are here. So now it becomes about you. Everything becomes about you. And if you are able to change your thought patterns enough to reflect that, your energy will rebuild very quickly.

Another reason you have been tired most of your life is that, as a soul, you did not rest between incarnations. You wanted to be here now so badly that you jumped back in as soon as you left the last one. And, although time is different on the other side of the veil than it is here, there is a replenishing of energy that did not happen with you. So, you have felt like you have been dragging a body around most of your life. Now the body will have a chance to dance, for you will find the energy returning slowly at first and then more rapidly. The next two years will be very big for you, dear one. Enjoy the ride.

FAMILY OF LIGHT

Spiritual Family

Triality, #009, Zeist, Holland

Question:

Are the ones here today the only ones who belong to this group or are there more people over the world doing same thing that?

The group:

The family is growing very rapidly and no, the people in this room are not the only ones, but we tell you, those in this room have direct connections to so many more pieces of the family, so many more parts in integrated pieces that now this energy will spread very rapidly and a field of Triality will soon inhabit the Earth. We tell you with that, you will move very quickly. It is not limited to those who even listen to our words. There is a family of healers that is gathering. Our greatest desire and soon yours, will be to be there to help a human awaken from the dream. That is the family of Light. The family is gathering now. That is why we thank you for the opportunity for us to be of service. It is such a wonderful question.

Spiritual Family of Light

Cosmic Winks, #059, Mt. Charleston, NV.

Question:

I know of at least one person here who's had some difficulties in accepting what he's beginning to experience, feel
and awaken to. And I'd also like to know when this specific
group of souls was last together.

The group:

There is a heart vibration that vibrates within each one
of you. Each one of you carries a singular vibration that is
your "unique beauty." It is your unique part of god. You carry
that vibration and, every time you breathe, every time blood
goes through your body, you send it out without knowing
it. It happens on the electromagnetic energy field of your
body. It sends out a beautiful image of god, and it looks just
like you. When you do that, you have a tendency to send
out these vibrational waves that sometimes take time to get
somewhere.

Imagine, if you will, it is like throwing a stone into a very
still pond. Those waves start as a little ring in the beginning
and spread out, and spread out, and spread out. As that ring
spreads out, and as those waves continue to go out, they resonate with certain hearts that have a similar vibration. And you
are in a constant motion of reuniting original spiritual family.
It is much larger than you think. The new family of light is
now forming and, in order to accomplish that, it is helpful to
come back in contact with members of your original spiritual
family.

We are having another dialog. The Keeper is saying, "It's
about time," for we have had him write in many people's

books, "You are part of the Original Spiritual Family of Light." They then ask, "What does that mean exactly?" and he responds with, "I don't know."

The Original Spiritual Family of Light is the small faction of healers who intentionally brought the Light from Home to use for healing. Most of you in this room or reading this are part of the Original Spiritual Family of Light. You are one of the clans that are so important, for each one of you makes up a part of that resonant group, and it is huge. When Adolph Hitler left the planet, there was an opportunity for change that started rippling throughout all of humanity all over the globe on all dimensional levels. And humanity said, "We will never give our power away like that again. We are now ready to start holding our power and the responsibility that goes with it."

A new thought pattern came out and the Second Wave of Empowerment became a ripple just like throwing that stone in that pond. But, instead of following the leader, you started looking for ways to follow yourself, for that is the Second Wave of empowerment. And even to this day, some of these concepts are not fully grasped. It is very difficult, for you are so accustomed to following a leader instead of following your heart. And you say, "I would much rather follow someone who can show me the way." [laughter]

So we tell you, as we speak of the Original Spiritual Family of Light, every one of you in this room knew somewhere in your heart that you were part of this family. It is not an exclusionary thing, for anyone can join this family. What you are seeing here are the people who have been in it over and over again, and they recognize each other. You look each other in the eyes and you say, "Oh, I know you! You are wearing a different body than the last time I saw you, but you are the soul

I love so much. I may have to learn how to get used to these customs, this language and this dress, but I know your soul and you know mine, and it is good to see you."

You then start connecting and meeting people in environments like these, where you can open your hearts, be vulnerable, and express even your doubts. How wonderful, for these are the people who can empower you the most. We ask you to put yourself around them any opportunity you can. Find the people who empower you the most and experience them, and then take that energy as a Human Angel and touch someone else with it.

The interesting part is, as we are telling you this story, many of you are saying, "Yes, I know that. I know that, and is it not fun? And we have done so many lifetimes together. I can now look around the room and see I have known these people for eons."

The interesting part is when someone from out there walks in and says, "Oh, this is interesting, tell me what this is about." And when he is not a member of the family lifetime after lifetime, but a newcomer, it excites you even more. Now you have a fresh opportunity to practice your empowerment. Now you truly have an opportunity to welcome someone into the family, to bring them in. By that nature, it is not exclusionary, for this is about expanding the Family of Light. The interesting part is the last time this group was together goes all the way back to Lemuria.

Most of you have gathered and have been together twice since that time. But there are some of you on the fringes who did not honestly think you were coming to this gathering this week. But at the last moment, you got a nudge, a door opened up for you, and you had an opportunity to be here. A last moment call went out from the members who were already gathering to get the rest of you together. You got most of them.

This gathering was a clan of high level teachers in Lemuria. You got together and worked in a way to help each other to find the truth and to spread that truth in any way you could. And you were highly sought after, for there are no drag-alongs here. You are here by design. You are here by your choice, for even as that call went out, you did not have to listen. You could have said, "I am going to my cousin's birthday instead," but you are here. Now you are gathering again and in this group of people, and you are triggering each other to walk out and teach one more time. By coming together one more time in this fashion, you are giving each other a level of soul confidence that you will never lose, even when you experience the doubt of, "What am I doing here?"

There was the wonderful time when the Keeper asked us, "Am I making this up? Who are you really?" And we said, "Yes, you are making it up. Please continue." For it will always feel that way. And we tell you, even though you will have the doubt, you now have a part of soul confidence by coming together as part of the Original Spiritual Family, for you are part of the first 500 souls that came to Earth. You were there when 500 beings took dense physical form from the ethereal and became human on the first pass. All of you here are descended from those 500. That is why you look over here at someone and say, "Boy, that person really acts like my brother. Is that not strange?"

Well, as you humans like to say: We have good news and we have bad news. The bad news is that you are going to run into yourself all the time and that is not easy. The good news is that you only have 499 other people you need to get along with. [laughter]

The Original 500 - Starseeds?

Dragonfly #060 Las Vegas, NV

Question:

My question has to do with the original five hundred, how it relates to "starseeds" and how I fit into that picture. [The Original 500 refers to the channel "The Original Family of Light" #021.]

The group:

We will address much of that, except about how it fits into starseeds, for we have asked the Keeper to not read other material on similar subjects. But what we will tell you is, you came from somewhere. Energy is never born and never dies, so it simply transforms from one form to another, and back again. You are certainly energy. And what a beautiful energy you are.

The reality of it is, you did not start here to create Earth. Earth herself was a fragment of rock thrown off into space, spinning and heating up very drastically. It was actually a fragment of molten rock at the beginning of its life. But that rock was part of another rock that was spinning and heating up at one point itself. However, it is not imperative that it knows where it came from, for its expression is unique, now that it is off on its own. For even though it is an illusion of separateness, it is that illusion of separateness that allows you to see who you are today, which is much more important than where you actually came from. So one thing we will tell you is, all of it is traced back to the One. At one point, everyone in every dimension of time and space you can possibly imagine was part of the whole you call God. That is the illusion of this God many of you have dreamed up throughout time, – a very tall man with a white beard who, when he is angry, makes the weather change patterns. And he is someone to be feared. Oh well, no, we are not going to fear him now.

Maybe he is a God of Love, so maybe that is okay. And your own evolution of your belief systems and what your needs were allowed that whole process to evolve. The only important part to re-member is that you are God incarnate. And, of course, the other challenge about that is that when you put on the veil, it is important to have a part of the ego that allows you to see yourself as separate from one another. However, your first thought when we tell you, you are God is that you are the only God and that is not the case, so getting along with the other Gods often becomes difficult (laughter).

You are here and yes, the original 500 were here, and they had a very difficult time in that first incarnation on Planet Earth. All of you have a direct reference to those original 500 even if you, particularly as a core personality, were not one of the first 500. You feel as if you were, because you are a direct descendent of each one of those. So when we talk about the original 500, it is not so important that you find out if you were there. In some way, you were all there, so take pride and hold that reflection of that unique beauty and that unique light that shines out of your eyes. And hold that, for you are a wonderful and unique expression of one of those original 500.

Did we answer your question? Actually, we did a very good job of dodging your question, did we not? Now you have nothing to write down, which simply means you will have to make it up.

FEAR

New Sexuality

Jacob's Mirror, Elspleet, Holland, 9/17/05

Question:

Hi. I wondered if we would be teaching spiritual sexuality together and if you could say a few things about that.

The group:

You have a strong connection through the physical body. People channel different vibrational ranges, and many of you connect to the animal kingdom very easily. You know you feel very comfortable in that vibrational range. Others of you feel comfortable bringing in the higher angels of Heaven, you call them, and love to connect on that level. Yet others connect to the crystals of the Earth and the actual mineral kingdom itself, the most densest form, and you can hold a crystal in your hand and tell a story from that crystal.

However, one of the most difficult things for you to see is your own reflection in human form. And one of those vibrational ranges when you open all of the chakras and carry all of the energy is sexuality. That is the expression that actually reminds you of the similar vibration we live in at Home. So that form of expression has been greatly feared on your planet and has been held within its place. "It only has certain uses within certain realms and must be treated with the greatest respect and honor. Quiet, don't talk out loud about it."

Because of that, you have actually cut off a part of yourselves that will be needed to move forward into this area. Now let us explain further, for that does not necessarily mean always relationship, for there are many different ways of expressing that energy besides the actual act of sex. There are many ways of bringing that energy through you completely to share with others. You have seen it done in this room many times this week, for there has been much sexual energy flying all over the place ... and you enjoyed it tremendously. Some of you took that energy and reflected it back to your partners and grounded it in the act of sexuality itself. What a wonderful way to do this. But it is a natural energy. We ask you to understand that all of your connections have to come through your emotions, and that some of the greatest emotional clearing can happen with the sexual energy. We ask you to embrace that energy, play with it, expand it to yourselves. There are many uses of this, so work with it.

The more you speak openly about it, the less whispering will have to happen, and the less power it will have in a negative way. Fear is only a lack of information. Fill in the information. That is what the two of you have decided to do. And you have done it six lifetimes already, so enjoy the ride.

Belief Systems

Are You Ready? #D030903, Baltimore, MD.

Question:

I'm going to ask a somewhat personal question. Being a Catholic, I have been exposed to a terrible crisis of faith, I think because I've had such expectations for myself. I am seeing a future in which I am responsible for creating everything, but perhaps this has put me into overwhelm. I'd like some insight. I've really worked on this over the past several days and I think I've finally hit on what I had to be afraid of. I think I'm afraid of being humiliated. And I was wondering, is this from a past life that I'm projecting forward, or am I truly just afraid of, as you say, having the quill in my own hand and me now having to write my own script?

The group:

You have asked an excellent question because it typifies what many people are feeling all over the world, and we thank you for having the courage to ask it. There are many – not just in this room but on the planet at this time – who feel something very similar, so we will address this. Yes, you do not see your own power, but there are also things in place you must understand.

Number one in this situation is the Seed Fear. All of you on this planet have taken lifetime after lifetime after lifetime, and have even played other Games before throughout the Universe. In those areas, you bring back cellular memories that are actually stored in the physical cells of your biology, each and every time, and those are chosen by you in the first stage of life, the planning stage. The seventh stage of life is an acclamation stage where you review all the things that happened to you when you were pretending to be human. You then decide which experiences incorporate into your core personality and make up part of your integrated self, and which ones you release. The core personality is the essence of who and what you really are, and the accumulations of all experiences of the soul in all dimensions.

But we will clarify this. Imagine you have set the Game so that you "fall into power." We have chosen those words very carefully because, typically, it is not something you create yourself. Falling into power means exactly that. Someone finds themselves suddenly in full power, and in a field of polarity with duality firmly in place and the egos trying to balance that and helping to ensure your survival, many of you have abused your power. You have found a wonderful saying, "Absolute power corrupts absolutely," but it does not really. It is the absolute use of absolute power that corrupts absolutely.

Many of you have experienced some form of that yourselves. You have been great healers, leaders, shamans and priests. You have found yourself helping other people in many ways, and sometimes the temptation is simply too great. You abused the power, and used it for personal gain in some area. You used it for money, sex or in a search for some elusive power you believe is going to make you more complete.

There are also the times when your energy affects many. The days of Atlantis are a perfect example of this. For those of you who were there at that time and who are even partly responsible, you carry a huge chunk of the seed fear in your own biology. When you got close to stepping into your own power in any lifetime after that, the moment you awoke and started feeling the energy of who you were, you had a great big fear coming up in the back of you warning, "You had better not do that."

It was the Guardian at the Gate who you, yourself, put there, for you took the scariest monster you held inside of yourself and told him, "You sit guard at the gate here and if I ever start moving into my power again, you scare the heck out of me," and he did … and still does.

That is part of what people experience as they move into this. So even though they set their intent to step into their power, they find great resistance. They may even look at their own actions as self-sabotage, for that is what it looks like to an outsider. It looks as if you are tripping yourself up, when, in fact, it is the Guardian at the Gate who does so.

We ask that you, number one, make friends with this Guardian at the Gate. Recognize him for the job well done. He is a part of you, so implore him to become a part of your energy again, for he is not outside of yourself. That is number one.

Number two is, you have an energetic tube that runs in front of your spinal column, which supports the energetic structure of your body. You bring things from the ethereal realm through that tube into your reality. This is the simple process of human creation. If you think about it, any man-made creation first began as a thought form. The energetic process is less complicated and you will be using that in the future.

Now about this tube, there are two ways you work with a life lesson – energy matrixes and energy stamps. Your energy matrix is the way you are wired energetically. You cannot heal an energy matrix, for nothing is truly wrong here. An energy matrix can only be mastered, not healed.

An energy stamp is an event that happens to you while you are here, and it can be healed. But an interesting phenomenon takes place when you heal an Energy Stamp. When that miracle happens, the healing goes forward and backwards in the timeline. You heal your grandfather, your father, your children. That is why the work is so honored, but those Energy Stamps are actually stamped on the outside of that energy tube. So, as you can imagine, this is much like a stamp that is crimping the tube and restricting the flow of creation energy. Even when you heal an Energy Stamp, there is always the remaining scar tissue, very similar to scar tissue in your physical body.

So, you have passed the marker, are stepping into your power, moving into evolution, and changing your own biology and energetic structure to carry more of this energy, and as you do, you carry a tremendous amount of energy through this tube, so the tube must expand. But, as the tube expands, the normal tissue begins expanding at a normal rate until it reaches the scar tissue. But the scar tissue cannot quite expand at the same rate, and you find perplexing things coming up.

It is a common scenario: You make your intent to be a Lightworker, to move back into the healing work you know is in your heart and, all of a sudden, your entire life falls apart. So you ask, "What am I doing dealing with this? I dealt with my father issues five years ago. I thought I was past this."

What you are doing is stretching that tube, including that very difficult scar tissue that has been a part of your experience. Even though it is healed, this offers one more chance to really look at what caused the scarring in the first place. What we tell you is, those scar tissues are your credentials. That is what gives you the possibility of mastery we spoke of yesterday.

It is very typical for you to step into Lightwork and watch your whole life re-arrange or even disintegrate. Build upon it fearlessly. Know that you may have been stuck for some time, for there are many things that seem to give you that illusion, but no one is ever really stuck. There may be times when you are waiting for the rest of humanity to catch up. When you feel the passion, the love, the energy of who you really are, and that no one can stop you, re-member you hold the power. You have been entrusted. You are the Guardians at the Gate. Turn it around. Use it well. Do not fear. Do not judge yourself in this process. Rejoice. Say, "Oh, goodie. I have been stuck."

Embracing the Darkness

Triality, #009, Zeist, Holland.

Question:

So, I have a problem with fear. I am very afraid at night, especially when I'm alone and I'm afraid it will prevent me from moving on and stepping into my passion. Maybe you can say something about it.

The group:

First, we applaud you for your courage. To speak of fear is not something one normally does in this situation. We tell you, you are courageous beyond your understanding. To be here on this planet after having two opportunities to go Home in the last six years is a very big deal. You are applauded for even standing where you do at this moment. You are never alone, dear one. What is now before you is an opportunity to experience challenges that show you your dark side. That is all it is. We ask you to look at that as an opportunity for mastery, as a dip below the line, something that challenges you, something that makes you afraid of the dark. Dear one, it is your own dark side you are afraid of. You have never been taught to embrace it. You have never been taught to look at it and say, "Yes, that is a part of me. I am not sure I like certain aspects, but it is me."

The darkness is only a lack of light. You can look upon darkness with understanding and see opportunities for light or you can look at it without understanding and go into fear. Know that much the same way that darkness is simply a lack of light, so too is fear only a lack of love. You will claim your mastery through that process of holding that dark side of yourself. There will come a time in the next year when you will open your eyes in the dark and enjoy every moment. We promise you.

Lots of GOOD Mistakes

What Color is Love?#042, Tel Aviv, Israel

Question:

Fear is blocking my view. I feel I am now facing major decisions in my personal life and it is blocking my credibility as my work is concerned. My question is, how do I get over the fear? How do I remove it?

The group:

Fear is nothing more than a lack of information. By definition, you can only be afraid of the unknown. If you have this great hole here that sucks up everything and all your energy because it is empty, find ways of filling it up. Ah, but at first, you do not trust yourself to do so because what if you put the wrong information in there? We tell you, it doesn't really make any difference because it stops becoming a vacuum and that is the first order of importance. You can fill in the correct information after stopping the vacuum. Action of any kind can also release the fear. You strive to become godlike humans and have a belief system that this means not making mistakes but, by definition, you are here to make mistakes. Please make lots of good mistakes. Find ways of putting something in that vacuum.

Let us give you another example, to clarify. The Keeper once had a job where the people around him did not understand him, and he was responsible for planning entire projects. In his staff meetings, he would review all of his plans and ask one important question: What is the worst that can happen? Once it was identified, he could simply say, "Oh well, that's not so bad." Some thought he was engaging in negative thinking but he was only filling a vacuum and removing the possibility of fear.

You have great work in front of you, and the challenge is, you have an opening in the veil that you have seen through. Very few people get to see the difference they are going to make but you have seen that. That is why you are trying to make every step perfect. You feel you owe it to all of those you are going to influence, but none of it will happen unless you are willing to take the steps and make the mistakes. Your way will be well lit. Enjoy the ride.

GRIDS & GRAVITY

Gravity

Amor—The Emerald City #D041402, Bemidji, MN.

Question:

Can you explain why we created gravity?

The group:

Gravity is a strange thing to you beings, for gravity does not normally exist. Gravity is something that has allowed you to play your Game on the surface of the planet. When you were in ethereal form, you did not have a need for gravity. What you have done, dear one, is come back with a lot of the restrictions removed, for you have worked very hard to forget many of the lifetimes you have had where gravity has played such an important part in your field.

Gravity is your friend. It is a part of you even though you feel that after a certain age, it takes over your body. [laughter] We tell you that all your energy is about lightness. We highly encourage you to enlighten up whenever you can on any level you can. The levity of your situations, even in your own humor, makes you ten times lighter than you were in relationship to gravity. Why do you so wish to move into Lightbody? Why the fascination with light everything? It is because you have a direct memory of when you moved around without the need of gravity.

You have a purity of soul, dear one, that all can see when they look at your smile. That is part of what you have been asked to do, for there are healers on this planet who heal in many ways. Twelve of you here in this room heal with your words; four of you will come out with books along those lines in the next two years. And there are those of you who heal with your magic touch. Others heal with energy, and two of you even heal with your laugh. But you, dear one, heal with your smile. You fill a room when you walk in and smile. Do you not know that?

That is the levity, and the levitation you have been attracted to, for there is a connection. Keep it light always, and re-member, please, do not take yourselves too seriously, for it is just a Game. If you are enjoying the Game, you are in your passion. If you are not, find a way to be in your passion, for that is what will allow you to enjoy the Game. And if you are feeling sad, if you are feeling disconnected in any fashion, simply walk over to this one and get her to smile ... and that will change the energy in the whole room.

Now we will speak to the other aspects of gravity. Gravity, as you know it today, is not the energy form you believe it to be. It is the effect of magnetic fields created when you crossed the veil to enter into this world. An orthogonal matrix is the best way to enter other dimensions. When something crosses that line and becomes finite, it picks up an electromagnetic stamp that determines many attributes of the soul experience. It is the basis of what you know to be astrology but much more, including physical and emotional attributes. The challenge of magnetism is that it exists in both the finite and the infinite. What you call the electromagnetic spectrum is what we call Light. In your sciences, you see visible light as only a portion of the electromagnetic spectrum. From our perspective, Light is much more than even science has hoped. From the spiritual perspective, Light is the one energy that is easiest for us to use to communicate with you.

Magnetism and gravity are actually an individual trait that affects each one of you differently according to the stamp you received when you crossed the veil. Some people will work easily with gravity, and to others, there will be more gravity to ground them. This will also affect the body type they choose for their journey. We think it very interesting that the subject of gravity would come up as a question, as your sciences have never been able to define it correctly, yet.

New Grid System

Hearts of Atlantis, #D101802, Mt Shasta, Ca.

Question:

I'd like to ask a question about the grids. I've been doing some work with them and there's all sorts of ideas out there. I've come to some tentative conclusions, but I'd like to ask the group about the aspect of three grids. Is the correct geometric shape for the light grid the double dodecahedron?

The group:

We ask you to keep in mind there is one aspect of human form that frustrates you endlessly. That is the inner knowing you receive from Home so strongly that even if we said it was incorrect, you would not listen to us. You are always reaching for answers to everything, and the most frustrating part is you cannot understand it all.

But we love you trying. We love you reaching and asking the questions. We will place only what we think you can grasp in the reality you are in, for until you understand the difference of the light grid and understand what light really is, you will not be able to understand fully the connection between the grids.

Firstly, yes, you are on the right track with the number three. Yes, you are working very clearly with your understanding of the geometric shapes. It will evolve, so please do not limit your belief system at this time, for not only will your own understanding and belief system evolve, but the grids are evolving. And even though they are strengthening at this point, they are in a state of transition just as your own DNA is in a state of transition at this moment. So connect it with your visualizations, for what you have envisioned, dear one, is right on target. And by helping other people to envision it and by passing it along, you are helping strengthen the core energy that will help the grids to evolve and, more importantly, to connect as one, for that is the magic.

The three grids you have are now separate from each other to some degree, but the connections bring all dimensional realities of time and space together as one. And we tell you the key to that connection point is very simply something you already know – what you call the Golden Mean. That makes up everything you see as real.

We love your human aspects of things, but you have one confused aspect of reality. You think it is real and it is not. But you know in your hearts what is real. That is why you have the emotion of love, because it helps you transcend your own belief system.

We also ask you to watch as another grid forms on the planet, a grid that all of you are aware of yet none of you have seen as a grid, but we do from here. Let us explain. From our side of the veil, we see all the wonderful changes you yourselves as human beings have made to these grids, and there is a grid forming more energy than you can possibly know – a grid of communication.

It first started in many different ways. Is it not interesting that the first of your radios were made out of crystal? You moved a little wire around on that crystal, and when you touched different places on it, that allowed a harmonic resonance to come through with what you call a radio signal which is a form of Light. You worked all day to find exactly the right spot on that crystal to bring through something you could hear in your ear, and when you finally found something, you did not even want to breathe because you wanted to hear every word. Oh, we laugh at that because, now, here you are with your satellite systems, your cell phone networks and your cable networks where you have so many channels you cannot even decide what to watch. Is it not wonderful?

The communication grid is connecting hearts, for the more communication you have as individuals, the more you see you are part of that whole and are not separate from one another. That, together with the magnetic adjustments on the Earth, is the reason you are evolving and assimilating the new energy so quickly. Only when you can see into each others' hearts will you understand that some of you cannot ascend while some of you stay. You are one. The lowest vibration may determine the speed and comfort of this transition.

This has evolved to the point where it is a light grid, indeed. Now let us tell you where it is going for, as you have discovered the Internet, it has expounded upon your communication capabilities. Ah, we get so excited, for we see two hearts sharing with one another across the Internet, and they talk for hours, and finally they discover they are in two different countries. That is the hearts of Atlantis. That is the way you connected then, for you did not even know you had drawn lines in the sand at that point. This is the connection of the intentional light grid. It will not be long in your own reality before that elevates to a more uniform grid, and you will see that as light, similar to what you call 'lasers.'

There is an evolution of what you call laser, for laser is simply coherent light beams. There are actually ways you can control, direct and bend light that you are on the verge of discovering. As you do, you will form an intentional light grid above the clouds in the ionosphere. From our perspective, you will have created a wonderful light grid of your own design for connecting hearts.

Can you see the joy we will have when you do this? You are taking your power as creators. And then as the Crystal Children come in, you will find that what you have set into motion as your own intentional light grid will evolve to the point where you do not even need the physical grid for communication. You will only need the imprint of the grid. One thing Crystal Children are born with is enabling communication, one heart to another. When you can have strong enough communication, the illusion of being separate fades. When you truly know you are part of each other, there can be no more war.

Grid Systems

Human Angel, #D101902, Hilversum, Holland.

Question:

My question is simply to ask about the energy network being placed around the Earth.

The group:

What can you expect? Expect miracles in your lives. Those of you have been feeling stuck for no reason may be waiting for the collective vibration to reach a trigger level. There has been an alignment of many dimensional realities, including the magnetic grid, that has been moving all of this time. The one you call Kryon has been working diligently to shift the magnetics of the Earth to incorporate the higher vibrations and to support the higher vibrations within the physical bodies you now inhabit. That is what makes this possible. There has also been an adjustment of the decrease of magnetism on the planet to make this possible. That allowed the new alignment of the magnetic grid.

There is a magnetic grid, a telluric energy grid, that has been on the planet for a long time, an electrical grid, a light grid, a crystalline grid and there is the most wonderful grid we wish to tell you about, for it is man-made. This grid is the intentional grid. Once again, you do not think of yourselves as the creators so you think, if it is made from heaven, it is divine but if you made it, it must be junk. Oh, we tell you, you will learn to trust your creations as you learn to trust yourselves. This grid is a grid of communications, and it has been forming since the very early days of the telegraph.

The magic of your communications grid is, as two beings talk to each other on the phone or in an Internet, they may not know they live in two different countries. These countries may even be at war with each other yet when one heart connects to another, there is no division. Dear ones, the joke is on you. For when you pull aside the veil, you will find you are all the same. You have different belief systems, different habits and customs, you eat different foods, you dress differently, you speak different languages, and somewhere along the line, you thought you would draw these wonderful little imaginary lines in the sand and call them countries.

Ah, so interesting the Games you play, yet if ever you were threatened by an invasion from outer space, you would all become proud citizens of Earth very quickly, would you not? What will happen, dear ones, is, as you communicate more, you will activate Unity Consciousness. The Children of Crystal Vibration will enter and take over the communication grid when the time is right, for they do not actually need the beams of light at all. It is here. But it will only happen because you have built it. That grid is a communication grid of light that will also light up and recharge the rest of the grids and, as it does, we will see the magic upon your planet. When will that happen? You did not think we saw that. When will it happen?

Understand, dear ones, we cannot see the future, for you have not written it yet, but we can see the direction you are traveling. We can see a little further down the road than you can, and tell you, if nothing were to change, this would happen in the year 2021, for that is when you replace all the physical communication grids by beams of inner light. Do not bet on it, however, for every time we have given you a "guestimate" like this, you have moved it up. That which you had expected for the year 2012 has already happened, and much of what you have already experienced here has already created that.

HOMOSEXUALITY

Communication

What Color is Love? #042, Tel Aviv, Israel.

Question:

As far as I know, for now I am a gay man and have a very difficult time creating a loving and supporting relationship. I would like your help in knowing how to create it.

The group:

The interesting part is that you have come here to work with a life lesson of Communication. The way you have grown up and have been taught, it would be very common for you to speak your thoughts but very difficult for you to speak your feelings. However, just asking that question shows that everything is changing now. So even though we think there are many opportunities for us to share things with you, you have already begun to turn the corner.

Now let us bring out one more point here. It would be easier for you to share your deepest fears and your deepest desires with this entire room full of people than it would be for you to share those same fears with someone very close and intimate.

Question:

I am speechless. It's true.

The group:

It is part of the wiring that comes with the lesson. Is that not fun?

Question:

I have turned the corner. Thank you very much.

The group:

What we will share with you is, you have already turned the corner. You are asking the question and that is big. People who refuse to step into mastery never ask those questions. Instead, they say, "Oh, this was wrong with him, or this was wrong with her," but you understand there seems to be a mystical force that pulls you in the direction of your lessons. It also just seems to miss sometimes.

You have a deep heart, friend, and the great capacity to love and that will not go unused in this lifetime. Or you will create it when you can turn around and speak those greatest fears to one person. And you are closer than you think.

What Is It?

What Color is Love? #042, Tel Aviv, Israel.

Question:

What is homosexuality and how does the fact that she loves another woman connect with her spiritual pathway?

The group:

First we will address the unspoken question about the appropriateness of homosexual relationships.

Love is love is love ... end of subject.

Question:

So why is it so difficult for me? What's this shame?

The group:

Ah, now you are addressing a life lesson. At first, you asked the higher perspective, which is very simple, but now we get into the fun stuff. In reality, you have come in with a certain type of wiring, and you have come in to help facilitate a life lesson of Truth. For the hardest thing for a person in your situation to do is to speak your truth, but you did wonderfully just a moment ago. And yet sometimes it is difficult for you to speak your truth with those you grew up with, those in your family. You just stood and spoke it in front of more than 300 witnesses.

It will not just be about relationships or in just one area; it will be in many different areas, for mastery of a Truth life lesson is very challenging because it is often misconstrued with a life lesson of Trust. It really means trusting yourself to speak your truth. But you have a beautiful energy emanating from you and you are a very bright star. The steps you have made over the last three months have opened tremendous doors for your light to get even brighter. And when you stand with that soul confidence you are just now starting to really feel, you will find something that is hidden from you with the life lesson of Truth. Even though we will tell you the secret, you will still have to experience it for yourself. You will be shaking and scared to death when you first do it but, when you have love in your heart, when you speak your truth from your heart, and when you place a smile on your face, you can tell anyone anything. There you have it.

HUMAN ANGELS

View from the Angels

Dolphin Flow, #D031702, Syracuse, NY.

Question:

You said we are the entities who have left Home, and Home has not been the same since. You also said that we're creating a new Home. Will we ever be together again?

The group:

Hear this well, for as it enters your ears, it sets up a vibration that is only possible to hear in human form. Yes, you are fully connected now. You will always be together, not only with us but the rest of it. It is only the veil and your actions that make you think you are separate, that keeps you from re-uniting with us. We tell you, Heaven is not quite what you think it is, dear ones, for what you see in the reflections of the angels in Heaven is a reflection of what you have on Earth. For all of this time, you have had it backwards. The way it goes is: "as below, so above."

You have made the essence of the Earth, and that which you have considered to be Heaven is only a reflection of what you are. There are times when it has been very difficult for us to keep up with your reflection, for you have such imaginary Games. There even came a time where we had to reflect polarity and give an illusion of polarity in Heaven where there is none, for there is no good or bad here. That was what you term the Lucifer Experiment, for it was a reflection of polarity in Heaven where there is none, so we could relate to you. In order for us to relate to you and reflect the magnificence of humans, we must get somewhat involved in your games. Such fun they are.

We particularly like the one you call the stock market. [laughter] It is a game within a game within a game within a game within a game, based on a perception of a perception of a perception. It has no basis in reality. We love it. [laughter]

However, you are changing your games and are coming closer to the true essence of Home, in the creation of the New Planet Earth. And in essence, yes, we will join you at Home for we have never left. We know there are times when you feel the longing of Home because, even as you come into groups like these and share the energy of all, we share that with you to help you re-member who you are and why you came here. You feel the longing, and we tell you the pull from Home is strong. There will come a time when you will have a chance to return if you so choose, and if you so choose, you will be greeted as a hero. And if you choose to stay and create Home on your side of the veil, that too is honored, because the illusions of what you think is Heaven in the angelic realm will be known to you as you step into that role yourself.

You are becoming the Human Angels and we could not have picked better students. We must remove the veil slowly, for you have seen some of the reactions that have happened among those who think they are in power upon your planet. If the energy moves in too quickly, they feel threatened and will grab at the old ways. Sadly, we tell you it is not over, and you may have more of that yet to come. But do not labor in that; do not look for that part, rather look at the lessons and the gifts that have come from what you have gained so far. Look for the opportunities you have had in this period of darkness to hold your light and strengthen that light within. For it is not outside of you, it is not about world events or world leaders, dear ones. It is what is in your heart that makes peace on Earth. And you have had an opportunity to go within and strengthen and brighten that light. This is where the magic has been and we re-mind you once again, those who cannot go within will go without. Find it within you, have the courage to create a good Home and we tell you, we will be there to dance with you. As you raise your vibration and begin pulling the veil even further, you will see us, for as we hug you and hold you unto our breast, you will be able to see it and feel it. We cannot wait for that day.

Autistic Children

Dolphin Flow, #D031702, Syracuse, NY.

Question:

For those of us who work with autistic children, will they recognize the sign of the Human Angel? And secondly, is there anything else specifically you can do to assist these children?

The group:

An inter-dimensional being can sometimes get locked in between dimensions. This is very confusing, not only to the being locked into that dimensional space, but also to the teachers, healers and also the parents. Anything you can do to get the attention of that being, if only to bring a smile to their face, can link your heart with theirs to understand the purpose in this life. But, of course, sometimes you are only looking at a small fraction of what is happening. Now, we have described that the crystal energy has gone through the focus lens of the Central Sun, onward into a beautiful rainbow. You are dealing here with an autistic child yet you are only dealing with a small fraction of that angel, and you cannot see the rest. These are most often multidimensional beings who have part of the veil removed and exist in two dimensions with the same reality. In yours, they are born autistic and they experience frustration. In the other dimension, they may be in their passion.

The child is not limited to that one dimension. The other dimensions are simply not seen. They are multi spectrum beings, and not just always in your single dimension. You will find ways to connect to them through other dimensional beings, like many animals. And look for ways of connecting with them through symbols. Other inter-dimensional things such as crystals will help here. Yes, play with the Human Angel by all means. That symbol is seen as clearly from Home as it is in your mirror. You are liable to walk in one day with something hanging from your neck and have a conversation with one of these children, and they will not talk to you, but they will talk to your necklace.

Lightwork at Work

Stitching the Hearts, #D102002, Leeuwarden, Holland.

Question:

I experience problems with my personal Lightwork when I'm doing my job. How can I concentrate on my regular job?

The group:

You, as beings of vibration, look for harmonic resonance of vibration. When it comes to working in a job, most of your jobs are classifications, assignments of duties that do not grow as you grow. You are in a great time of advancement and movement of spiritual vibration so, as your vibrations increase, your relationship to your job changes quickly. Here is what it looks like. Typically you look at a job, and it is vibrating at let us say 22.3 kHz . You try to come in somewhere down here when your vibration is about 20 kHz for you love to pad your resumes and say you can do things you have no experience doing.

We watch you and we enjoy it. And we see you trying very hard to accomplish your job, but you literally have to challenge yourselves and move to raise your vibrations enough to do your work. Then you start getting very good at your job; things start happening and you get into harmonic resonance with your job and your vibrations are equal at 24.3 kHz. You do your job and love your job, for you are now at the top of your game with this job.

The challenge comes when you continue shifting but your job does not. You are a 25 kHz kind of guy doing a 22.3 kHz job. As you continue shifting, you get to such a vibrational difference that it is necessary for you to intentionally lower your vibrations just to go to work every day. When you need to do that, we tell you, dear ones, you will either change your job or it will change you. And the latter is no fun at all, for it will show up in your physical being because that stress can only be tolerated for so long.

Your fathers, your grandfathers, and all those who have preceded you, talking of sticking it out until you reach retirement, walking away with a gold watch, and having a heart attack, for that was their truth, for a different vibration.

As your vibration raises, you will return to more of the days of Mu, for in those days, you had differing job assignments. But there was a custom, for there were no laws in the days of Mu, that every three years, you would change your job. Although it was not mandated, it was highly suggested that regular change would engage the spirit within the human.

You might say, "Ah, but what if I love my job? What happens then?" Every three years, you would change your job and work at another one for three years. If you so desired, you could come back and do the first one again. Ah, and you kept the excitement alive, and it gave you the courage to make changes when you would not normally change, for humans resist change at all costs. You love to get stuck in a loop, but that loop becomes painful. However, even the pain becomes familiar and therefore you think it is comfortable. Can you imagine such a wonderful thing as comfortable pain? We have a lot of humor on this side of the veil over that paradox.

You say you have trouble doing your Lightwork at work, so how can you do more of it at work? We tell you, it is not important that you all do your Lightwork every moment of every day. You can do more on the weekends. The more you can teach during the weekends, and share your love and your connections with others around you through your own writings, your artwork, your teaching, your music, the more comfortable you will be going to a job where you have to lower your vibration. Finding expression of your passion will enable you to prolong the inevitable but ultimately you will change jobs.

Do not be afraid of change. Do not be afraid of going to the next level. Do not be afraid to go after what is in your heart. That is when everyone who comes in contact with you has the courage to change.

When you get Home, you will understand more of the definition we call Human Angel, for that is becoming your role. The role of the Human Angel does not need to be metaphysical at all, and can be very practical. You make a commitment to be there and to be tapped on the shoulder by your own higher self and say, "If I am ever in a position where two paths cross and I can be in exactly that juncture where I can make a difference in another human life, I will do it." That is the role of a Human Angel.

The call of the Human Angel is, There Before The Grace of You Go I. There is much to this, dear ones, and we will be talking much of this in the days ahead for you are becoming Human Angels and your greatest desire will be to reach out and lend a hand. When you see another angel falling, you stop and help them up. You give them something, be it confidence, money, a place to stay, a hug or a smile.

There are junctures in every human life where two infinite timelines cross, where some seed can be planted perfectly. When you make a commitment to be a Human Angel, you commit to being a planter of seeds, and sometimes that does not always reflect Lightwork. Sometimes, you bide your time to say the perfect words at the perfect time.

When you get Home, you will see what this looks like. You will see the many people on your planet who are becoming Human Angels, who are making commitments now. You will see those on this side of the veil who are being called Home so they can help you become Human Angels. And we tell you where it is going, for it is no secret. You are no longer the only Planet of Free Choice, dear ones. Because of your choices, because of your courage, because of your love, another Game has started on another timeline within your own dimensional realities of time and space.

So what will happen to the First Planet of Free Choice? You will move to the next level for, as you become Human Angels and learn how to help one another to trust, to love themselves, to see who you are, and to move into your own passion, there will come a day when you will now be the angels to the Second Planet of Free Choice, for we all move together, dear ones. All vibrational levels go through this thing you call "ascension," this evolution on all levels. Only when you have the courage to step into it in the most difficult places, which you call your job, this happens. Thank you for asking the question.

INDIGO AND CRYSTAL CHILDREN

New Schools for New Kids

A Day of Rain, #057 Oostmalle, Belgium.

Question:

I'm starting a new school, and we follow the Sudbury concept which started 37 years in America, but still I feel something is missing. I don't know what, but it's not there yet. Do you have any suggestions?

The group:

You are on track. You are finding a need in all of your energies, in all of humanity. You are finding a need to address special situations the new children are calling for. You are finding these children do not work well in individual classes with set standards.

Let us take you back to a larger perspective and then we will come back to your personal question, because you are really asking us if you are on the right path and what is missing. Well, you know you are on the right path; that is a given. There is a side door you have not found yet that will fill in that piece you know is there. But when you are working with a life lesson of truth, as you are, that piece you feel in your heart is the most difficult piece to find. And even when you find it, to speak it and to share it with others is rather difficult. That is why you have set into motion your individual dream of a school that will engage the new kids. That dream is in motion and will manifest. You will do well with this.

The Sudbury is one of many concepts of higher learning and higher opportunities for individuals. The biggest challenge about all of how humans educate and raise their children is, by very nature, you teach the children how to become like each other. Without even realizing it, the fact that you bring them all together in one school, put all of them in one classroom, send them all to lunch together, bring them all back, give them all the same assignment, and give them all the same measuring tools to gauge their advancement means basically, you are teaching children how to be alike. In fact, it is the child who is different, who is made fun of in school, not by the teachers certainly, but by the other students. The essence of what you teach children in the early stages of life is how to be alike. In fact, it is their unique abilities and differences that make them special. More and more schools will be looking for ways to engage the new children. In general, all of humanity is moving into a state where the empowered human can thrive. This is the "Age of E." Institutions of all kinds, including schools, will only thrive when they make space for empowered humans.

Look at some of your greatest teachers, and at some of your greatest entertainers. There is one the Keeper loves to point to. His name was Jimmy Durante, and he had a very, very big, odd-looking nose, and an odd way of talking to people. Although he was a singer and a dancer, he really could not sing or dance that well, but it was his uniqueness that showed his heart and reminded people of Home. Now do you think that perhaps he was made fun of in school? You can bet on it. For that uniqueness made him physically different, so therefore he felt apart. He did not feel like he was even a piece of the entire school system, because the school system was teaching people that success was being alike. Had he bought into the be-alike theory of success, many humans would have been robbed of the gifts of his unique beauty.

The schools you are speaking of greatly encourage unique beauty. Each one of you has a piece of God, and you can look in the mirror and say, "Gee, I don't think I'm as attractive as this next person, I don't think I'm physically as beautiful, I don't think my soul shines quite as bright," or, "I'm not as articulate as the next person."

However, you have something nobody else has. You have got a spark of God that shines brighter in one area than anyone else's. And your entire life is about finding that spark, which is what we call passion, which is what we call joy, which is why we tell you, your mark of mastery is finding happiness. Because when you find it, you walk with a smile on your face. You walk with love in your heart to all things. You vibrate the highest you can be and attract only the highest to you.

You are confused, for much of your movement in the direction here can be determined to be segregation rather than connection. But we tell you, if you simply do everything you can for your children, no matter who they are, no matter what they are, to help them find that unique beauty in themselves, they will walk with pride throughout all of life. That is what it is about. And if Sudbury can do it, that is a perfect place to start. Yet keep in mind, you have a part of this puzzle. Find and share this piece, this box, that is buried deep within you, and you will be on purpose. Then you will find that unique beauty, not only within yourself, but allow yourself to teach and treat the others with the dignity and unique beauty everyone deserves. This creates a space for true empowerment.

Indigo Energy

The Smile of Spiritual Confidence, #013, Edmonton, Alberta, Canada.

Question:

You once told me I was a pure Indigo through and through. Is that why the talents and skills I have are present and have been known by me since I was a child? And yet as I get older, of course, we have our culture, our community our belief systems put in place and saying, "No, you can't do that," and that's kind of spooky. So as an adult, even though I know the skill is there, there is a hesitancy to just step forward. Is that part of the Indigo resonance?

The group:

Part of the challenge of what you speak is the fact that you had such a strong energy even as a child. You came in with this energy, and you have had to learn to try to fit in. Being an Indigo who is not around other Indigos, you have felt yourself different so you had to make adjustments to your energy just in order to fit in and not be labeled different. Now you are in a situation where you are trying to amplify the difference because that is where your real strength has been all along. Being a forerunner the way you are, it was more important for you to protect yourself so you felt safe. And now we are ready to push you off the cliff and all we say is: Enjoy the ride.

Where Are the Crystal Children Now?

Clan of the Bright Eyes, #037, Baltimore, Md.

Question:

I would like to hear more about what's happening with the Crystal Children now.

The group:

The Crystal Children have been entering this Earth, pre-paring the way for those to come with the full crystalline attri-butes. If you understand that a Crystal Child is one who can see in your heart and see what you are thinking and feeling, you will understand they can cause great fear on this planet. They have the magical abilities everyone would talk about. It is very simple for them to move a chair across the room with their thoughts. You can see this world is not quite ready for Crystal Children. Therefore, there is still shifting that must take place in order to make that happen.

The Indigos and the magical children are here already, causing great turmoil. Is it not fun? And having the time of their life doing so, because they are here for change. They are here to help open these doors to have humans start thinking of children in different ways, for that is what is opening the door for all the full crystal vibration to come in. And as that happens, there will be much ahead with this, for as that hap-pens, you will see even more change in the way of children. But before that happens, we tell you there will seem to be somewhat of a lull in the action. For you have had a great interest in humanity with what is going on with the children of Earth. The Crystal Children have even started to come in, yet most of them are not actually carrying full attributes yet.

There is a natural underlying competition that goes on with all humans in some form, for they want the best, so therefore, when their children come in, they all want to see crystalline attributes, thinking that somehow crystalline is better than something else. It is not. In fact, those who have the first Crystal Children on their block may want to think twice. You think the Indigos were a handful —watch this. So the reality is, they are coming in with different attributes, not better, not worse, simply different attributes. As evolution of humankind continues, many things will begin changing and you and those like you will already be in place to help usher in the age of the Empowered human.

The first Crystals will not be seen. You will not see them on CNN. You will not have Crystal Children gatherings. You will not generally have Crystal Children seminars to teach the children or teach the parents of the children. For the very first Crystal Children will be well hidden. It may actually be several years before this information starts really becoming public and validated from the other side of experience. But in the next few years, they will start coming in more often. Sooner or later, you will begin to hear strange stories that match our description of them. Ready?

Helping Them Integrate

The Small Step, #029, Atlanta, GA.

Question:

I want some information on how I can help integrate my Indigo Child with her environment at school. Also, what information you can offer for the Crystal Children coming in, particularly those who are having difficulties with the autistic qualities? What we can do to help them integrate?

The group:

Such an excellent question. We start by saying that the work of the transition teams does not stop as the person goes to the other side, for that soul is in an evolutionary cycle. The transition team's final stage is actually when they help that soul back in through the birth canal.

The Indigo Children who are experiencing difficulties in your schools need understanding more than anything else.

We must take the expectations off of them, and try not to put a square peg in a round hole, for they do not fit the same way, and feel outside of everyone else. They feel different from everyone else and that causes frustration inside that will ultimately build into an anger. They have a thin veil and sometimes overreact in their anger.

The idea with an Indigo Child is to not only help them understand they are different, but also to help them understand they are not less than just because they do not fit in. Help them understand that, in fact, the very difference that makes them feel less than is an opportunity of greatness, of mastery, where they can take something that dips below the line and use it for something positive. In fact, those attributes they carry can be something special indeed.

Some of you have asked about the labels. One reason for the labels is to help them know they are special, that all the difficulties they have in their school where they feel less than, where they feel they are hitting a brick wall, can, in fact, help all of humanity rise to the next level and will ultimately help to change their schools.

What can you do? You can love them. You can give them the guidance. Do not revere them, for they do not need to be placed on a pedestal. Know they are children, just like you were. Know that they need your guidance, your understanding, and your education. Love them, give them the confidence, even though they may not fit in where you did. They have a spark of greatness in them that even some of the other people who fit in that round hole do not have. And that they have an opportunity because of their differences to help change the evolutionary cycle. Challenge them to grasp that opportunity and make something of it ... and watch the miracles happen. Find a way to engage them by letting them find their own way of doing things. That will stimulate the creativity within and engage them in life.

What do you do for the Children of Crystal Vibration? Oh, you are going to have your hands full there, but you will do well. The Children of Crystal Vibration are also children who need your guidance, your love and your understanding.

Talk to the Crystal Elders who are in this room, and ask questions of those who have dealt directly with this, for you will find there is already a base of energy in place on your planet that will help assimilate them. There is a network already in place, and you strengthen it every time you ask these questions of someone who says, "I believe I am a Crystal Elder," "I believe I am a Crystal walk-in," or, "I think I am a Crystal scout who has come here early with some of these attributes."

The difference between the Indigo and the Crystal is marked, but the Indigo Children are a special breed of children, whereas Crystal Children are, in fact, all of you. As the Indigos help you to change your environment, the Crystal energy within all of you will awaken. So there will come a time very soon when there will not be much difference between the Crystal and what you call "regular people." It will become less and less as time goes forward.

You will see opportunities here to awaken crystalline structure, crystalline energy, crystalline attributes within each one of you. In fact, when it begins to happen, the transition of the Crystal Children will be much easier than the adaptation of the Indigo energy.

Children of Crystal Vibration will create the reality of their own choosing once into adulthood. The hard time will be the first thirty years or so. They will do so quite well. In fact, they will heal you if you ask. Offer them your guidance, your love and your parenting skills. You are wonderful at it. Offer them confidence. That is something only you can do, and you will do it well. We thank you for asking the question.

What Can We Do?

Magic Hugs, #D031002, Baltimore, MD.

Question:

Much has been written about the Indigo and the Crystal Children. I was wondering what we could do to help pave the way for the gifts they are coming to give us?

The group:

That is an excellent question, for they have waited this long for humanity, the collective vibration of humanity, to reach a high enough state to where they could actually survive. The Indigos are here, and have come in with a force. They are doing tremendous work and will continue to come in. They are wondrous beings, and have a clean slate as far as karma is concerned. It is necessary for them to come in completely free of attachments, so any energy stamps that have carried forward with them have been erased. It does not mean they cannot create karma; they can, but they are starting from a fresh slate. The Crystal Children will do the same, for it is important that they come in not carrying the baggage of the "sins of their fathers," so any longstanding karma has been erased.

They are a new evolution of human beings on the planet, so what can you do to make way for them? You can find space on the planet for the empowered human, for when one amongst you stands empowered, typically the rest of you fall into fear. When someone stands up and says, "I have something of value," you have a choice. You can find that something of value within yourself and stand up with them, or you can try to knock them down.

Fear of change means you have often tried to knock them down, but we tell you, every time you can help someone build, you all get higher. There is a misconception of human advancement, for each of you has reached for higher vibrations thinking that one vibrational level is better than the next. It is not. We have given you the example of the schools you place your children in. As you go through the grades of your own schools, you have a belief that twelfth grade is "better" than third grade. It is not; they are only different vibrations to accomplish different tasks. To illustrate this point, imagine you are in the twelfth grade helping the third graders. Ah, but through your own free choice, it is the magical third graders who have changed the paradigm of All That Is.

As you move toward the fifth dimension, it will be necessary for you to understand that what you have seen as a field of polarity has been an illusion. Beliefs you have built upon, such as competition, have been an illusion. You have a belief that you are finite; you are not. You are energy, and energy is always infinite. You are part of the overall you call creator. Your energy is boundless and limitless. That is difficult for you to understand in the form you are in. But as you start reaching for the higher tools that will support you in the fifth dimension, you will see the results. And as they start beginning success, you will use more and more of them, for that is how it works. That is when you will uncover the magic within yourself, for that is where the magic really lies. And in doing so, you will grab more of the higher vibrational tools and use them.

Each time you do that, you will see more of the opportunities to not only reach within but to pass it on to other people. That is where the collective vibration rises as a whole. We tell you, the ladder of human advancement is not to where you find each step of the ladder, and when you reach the top, you go off to some other state. That is no longer possible. It is something you tried once and it did not work. When each person takes their step on the ladder, the whole ladder moves. That is where the magic is. So when you see an angel fall, stop and help them up.

You have felt part of your own energy through us. We have asked you here to experience the vibrations of Home in this time we have had together. What you do not understand is that since you have left, we have missed you. You have added to our vibrations, dear ones, and for that, we are eternally grateful. For we are in the twelfth grade and the distance between the twelfth grade and the third grade is so distant we cannot even touch. We ask you to touch each other, for with the touch of a human, you will re-member who you are and hold that power.

You are the magical masters of the Gameboard. You are the Human Angels who are now moving to the next level. We are so honored to be in your presence. All eyes are upon you, dear ones, watching you with such love and such support.

Support each other. Find ways of helping others move to the next level without taking their power. What can you do to make space on this planet for the Children of Crystal vibration and the Indigos? Make space for yourselves to be empowered. That is what we need the most. Take your place as a Human Angel. Stand up proudly, and hold your light high. Then there will be no more shadows on Planet Earth.

Higher Communications

Dolphin Flow, #D031702, Syracuse, NY.

Question:

Is there any way we can help the Indigo kids to communicate with us, maybe through music? Then they would be able to communicate and make it a little bit easier for them to relate to the rest of us, whether it be in the third dimension or the fifth.

The group:

The most difficult part about communication is that you are not accustomed to the type of communication they do naturally. The Indigo Children have come in with a higher vibration. They feel "on the outside" and have difficulty. They feel much like sometimes they are observers instead of participants, so it is difficult for them to communicate.

What can you do? You can accept them for who they are. Instead of placing them in separation, instead of labeling them this or that, simply accept them for who they are, and encourage them to go forward from this point on to be the best they can be.

Challenge them, for they will rise to the occasion. Do your best to keep up with them, for their brains move a little faster than yours do. You have seen this as a problem but it is not. It is an evolution and, as you move even farther into this, you will understand the great role the Indigos have come to play. For even as the Children of Crystal Vibration start becoming part of your daily life, even as your reality begins to change, and as what you call "magic" on the planet becomes mundane everyday occurrence, then you will always re-member the Indigos, for they came in to change that which was, to open the door and make room for the empowered human within your own belief structures, your schools, your churches and your organizations. That is the essence of Crystal Children but you will not use the label "Crystal Children," for there will come a time when you will simply call them "us."

The Indigos have had the challenge, so we suggest something else you may connect with. Provide a space for Indigo Children to talk to other children in a safe environment. For when two children start comparing notes about the difficulties they are having growing up, magic happens. And if you put an Indigo Child with a non-Indigo child, you will see similarities that will not only help the Indigo but will help the rest of humanity move very quickly. Provide a safe space for them to talk and for them to challenge each other. Give them the opportunity to create their reality and their ideas in their hearts, and you will see magic unfold very quickly. You are well on the way.

The other part to which you intimated has to do with vibrational healing. That which resonates in your heart is that you are a master healer who works through tone, and you do it well, for you have blended tone and words to find your true modality, which is only now beginning to really emerge. Yes, they will emerge through music, and wait until you see what the Indigos bring on to the planet.

It is not long before the early Indigo Children begin moving into senior management positions. They are getting old enough now to move into your governments, your corporations, your churches and your schools. Wait until you see what is in store.

Also, they relate differently to your integration than you do, but you have experienced that before, for many of your own parents thought the music you listened to was noise. [laughter] They can communicate on many different levels through vibration and they will do so. Vibrational healing itself in all the forms holds the key to healing, facilitation and health in the higher vibrations of the New Planet Earth. You will quickly find it is becoming more important.

It will also hold the key for communication where no other communication has been possible. There are times on your planet when your world leaders lock heads and cannot talk, but if only you could find a way to introduce a vibration that can span that gap, you would unlock the situation. It is not long, so experiment with it, play with the vibrations and the signatures of the vibrations, and find new ways of enjoying it. It is all held within the heart, and is unfolding as we speak. Enjoy the journey. Follow the passion.

Electricity and Crystal Children

Wings Over Mu, #D032603, Kona, HI.

Question:

Regarding the Crystal Children, are they going to be uncomfortable with the electricity we use in our homes? And if so, what can we do to make it less uncomfortable for them?

The group:

Such an excellent question. We spoke the other day of how, when you lost the opportunity to move forward in Atlantis, you stopped time. There was a meeting of all souls everywhere of Lemurians, Atlanteans, whatever label you put on yourself. You stopped time and all beings who had ever played this Game of Free Choice met and made some choices. One of them was to hide the crystal energy from yourselves. You did not say it would never be found, but that it was going to be very, very challenging to see it and never use it again. Therefore, you simply had to come up with different forms of energy to use. We actually think it is quite humorous, because the form you now use – alternating current – was actually developed by a Crystal Child named Nicola Tesla. He came up with a form of energy that was as close to the crystal energy as could be developed in this specific realm, in the three dimensions.

As the Children of Crystal Vibration come in, they are still looking for the higher attributes of the crystal energy. They do not know this form of energy within their own structure of energetics so this is foreign to them and they will be confused about it more than anything else.

For anything a Crystal Child has not had a reference for within their own energetic structure, they will have a tendency to reflect it back. The challenge about that is, if they reflect anything back, they naturally amplify it as they do. Your electrical circuits can be very confused by that. Therefore, it is quite possible for Children of Crystal Vibration to reach over and touch a television set only to melt it. They may flip a wall switch on, and all the electrical circuit breakers in your household may trip.

So part of what you will be doing is helping the child to acclimate to an energy form that is strange to them. First, you may tape "Do not touch" signs to appliances, and tell your children. "Please not to touch this." Oh, it will be very expensive but soon they will understand what that is.

They will learn how to let that energy move around them without having to reflect it back and amplify it as they do. It is simply a matter of training. They do not come in knowing how to deal with gravity, or walk in two to three dimensions, and now five dimensions. And, therefore, they have to adjust their physical bodies, balance and everything else to learn to walk. They will also do this, but a little later in the training most times. It will be something they will adjust to very quickly. Eventually, it will also lead to the discovery, or re-dis-covery, of the crystal energy when the time is right. All bets are off. They will be back-ups to change the energy. And that is exactly what is coming later.

Loneliness

Cosmic Winks, #059, Mt. Charleston, NV.

Question:

This life has been extremely, extremely lonely for me and it is very hard for me to stay here. I am wondering why.

The group:

This is about beauty, the beauty of Home, the beauty of god incarnate in human form. There is a time when people can carry an energy and radiate it outward which is often mis-understood. Yours was clearly misunderstood for quite some time, for we tell you, you are a Crystal Child, dear one, and that beauty can be seen way beyond your knowing. And no, it is not about the artwork you do with people helping them to see their own beauty; it is about the inner beauty and there are times when seeing that much beauty scares people. The ego places them in competition with you; or tries to control you. You have felt it from your own family, and it is difficult. When you try to hide your own light, and not look people in the eye, it becomes challenging, for you cannot have a full relationship with them.

There is only one way you can feel comfortable here on this planet, and that is to take all the blinders off and let your full beauty shine in all situations. Is that scary? You bet it is. Especially if you are working with the life lessons you have been working with, for that beauty has been misunderstood throughout most of your life. That beauty and that radiant energy coming from you have been taken the wrong way and misinterpreted. We tell you now, it will no longer be misinterpreted, for you no longer need those lessons in the way you needed them before. Now it is about taking the blinders off, about letting people see your heart, and letting you see who you are.

We thank you for asking the question, for you are not the only one who had that question.

Drugs and the New Kids

The Smile of Spiritual Confidence, #013, Edmonton, Alberta, Canada.

Question:

Greetings. I am honored to be here in your presence. With regard to the children who are coming in who are diagnosed with different "diseases," many of them are being drugged in schools. Is there something you would recommend we could work on because it is really sad and many of us feel helpless that there is little we appear able to do?

The group:

Your question is aimed at the drugs given to slow the Indigo Children to help them fit in. Indigos function and process at a different pace than others. It is not better or worse but they process much faster. Most of the time they are waiting for you to finish your sentence so they can say what they have been waiting to say. Their biggest challenge is boredom. When they are disengaged with their activities, they appear to be distracted and thus many times are diagnosed with Attention Deficit Disorder. Then they are drugged to help them fit into the "normal" environment. It was either that or drug the teachers to speed them up. We jest. It is already beginning to change thanks to many people within the teaching professions who have been quietly shifting the energy to make it work. There are many more of them than you know, and many of them carry some of the attributes of the Indigo. These are the Indigo Scouts. They, together with teachers who are working from the heart, opened a space for these children to fit in.

There is also the case of the Crystal Children who get vaccinated and suddenly develop autism. Yes, there was a connection but already many of these items have changed as well. If you are unsure, then get more information from local sources about local conditions.

We are going to say something now that will not be popular, so take a deep breath before going further. You have asked about drugs these children are given that are potentially harmful to the new children. We will now speak of one that will not go away easily. But if you look at your societies, one time, only about 15 – 20 years ago, you were highly attached to cigarettes. Then you became aware of what they were. Even though they served a purpose of grounding, ultimately they generally do more physical harm than good. Even with that knowledge, you continued using them for they allowed you to feel that, for a brief moment, you were whole in some way. A being hiding in a bubble of biology who is completely finite is always looking to complete itself in some way. So that was a natural attraction.

Now, even as the Indigo Children started coming in, you became intensely aware that it was not good for you and even you are making great strides in helping people understand how deep it runs in everyone's veins. It is not bad; it is simply not healthy for your body.

You will find the same true with alcohol, so even though that level of pollutants in the mother's body has not changed in a very long time, the children's sensitivity to it has. So, therefore, you are seeing more cases of what you call Fetal Alcohol Syndrome than ever before. And you will continue. There will be a time when you will have anti-drinking campaigns much the same way you now have anti-smoking campaigns.

Parenting Tools

Masters of the Gameboard, #D101302, Oostmalle, Belgium.

Question:

I have one question for the children of the Earth. What is very important for them? What can we do that we don't do now?

The group:

Oh, we love your questions. "What is it that Spirit wishes me to know? What can we do for the children? What can we do for all people on the planet?" There is one thing you may not have expected that you can do to give the greatest gift to your children and all children who follow. There is one gift you can give all of humanity that extends far beyond anything else you can do, and that is to stand firm in your own truth. Hold your light high for, in doing so, there will be no more shadows on Planet Earth.

Then find your own passion, for it is when you find your own passion and your own joy that you step into creating the greatest role models for the children to come. Have the courage to place yourselves first in the energy flow, even before your children, for they do not learn by your words. They are much smarter than that; they learn by your actions. Give them the courage to do this. Oh, yes, give them the courage to step forward and put themselves first by placing yourselves first.

Four of you here in the room have made monumental changes in your own life by having the courage to step off the bridge, to walk out of relationships, or to change the energy of a relationship and have the courage to say, "This does not work for me anymore. And as much as I love you, I have to move forward."

You have no idea what you have done, for the applause from this side of the veil is tremendous when you do that. Some of you have set yourselves up in life lessons you cannot see, and finally at some point you say, "Wait a minute. This is my energy over here and that is your energy over there and, as much as I love you and as much as I feel your energy, I am responsible for my happiness and you are responsible for yours."

Again, when you do that, you have no idea how you set the energy, for you become so much of an individual at that point that you begin connecting to everyone else. Even though you think you are pulling into selfishness, you are actually connecting into the 5th dimension. That is the one thing you can do for your children.. The greatest gift you have to give them is to share in your experience as an evolving soul pretending to be a human.

The other thing we have spoken of is to simply eradicate your own fears. Come face to face with your own fears as humans. Dare to claim them as part of your power, for these are definite gifts below the reality of what you call the norm. And instead of healing them and bringing them back to the norm, dare to face those fears and claim them as your mastery. You will wear them proudly as badges. And as you come Home, you will be applauded for those badges because you will wear them for all time. You have no idea the courage you already have to simply be on Earth at a very difficult time on your planet. Many of the old ways are surfacing for, as the blended crystalline energy comes in, the blend of male/ female energy threatens some of the old male leaders. Some of them wish to strike back in whatever way they can justify.

What does this have to do with you? Where do you stand in this? You stand in your truth. Do not only speak it when it is time but more importantly, hold the truth within your courage. Hold the truth of who you are and know that none of this is really about you. It is simply some of the Games being played out on the stage. Do not get too wrapped up in it, dear ones. It is only a Game. Enjoy the Game you play. Have the courage to go after your own passion, to go after that which suits you. Have the courage to be the best you can be. We will be with you every step of the way because we are right over your shoulder. If you doubt that, simply look over your shoulder.

MANIFESTATION

Manifestation in the 5th Dimension

Crystal Walk-Ins #D0402, San Diego, CA,

Question:

I understand we have moved into the fifth dimension and are creating very quickly with our thoughts but sometimes it seems as if nine out of ten of my thoughts are the positive, abundance ones or whatever, and the one thought in ten is of fear, and the latter seems to manifest more quickly than the nine thoughts of the positive. Please tell us about that.

The group:

The Keeper uses a very interesting way to illustrate this process. He is hesitating because he hates it when we tell stories about him (laughter) but we are going to do so anyway. There was a time early in his training as a young adult when he studied hypnotism, when he studied different healing techniques and he did so, not to help humanity but to help in his sales job. He learned positive affirmations and the power of positive thought. He used to tape on his mirror a little saying that simply said: "I am wonderful. I am beautiful. Everyone loves me." [laughter] He would go into the bathroom early in the morning and read that ten times to himself. "I am wonderful. I am beautiful and everyone loves me."

He would read it over and over and over again, for he read somewhere in a book that if you did that, you would be wonderful and beautiful and everyone would love you. Ah, but we tell you something else, for all creations are not as simple. As the Keeper soon found out, he would stand there in the morning, some times with his eyes half-awake saying, "I am wonderful. I am beautiful and everyone loves me," but a little voice in the back of his head would say, "This is bullshit!" Which do you think manifested? The one he repeated over and over again, or the one that had the emotion behind it that said, "This is bullshit!"?

So please understand, as you manifest, it is your emotion that mixes with it. That is why we tell you, you always create your greatest fears. You cannot help it. It is one of the most powerful emotions you have on the planet. So eradicating the fears sometimes becomes the most important part.

Now we will tell another good story about the Keeper [laughter] just so he remains happy. [more laughter] As a contractor, he had opportunities to work with energy. He had opportunities to bid on jobs to decide if he was going to do this job or that job, or maybe he wouldn't do that job because it did not excite him. So he had opportunities to choose his work and which job his company would do. We tell you, there was a very smart thing he did back then. In each of the jobs he would consider, he would ask himself, "What is the worst thing that could happen?"

What he was actually doing in that field was to shine light on a potential fear because if he never addressed that fear, that possibility would always be looming in the back of his mind. "Oh my God, where could this go wrong?" But if he knew exactly the worse that could happen, then it was not so bad. He could grab hold and move forward at that point. So creating the opportunity for him to move forward into words and into his own creation became very important.

We have spoken much about the words of creation. We will not spend time here for it is in the writings of the first book. We will tell you that your words play a very important part, for that is what your Spirit hears – the vibration. To give you an illustration, asking for anything is actually a statement of lack. What you will do is create more of the lack. The greatest words you can use for creation are the words of gratitude. "Thank you."

We will also speak very briefly of a process you need to understand. For even though you have stepped into the fifth dimension as you have spoken, even though you are in a state of enhanced creation, there is still a short time lag. It has grown very short but it is a safeguard. And the reason is, you are not yet masters of your thoughts. If you manifested every thought that came into your head, there will be big trouble on Earth. [laughter] So there still is a short time lag. Learning to use that time lag is how it works.

We also tell you at this point that you do not have control of what comes into your head. You are part of a Universal subconscious mind, a thought stream that carries many thoughts through it. Nor are you even responsible for trying to focus only on positive things. For if you do, that little voice in the back of the head will pop up and tell you, "This is not going to work." So we ask you to not worry about trying to control the thoughts going through your head. Experience the wide range of beauty and emotion that will go through your head. Allow yourself to experience it all, for you are Spirits in human form. You are Spirits inhabiting these temporary bubbles of biology. That is the beauty of what you can do. Experience all. We ask you to become masters of your thoughts. That does not mean you limit what goes through your head. It means choosing carefully what stays there. And if, in any moment in your reality, you are not happy with what you have created, have the courage to choose again. We thank you for asking the question.

MULTIDIMENSIONALITY

Meeting Myself

Breath of Spiritual Confidence, #074, Genk, Belgium.

Question:

We have multidimensional beings of ourselves here on Earth and in dimensions. How can we find them and meet them?

The group:

When you do run across yourself in another dimension of time and space, we tell you it will be very weird. Actually you come close to it every day. Like two magnets that are the same polarity, there is a field that keeps you from running into yourself. That field actually defines the boundaries of each dimension. If you did happen to penetrate that field and come face to face with yourself, you would most likely not recognize the person in front of you. One of the main reasons is because of the way everything is made up of threes in your reality. You would need to have two separate points of view to activate the third. Even when you look at yourself in a photograph, you believe it might be someone else. You have to actually consciously imprint that picture of a photograph in your brain as being yourself. Looking in a mirror sees everything as reversed, so you see the mirror image of yourself much the same way you see the mirror image of god every time you look into someone else's eyes. Interesting concept ... we hope you keep that one.

When you step into multiple dimensions, it does not make that much difference any more about meeting yourself. You will do that at some point but it may disappoint you, as you will naturally be very critical of the other you. As you begin to awaken to multidimensionality, you will go out of your way to polarize yourself in this way to keep things straight. You have no idea how complicated life can get when two timelines cross. It is more important for us to build your confidence about who you are on the inside rather than who you perceive yourself to be. That way, when you change, when you meet yourself in other dimensions of time, which will happen eventually, it becomes much easier to deal with. We leave you with more questions than you had intentionally.

New Time- New Space

Triality, #009, Zeist, Holland

Question:

I had an experience that there is no future, and I wonder if there is only my own imagination.

The group:

And such a wonderful imagination it is. It is not that you have not experienced the future but you have experienced the way things really are, for there is no future because you have not written it yet. Many seers of times past have seen into the future. They get their wonderful little crystal balls, oh yes, we love to play with them. Quite often, we crack them just to see what happens. But they have done well because they have helped other people to see there is more beyond the physical reality you call life. It helps people to see that you are spirit and not just physical beings, so they have done quite well. But those who have told the future have done so very rightly to help pull other people around you, and sometimes the mystique was necessary to get your attention. We tell you, it is not in place at this time and no future is written. You hold the pen and you wait to write it. Script your contracts well for they are about your passion, about your joy, about what you are going to move into next, and we cannot wait to see what you are going to write next.

Simultaneous Dimensions

The Smile of Spiritual Confidence, #012 Edmonton, Alberta, Canada

Question:

If we exist simultaneously in other dimensions, how does evolution progress? Is every dimension moving on, or is each dimension progressing separately?

The group:

We love it when you ask the technical questions. If you can imagine harmonics, we will go back to the keyboard of life and put you on the keyboard. When you strike a note, it resonates with other notes there. And when you play two notes that are very close together, there is disharmony or discord as the two vibrational tones fight each other instead of blending and adding to each other. Those vibrational tones are what make the different levels of inter-dimensional realities. And you will find that when you uncover what we are calling "the secret of light," you will know what divides those resonant tones of harmonic vibration. When you can understand that, you will even have access to the alternate realities you seek. Those that are in harmonic resonance with your own also rise.

Number of Dimensions

Masters of the Gameboard, #D101302 Oostmalle, Belgium

Question:

What is the difference between the eleven dimensions that are envisioned in physics and the fifth dimension of consciousness?

The group:

We love the complexity of the questions. This is such a simple question that has a simple answer. There are actually twelve dimensions. Physics has not yet found them all, but they are getting close. The revelation and the understanding of what you call quantum physics and quantum mechanics are blending the physical and the metaphysical together. Both the physical sciences and metaphysics hold truths, and when you blend them together, magic happens. This will be the alchemy of the new age. It is beginning now.

The fifth dimension of consciousness is now where you reside, for it is a new world out there. And as you go through different levels, it is quite a bit different than the physical levels of dimensional realities for there are actually even many more because there are inter-dimensional realities that span between this one and this one. We speak of twelve realities, of which physics is aware of only eleven. For now we will simply say that the twelfth dimension is the point of perception from which it is viewed.

The temperature has changed three times since we have been speaking through the Keeper. That is because many of these inter-dimensional realities have opened up and portals have come in to your reality as you sit here. There are many entities within the room that are sitting around you watching your every move at this moment. They are simply on inter-dimensional levels. Now if you wish to experience this, close your eyes for a moment and take a deep breath, and they will take a place behind you. Feel it as they put their gentle, loving hands on your shoulders. Feel it as your own guides sometimes reach around and hug your body. Feel it as they put their hand on the back of your heart chakra and rub it ever so gently. We tell you, it is quite crowded in here but they are enjoying the interaction as you sit still in your reality long enough for them to do that. You are honoring the other dimensional realities.

The fifth dimension in which you now live is not describable in terms you would understand so we use the simplistic terms of height, width, depth, time and space to illustrate your new relationship of living in the fifth dimension. But we will tell you a secret – you are already there. You just need to learn how to use it, to convince yourself that things have changed. You can see that, in the fifth dimension, truth itself is an evolution, not a standard. Do not cling too tightly to any one truth. Allow your truth to evolve to new levels, and you will find that you adjust very quickly. Many of you here in this room will help with higher fifth-dimensional attributes and helping people adjust.

Intention

Dragonfly, #060 Las Vegas, NV

Question:

Five of us went back up on the mountain after you did your channel and we climbed up onto a trail and just created a ceremony right on the spot. It was very beautiful and I think all of us sensed that this ceremony had meanings at many different levels. I wonder if you could talk about some of the other layers, or some of the other aspects, that we are not aware of consciously?

The group:

Oh, you have no idea of how many beings in different dimensional levels watch your every move. We think it is humorous that humans love privacy, for you have none. You are being watched every moment of every day in everything you do, and most of the time, you are being applauded for what you do. When you open a space consciously to connect in that way, you are literally calling Beings in. When you did your ceremony, a portal opened and you were surrounded by more support than you could ever imagine. It's as if you were shouted through a bullhorn: "If anybody is in the neighborhood and wants to come visit, here we are." Literally, Beings from all dimensions of time and space come and gather there to be part of your gathering. It has happened in many different ways throughout your history. That is the nature of prayer, of meditation. It has been shown in many different ways. Do Ouija boards work? Of course, they do. You are basically setting your intent to communicate in Spirit in whatever form it will take. And that is what happens.

Before we let you return to your seat, we wish to give you a caution. The call we just spoke of it can be done in the heart, in the head, through speaking, or through symbols. Many of you are starting to wear the symbols of the Sign of the Human Angel. But you must also be aware that this is the signal to the other side of the veil that you are one of the people who is asking to receive those assignments, and you will be taken seriously if you wear them. They are fully interdimensional symbols that are seen in all dimensions. You will be nudged on the shoulder if you choose to wear these symbols on your person. It means you are asking to become an angel in training and you will be given the opportunity to experience it. The nudge does not mean you have to do anything, but it will be very difficult for you if go to all that trouble and then not do it. But there are times when you will be chosen because of wearing that.

So when someone is having a difficult time out of nowhere, and they are hiding in the corner, and all these people are passing by in the street, no one would ever dream of going over there to that corner of that alleyway and touching a person or making a difference. Then, all of a sudden, you will get it just as clear as a bell that you are supposed to go over to that corner, tap that person on the shoulder and give them a hug. Oh, you will rationalize it, think it through and say, "Oh, that's not safe, I cannot do that." But you will get those nudges if you wear that symbol, for it is a signal seen throughout all the universe that spans all dimensions of time and space. It is a trigger, and you will be called and you will be honored as touching those people. You have done a great job thus far and we cannot wait to see where you go now, because you are going to start moving a lot faster than you ever have.

Enjoy the ride.

Espavo.

NATIVE TRIBES AND ABORIGINALS

The Role of Aboriginals

Tag—You Are It, #D090802 Las Vegas, NV

Question:

I would like to ask what part the Red Nation and Star Nation are playing at this time. I speak of the Native Americans, Aborigines, and the Ancients of that caliber.

The group:

The Aborigines on all levels of your planet have held secrets. They have held the energy of what the magic is within their own realms. So many of them have held it in so many traditional forms that most have forgotten how to put the pieces back together. Some have lost track of some of the truths they were guarding due to the fact they have guarded them so well.

We tell you, bringing this back together will be important for the planet, for it will help you move very quickly into the next levels, and there are many, many Aboriginal tribes that have held this energy in sacred places. You will find much of it held even outside of these tribes, for even what you call the original crystal skulls have held energy and vibration in the form of knowledge.

These are some of the magic secrets that have helped anchor your planet while you played the Game. These are some of the things that have held things in place. Now, recently a movement has taken place to bring back and honor the Aboriginals in all tribes, in all nations, on all parts of your globe. We tell you this is wonderful. The biggest challenge, however, is that you must keep the egos out of it, and that is hard because each one of these Aboriginals holding secrets believes he or she has THE secret. In fact, none of them has THE secret. All of them together have the secrets. They are the energy of Earth Herself, how it was built, and why it will go to the next level. That is in progress now. Work with each one as you can, dear ones, and find the knowledge in each and every level of Aboriginal training.

The word "aboriginal" simply means original, for it is the original tribes that have held the energy. You will find much of this passed down. You will find much that still needs interpretation, but these are important pieces of the puzzle. They are in many lands, on many continents of your globe. You will find them and eventually the egos will move out of the way, so you will be able to incorporate pieces back into a whole picture. As you do, you will help to set up some of the return of what we have called the government of Mu. The Aborigines can help if they choose, It is their choice.

PHANTOM DEATH

I Was Going to Die but I Didn't

Angela's Broken Wing, $D060301, San Diego, CA.

Question:

I felt very strongly for a long time that I was supposed to die in the early nineties. I came close a couple of times and, although the veil has thinned out a lot for me and I can see and receive a lot of information, I still have trouble separating what is coming from me and what is coming from the other side. I'd like to know if I was right, that I was supposed to "cash it in" in the early nineties.

The group:

Yes, it was a Phantom Death. Your life experience and all of your contracts were complete. You were complete in the energy, as are many others in the room. Eight of you here in this room have had this experience during the last year. Eight of you had the opportunity to leave. Your contracts were complete, your energy was settled, and it would have been perfectly okay for you to go Home. Yet you chose to stay. Why? Because you had something to do. What? You may never know the full contract, for it is not possible for you to see. But you would not be here receiving this message if you did not still have something important to do.

There are times when you may pass someone in the grocery store and, without uttering a word, you may look into their eyes and change their life. That may be part of the reason you are still here, to fulfill some of these types of contracts. And you, dear one, have touched many with your work and your love, for that love was completely opened in the early nineties. You are now a different person entirely than the person you were before the early nineties. All of the fears and expectation are gone. You are here to touch others and you are doing that work very well.

The Phantom Death is confusing to many. Simply know it as the reset button. Push it and then be ready for what comes up on the screen next. Thank you for staying.

Phantom Death

Portals of Lemuria, #D032403, Kona, HI.

Question:

Hello. Several months ago you told me at another workshop that my work would be going to the next level. I suspect that's true for all of us, obviously. Specifically I had two experiences. One was in the middle of the night, being asked if I was now ready to go to the next level, and I said yes, but wanted my lessons to be gentle. And I was downloaded with information all night. The next night, I had a dream, and it was a symbol of a blue sphere with pinpoints of potential eruptions all over it, and I was told that it was the globe of the Earth, and at all of those points were holders of energy to catch the negative energy and transmute it back into positive energy. And this was regarding Earth and it had to do with tectonic plates and the Earth. And that was regarding the decision to come here also. Can you explain what that brings me? And I think it probably is significant for all of us.

The group:

We wish to address several points of your question. First of all, let us address the first part of your question. No, it is not true for everyone. What we told you was specifically for you. And although many in here will choose to take their own work to the next level, we will address you individually. It takes courage to step off that cliff, even if you do not see the bridge in front of you. And having done so, you have put yourself through what we call the Phantom Death. For in order to reset the energy, it was necessary for you to re-align yourself to the planet and the new grid. You have been aligned in a certain fashion for a very long time, but the grids of the Earth have now changed and the final adjustments have been put into place, which makes many of you feel very uncomfortable. For all of your alignments, all of your feelings, have been moving. It is almost as if you have been doing the hula-hoop while someone is pulling the rug out from under you. Your final adjustments afforded you the opportunity to go Home six weeks ago.

There are many opportunities you have when that happens. You can push the button that says, "I am going Home." Or you can push the button that says, "I am going to stay and move into my passion, and I am going to do what I came here to do." Or, you can push the third button that says, "I will make my mind up later."

You have pushed that last button many times. This time, you pushed the middle button, choosing to stay and move into your passion, so things have begun aligning for you as a result of your changes. You are now beginning to align yourself to a new grid. But that requires changes within your own physical circumstances as well as your energetics, and more importantly, your relationship status. So the relationships around you are now lining up to help support you in the next level of your own work. As that happens, you have begun working with the inter-dimensional levels, which has shown up in your reality as dreams. What you are seeing is exactly what we described not more than ten minutes ago. For we tell you, there will be change again around the Ring of Fire, and you will see it happening. And it will trigger a new dimensional level of the Earth Herself, for it is only one of the many signs that things are moving on target.

It is also an opportunity for each one of you to intentionally move into place. How do you do that? What does that feel like? What does that look like? How do I make a living at it? Ah, we can see the questions. Your vision is clear, your dreams have cleared. And also please know you have been downloaded with information. Sometimes trying to interpret it and bring it into a reality which is not yet quite here can only lessen the message to the real essence of who you are. For now, trust that you have been receiving information that is very valuable, that will set you up for the next stage of your life. And understand that sometimes a cup of coffee is ... just a cup of coffee.

Stepping Off the Cliff

Seven Stages of Life, #004 Santa Fe, NM

Question:

Since choosing change, energetic change in DNA, in my life, everything has changed and there have been two situations that can involve death and life and a choice between them ... and I don't know how to choose. Right after asking for a change, a river suddenly flowed into the house I live in and acres of cliff washed away, so my home is now perched within a few feet of a 150-foot straight drop. And it's closing in. People have advised me to move out but I just can't make that decision. It doesn't seem it's the right thing to do. I don't know if it's a choice toward death. The second change is that my blood pressure is up to 217 over 211 and the doctor said I must take medication for it and he was surprised I hadn't had a stroke. Yet I feel I'm being told this is a part of the energetic change and to take medication would inhibit it, so it's my choice. I'm not making one of these choices and I just don't know how.

The group:

We will start with the second question first. Your choice is about your own health but you are exactly correct. It is a choice between life and death, for this is your Phantom Death. This is an opportunity for you to leave the planet if you so choose, but humans do not do change well. We love to embarrass the Keeper when we talk about him and we will do so now. Everything he has ever given up has deep scratch marks all over it, for human change is not something that is part of your make up. You strive so much to be comfortable and comfortable with yourself, so change is very difficult and we tell you, yes, you are exactly at the crossroads you believe yourself to be. Yes, you are making a choice between life and death.

Now please understand: All choice is honored. You can choose to come Home, dear one. We will greet you with the most celebration and wonderful hugs. If you choose to stay, we will support you, love you, touch you with the touch of a Human Angel when you think you are alone, yet from that point forward, you must choose to be on purpose. There is work to do, dear ones, and we tell you lovingly that rise in vibration has left you with a very narrow tolerance for misalignments of energy. In short, your bullshit tolerance is gone. That was the reason you stayed this long, for you have already been through one Phantom Death, The one you are in now is your second.

This is also the same illusion you have about the house. You can see very clearly that if you do not choose to change, you will simply drop off. We tell you, dear one, it is a wonderful way to go. Please know that we say this with the dearest of love for your choice is here. You humans have always been brought up thinking that death is wrong. In fact, death is not a problem; it is simply one stage of life.

You have also been brought up to think all illness is a sign of something wrong, but it is not. Let us also explain another illusion you have – an aversion to what you call your medical sciences. You will take the vibrations from aromatherapy into your nose and intentionally change your own vibration in order to facilitate healing. Yet when that same process is offered through a medical doctor, you will refuse it, thinking there is something wrong. Please understand, it is the blending of the metaphysical and the physical sciences that will release the genie in the bottle. That is where the joy and the magic is. Do not fear it. If it would help you to take the medication for a short time while you ease some of the other pressures which, by the way, happen to be causing the blood pressure in the first place, this would be very much appreciated and would not, in any way, hamper your spiritual advancement.

You have choice in every moment. Please understand that all choice is honored. If you choose to go Home, you will be honored. If you choose to stay, you will be honored. If you choose to take the medication, you will be honored. You get the idea? Choose well, dear one, and enjoy the ride.

PLANETS AND THE SOLAR SYSTEM

When the Sun Burns Out

Reflectors of the Light, #051, St Louis Mo.

Question:

What about the climate and weather and how the Earth is being affected by industrialization and the safety of our environment, land, water and air and the fact that some day, the sun will burn out. [laughter]

The group:

It is fun to see how you encompass about six billion years in one question. But it is a very interesting question, so we will take the larger aspect of the question first and then try to bring it down to some of the smaller aspects. Let's look at the big picture. What happens when the sun burns out? Well, the sun will not burn out in an instant. The sun will become hot before it begins to burn out and that will affect your game here on Planet Earth beyond your understanding, for it has happened before in a similar situation. But there are many options, many opportunities for you to begin to travel to new dimensions of time and space. And even though your research and your development up to this point have been in what you call space ships, rockets or spacecraft of some nature, we tell you it will originally be a combination of time travel and space work that will help you to understand how to move from here to here.

In a very short time, you will begin reactivating the life on Mars. For Mars will once again support life. You will find life on Mars in a very short time. You will find evidence not only of past life beyond recognition, but you will also find current life happening on Mars at this moment. And no, we do not mean space beings walking around with pointy ears. We mean evolution of molds, fungi and bacteria. We mean on very molecular levels, you will find actual life happening on Mars now. Shortly after that, you will know how to affect that process and how to evolve it, for it is the evolution of what you call "greenhouse gases" that will once again put an atmosphere around Mars and part of what you will see eventually will be a colonization of Mars or an attempt to colonize Mars.

We tell you this in a wonderful way, because we want you to see where the next direction of your own science will be heading, for you will be working very clearly in that direction because it is well known that the sun is changing Earth at this moment. Over the last five years, you have had major solar flares like none ever recorded before, which have started to reprogram Earth with a new hologram. It has opened up the possibility and that is the reason why we ourselves have imprinted and helped you to develop the idea of the hologram of the third Earth.

By you creating a thought form that will now become Earth, that thought form is moveable. Not only will it come to Earth but it will go to Mars or any other place you will. Part of the reason we tell you that you will attempt to colonize Mars is because the attempts will not be successful. The reason for that is very simple. As the sun begins to increase its heat, it will very rapidly overwhelm Earth, and Earth itself will start changing very quickly. But before you get the technology to go to the next level over here, we will tell you that scientists are already beginning to understand there is a place in your own solar system that will take very little effort for you to adapt to support life. Which can very easily house all of humanity. It is a moon of Jupiter you know as Europa.

You will eventually skip your colonization attempts to Mars and move directly there. That is the larger picture as we see it. Please understand, you are on the planet of free choice. You are jn the Game of free choice no matter what planet you are on. Therefore, all of this could change but that is the larger picture we are looking at in this moment. That is the path you are setting into motion and that is the natural evolution of the larger picture. You will make wonderful Europians.

In the meantime, you have other evolutionary processes going on, for the industrialization of the planet certainly has changed planet Earth but we tell you, you have actually made less impact on planet Earth than you think. Planet Earth is in a process of changing and evolving, anyway. Even without your industrialization, you would be experiencing global warming at this time for it is actually radiation coming from not only from the Sun but also other planets and is now starting to penetrate and change Earth.

Even though you certainly have had a hand in it, the process itself is necessary, for we told you here that as the Earth cooled, you had to gain density and actually intentionally lower your vibrations to be on planet Earth. Now you are raising your vibrations, and the Earth must once again begin to heat up. That is the natural progression of your cycle. The fact that humans have yet to learn to live in harmony with the Earth must also shift for this change to take place. If you keep polluting the way you have, it will be only a few years before irreversible damage sends all of Earth on a collision course with disaster.

You will not only see the weather patterns changing – which you are currently seeing – but you will see movement of the Earth. And we tell you, the next one to watch for is a volcano that will erupt in the middle of the Pacific Ocean. That is a trigger point and you have recently seen the type of effect this can cause.

No we are not predicting great global catastrophes. That is really not necessary for you to experience them as in recent experience. How you acclimate these actions is entirely up to you. But it is also no secret to tell you, as the Earth heats up, the polar caps will be melting and the rising water levels will make a difference immediately on your planet, even in as little as the next fifteen years. So prepare for that, watch for that.

You could have as much as three meters increase in your water level over the next fifteen years. And if you understand that three meters is not that much, the reality is, it can be a huge amount on your planet. And the collective of all coast lands everywhere will change as a result of that, causing other changes in your weather patterns. All is appropriate. Yes, it will look like the end of the world and in some ways, it will be the end of the world. But it will not be your end, for you are beings that have a purpose, your spark of god is being seen in each other's eyes. God is seeing god. And god is evolving and becoming self-aware as a result of planet Earth, the planet of free choice. Enjoy the ride.

Other Games, Other Planets

Healer's Healer, #065 Las Vegas, NV

Question:

I've talked to people about how planet Earth is a very hard school to be in, and a lot of times, people say to me, "Well, this can't be the only place like this. Are there other Earths? Are there other Earths out there?" That's what people think, but surely, if you're thinking that way, then you're thinking of it in duality instead of energy. What are your thoughts on that?

The group:

Bingo. You have the concept, for that is exactly what is going on. There are many other schools on Earth that are in a slightly different dimension of time and space, a slightly different vibrational harmonic that you do not exist in. Also, you have a misconception of what the universe is, so you look out into the night sky and think that it is 16.3 million light years away ... but it is not. It is very close to you, for there is a fold in time and space. Instead of measuring distance this way, you actually go around fold, so the two points are very close together. Yet that perception of being so far away allows you more freedom in your own mistakes, in your own schoolhouse Earth.

Earth is one of the most difficult schoolhouses, and when it began, you in ethereal form set up the possibilities. You argued with yourselves, saying, "Oh, that will never work. That cannot possibly work. We have to have some direction."

That was the purpose, to have some point of direction. The intent was not to make a difficult school, but to put a Game out there where God absolutely could not see God. You had no perception that you had any divinity in you whatsoever. You thought you were victims of circumstance. And you put on the veil tight and complete, and then you took all the rules off except one: Free choice in all matters. Many of you said, "Oh no, you have to at least give us some hints. You have to at least put some crystals on our path or give us some direction, or send some wonderful stones down from the mountain with the rules on them."

But, when you looked up in the mountains for the stones with the rules on them, you could not find them, so you created them yourselves. How wondrous. There are no rules except free choice in all matters.

We have called it "The Grand Game of Hide and Seek," but you carry the knowledge. Enjoy.

Tenth Planet

Carrie and Sam, #D042802, Fullerton, CA.

Question:

Over the last two days, I've been drawn to some of the writings of the Pleiadian/Sirian councils and DNA re-coding. Some of these writings mention the return of the tenth planet, scheduled for sometime next year. Could you tell us more? Why I am so drawn to this material? And how will the arrival of the tenth planet play out?

The group:

Thank you for asking the question. The first part of the question we wish to answer for you is why are you drawn to this material. That is no secret. It is something you know in your heart, for you have origins on that star system. Yes, you are most certainly an alien. [laughter] What are you all laughing at? None of you are from Earth. [laugher] You all have origins elsewhere. Your veil has simply been so thin from the stress you have received in the early lifetime that you have been pushed into realizing a time when the heart connected strongly and you have done well with it.

We will speak of your solar system, for you think you have a handle on it, but we tell you, you do not. There is more that is in an elliptical orbit that has been there all along. Please understand, your own technology here on the planet has only been here a very, very short time. You cannot see your full star system, even that which is in your own orbit. You will find at least two more planets which are part of your solar system.

We believe this is what you are speaking of that will happen within the next year. We will tell you, the pattern has been in place for quite some time and, in fact, has passed your way less than 500 years ago but you did not have the technology to see it or to know what it was. Much of that is now changing.

You, yourself, are a channel from the parental races of which you speak, one of six of what you know to be humanity. You have been an accumulation and mixing of many energies that have agreed to help plant the seeds of the First Planet of Free Choice. Many of those energies are around you now. They have come back to see what all the excitement is. "My word, they are actually winning the Game," they said. And we tell you, there have even been two of them come in and fight over who is going to help you the most. It is quite humorous from our perspective, for they have pretty much forgotten you up to this point, but now you are of great interest to them. There are many, dear ones, who will be here with information of what you will perceive to be of very high origin, and you will take all the information they give.

Watch for the love content, for that is where the key is. That is where the connection is, for there will be those who come to put you in fear. Hold your power. Hold your energy. Know you have more keys to your own existence than you could possibly know. And take all the information coming in and run it through your own filters of discernment. Do not take anything anyone says as complete gospel, including us. We do not want your power; we are doing just fine with our own, and yet you try to give it so freely. You are doing so well, though.

The veil is getting thinner. You will find much in coming years about the origins of your Universe and the very central sun around which the Universe revolves. You will start beginning to understand, and some of you are on the right track when you look to crystals, for they hold the seed of the energy now emanating from the central sun. It is not just your planet that is in evolution; it is All That Is.

All we have termed to be the Universe and all the Universes around it are in a state of very rapid evolution, and it all began here. Many entities watch each and every one of you in the smallest of steps. And you thought you could hide in the bathroom! [laughter] They are watching you in awe because you are changing their world, even the Pleiades. You have helped all to move to a higher vibrational level and therefore the changes are tremendous. There are so many entities watching your every move that in some of the overtone levels directly adjacent to the reality in which you live, there has been quite a parking problem. Fear not, we will deal with it. But the interest has been great and you will see more.

Such silliness goes on in the Universe that recently, two of these emerging races have even fought over who will take a place in the first overtone level. Find the love, dear ones. Go with the heart energy, for that is what you have learned. That is why you have won the Game. You are holding the energy of the love, and the greatest love of All That Is. And it is that love, that energy that connects each and every one of you to not only each other but also to us, and to each of these other entities. We are one. And your Game is doing quite well.

Watch your sciences for the potentials of not one but three recent discoveries of planets that have an outside elliptical orbit that are not actually a part of your solar system but that interact with your solar system on a regular basis. One planet you will find has an elliptical orbit that takes it outside of your ring and brings it back which is actually part of your solar system. And we hope we have answered your question.

NOTE: The following year (2003) astronomers and NASA found a new planet in our solar system as predicted in this channel. The second one was discovered in 2004 but was reclassified in 2006 by an international delegation of astronomers. They also agreed that even Pluto was too small to be considered a planet.

PLAN B

Free Wheeling

Are You Ready? #D030903, Baltimore, MD.

Question:

Could you please address the desire for abundance or the changes that the third dimension personality would like to put into play? How that juxtaposes with what the divine spirit's plans may have been beforehand, and any contradictions that may ensue? And why certain things may not come to pass because they may be the divine spirit's contracts or plans for the individual that precedence?

The group:

That is an excellent question, for you have chosen to separate yourself, as you did in the beginning of the Game. What you do not understand is that as we sit in front of divine spirit this very day, there is no grand plan in place. You have surpassed that plan yourself. You are the ones who scripted the plan in the first place. So we tell you now, you are in Plan B. You are ready to do it again.

As far as spirit's plan of where you are, spirit never had an entire plan of where you were to go. Spirit had a grand hope of what could be accomplished, but there is only one rule upon your Game board. It is a rule you have put there yourselves: Free choice in all matters. Having known that, you have been guided in certain areas, for you have asked for guidance. You ask in prayer, you ask sitting here in front of us, you ask in different ways when you read books to look for guidance. But you hold the key, and you decide what is going to be in your reality and what is not.

We re-mind you that you do not have control over the thoughts that enter your head, for you are part of a Universal Consciousness. When this one over here has a thought, it circulates and it is not long before this one over there has that same thought. That is the way it works. You share that Unity Consciousness, even though you live within a field of polarity and you see yourselves as different. However, you have complete control over what thoughts stay in your head, and that is what creates your reality and a collective divine plan which you, as spirits, are making.

For you to move into your highest evolution as spirits, at this point in your evolution, it is necessary for you to take the reigns. It is not easy for you to understand, because you have been living in a world of duality, where your power has always seemed to be outside of yourself, so you have always looked for answers or guidance from a supreme being.

Let us tell you an interesting story. As the baby lies on the table having its diaper changed, it looks upon its mother as this wonderful, omnipresent being who takes care of its every need. Any time the baby wants something, it cries out. It is the only way it can control its reality, as it calls out and its mother comes and takes care of it. It is necessary in that second stage of life to give your power away in order to sustain life in your physical bubble of biology. You must rely upon your caregivers at that stage to take care of you. It is also the stage where you get your ideas about god being outside of yourself and about heaven being up. Your first experiences are that of a loving being who takes care of you, where that being stands above you somewhere taking care of you below. And that is also why you think Heaven is up here and not right where you sit. So naturally, you believe your mother has a plan because she does things on a regular schedule. She knows where things are and she has a plan for you. Even as she changes your diaper, she has already figured out you are going to go to college and be a doctor. You look for the grand plan, and yes, Spirit has grand potential. As you set this Game into motion, there was the highest possibility that the Game of Free Choice would be that you started to awaken from the dream. And here you sit with your eyes wide open.

No, you do not have all the answers yet. Nor do you yet know all the things you have come to learn. You do not even understand that you, in fact, are Spirit. You are god, itself, incarnate in physical form. You have the same powers as god; you have just forgotten how to use them. Along with that comes the ego because it jumps in and wants to balance things immediately.

"Oh, but I cannot be god," you protest. Let us tell you something: It is not easy being god, for immediately your ego – a very important part to help you survive in your physical bubbles of biology – jumps to the immediate assumption that you are the only god. [laughter]

What you do not necessarily know is that you are changing your world with every thought you have, and that as you evolve into higher vibrations, you change the paradigm for everyone on the Earth. Everything changes. But it goes far beyond that, because this Game was never anticipated to go quite as far as it did. The reality is, the grand hope of spirit – what you call the grand plan – has already won the Game. Here you sit, having already passed the marker. You are not about to destroy yourself, even though your television programs may tell you so. It will not happen, dear ones, for you will not let that happen.

Do you understand how much humanity has moved in the last fifty years? Do you know what a miracle we perceive from this side of the veil as we look upon your Gameboard in the last fifty years? You are the magicians. You are the ones who have sat here scripting it, looking outside of yourself for answers when here they sit. We tell you, the rest of the Universe is watching you very closely. You are setting things into motion that will not only change paradigms of planet Earth, but also of All That Is. Your Game has been wildly successful, and we cannot wait to see what you write next. As far as any contradictions between what has been set in place before and what is setting in place now, yes, there have been some. And yes, when any being changes direction, and goes in a different direction, there will be seemingly contradictions of purpose, but they will be corrected.

Choose well. You are on a wonderful path. Thank you for the question.

RELATIONSHIPS

Pain in Relationships

Crystal Walk-Ins, #D042101, San Diego, Ca.

Question:

Can you talk about why relationships have to be so painful?

The group:

There is one other question we wish to address that has not been asked for a very intentional reason, yet it applies to so many of you here. It has to do with relationships. Sometimes this is a very difficult area, for you have come down and gone through the second dimension, and you do not know you are not what you see in the mirror. You do not understand you are not just male or female; but are part of a whole. You think yourself just half, or part of, and therefore you need something else to complete you. That is simply not true. We have told you already that a good relationship is much like life insurance. You can only get it if you don't need it. [laughter]

It is important that you hold your own energy within yourself and stand in your own truth, for there really is only one relationship – you with you. The person who was holding this energy actually fell in love with who she thought this person could be instead of who this person really is. This is a very common misdirection of energy. You see the potential and think, if only this person will grow with me, then we can ride off into the sunset. We tell you, that is very boring. [laughter]

You have much of your life to avoid pain, dear ones. Please understand that when you come home, when you get to this side of the veil and all energy is correct, you will even re-member that wonderful pain as part of the beautiful experience of life on earth. You have evolved your spirit to such a point that you can actually put a piece of it in those beautiful physical bodies you own. That you can actually take the spirit within your own hand and reach out and touch another angel. Do that now. See the essence of your own being reaching out and touching another Human Angel, another spirit hiding within the physical being of biology. Oh, it is grand indeed. That is your evolution.

Do not think of yourself necessary to have a relationship for, if you do, you will only attract in your field those people who you can lean against. And when two people are leaning against each other, trying to make a whole person out of two half people, it does not work. For two people never move at the same rate, and when one moves, the other falls. Find someone you can walk next to. Share your life. Do not worry about tomorrow; share your life today. Have the courage to stand and let them be free. Empower them to be the greatest they can be without the strings. Walk freely without expectation, and you will make space for empowered humans in your own relationships. Do not think that only long term relationships are successful. Just the beauty of your willingness to love yourself through another person deserves our applause on this side of the veil. And please understand that that applause is thundering.

Together on a Different Level

Angela's Broken Wing, #D060301, San Diego, CA.

Question:

I'm experiencing confusion around my marriage, in that we connect as souls so beautifully, especially when we go to seminars together. Even when I am in a seminar by myself, he is just right there, the communication is there, and it seems we are in step. But when he goes back into his normal life, he's just not there at all and it's like we are two incompatible personalities.

The group:

As you came through the first dimension, you passed through the second dimension in order to land here in the third. As you did that, you split off into parts of yourself you call the sexes. You choose male or female for each incarnation and as you do, you feel like you are not whole. Every time you come in, you feel as though you need to add something to yourself to make you whole, and you look at the potential of being whole through a relationship.

It is a misdirection of energy, an illusion, because only when a person is whole unto themselves can they actually have a relationship. You are finding that out. There is only one relationship and that is you with you. When you get that one right, you can have all the other ones you want. The biggest challenge, of course, is that you often fall in love with someone you think may have it. We ask you instead to focus on what is there and to fall in love with the person who this person is today, right now. If you can make it work today, you have the magic. If you can look at this person and find the things that drew you together – the support, the love, and most important, the communication — then you can make that magic work for you right now, today. If you cannot, move on.

Have the courage to release in love and center your energy on yourself, for only in doing that can you open to a new relationship. As far as where your partner is going and where you believe his systems are, we tell you he is moving into his own vibrational advancement; however it may not fit with yours. The two of you still have not decided.

There are misconceptions of relationships we wish to address here. All relationships are built on communication. Any time you can pull aside the veil and really see another soul, you have complete communication with them, and when that happens, you fall in love with that soul. It may be a fatherly love or a lover love or both.

On the keyboard that relationships are, it is easier to see for everyone is an individual vibration. Humans seem to be at first looking for someone playing the same note they are. When you do find them, it is very validating ... and very boring. So you pull in someone next who is playing a note close to yours, and you end up playing Chopsticks, which is tolerable but aggravating. It is not until you move a comfortable distance apart that you hit a chord. This is where two vibrations overlap each other at regular intervals, supporting each other. This harmony creates a third vibration, which is what you call a relationship.

Find the chord where you are now and you will have your relationship. Do not anticipate that he is going to move to the next note and it is going to sound great, because you are moving as well. Find the chord now and work with him on the communication, for that is what creates the chord. Two humans, once they find the chord, do not stay on the same notes. They are constantly evolving and there will be times you hit very awkward chords. The whole idea is to make sure you are playing on the same keyboard.

You are on a good path. The relationship you have currently is not yet complete. You feel that in your heart. Speak all of your truth to himl and allow him to speak all of his truth to youl and you will quickly find whether you are playing the same notes or whether you are playing something that is very uncomfortable. You are closer than you think, dear one. Enjoy the ride.

SPACE & THE COSMOS

Space Brethren

The Age of E. #017, Mt Shasta, CA.

Question:

Can you give me some insight on my role with Universal or Galactic information?

The group:

There are six parental races making up what you call human biology. The human race had always been in ethereal bodies up to that point in your evolution. As the earth began to cool, it was necessary for you to find denser bodies that would allow you to keep your full connection to the Earth. That is when six invited races or beings came to Earth to join together the form and the spirit in a physical bubble of biology. It was here that the species of ape was adapted for use by the human spirit. You did not ascend from the apes. You did not crawl out of the sea and later learn to walk erect. You literally took a physical vehicle and split off and adapted it for your use as spirit. This is not an evolutionary step, for you will see that the apes are still here and their line is still intact. Do you see apes evolving into humans? No, humanity is a very special case as the bodies you carry had to be hand-crafted to carry a portion of your spirit. We tell you that as critical as you are with your bodies at times, they are the perfect vehicle for your energy in any given moment.

After they were done, some of the parental representatives left. Some of them stayed; some of them have been here in other dimensional realities between spaces you cannot see, for they do not interfere with your Game. The Game was free choice, so it was appropriate that they would create and step back entirely. They have done so.

There were also those who, by special divination, were given permission to come in and not interfere with your Game, but to try to save their own race. They were here for some time, and some of them are still here, but they are not able to do what they were hoping for. Their race was dying, and they were limited in the human interactions needed to sustain life in a physical body. The one thing this particular race has done is they caused absolutely wonderful spaceship stories.

Are you alone in the Universe? Of course, not. How could you possibly be? You are great creators, yourselves. Even your thoughts will create a reality. Now that the portals are opening, you will see that you have much to do here. For there will be time when education becomes necessary, and many of you here in this room are holding that information, waiting for the time for it to come where others will be motivated to search for the answers that you hold.

You have felt so alone. You have felt as if you have had this knowing in here that you could not do anything with. You knew that a number of people would just roll their eyes and shut you out. That was the difficult part, dear one. Now it is time, for people will soon come to ask the questions you have waited so long to answer.

Many of you have had very few incarnations on Earth. You are here in preparation for what is to happen. You are special inter-dimensional beings yourself, and that is why you came here at this time. You can spot these new souls as they have a refreshing view of the newborn child, wide-eyed with excitement, waiting to experience everything. They will help with the transition that is ahead and they will validate what is in your heart.

Second Planet

Seven Stages of Life, #D071902 Santa Fe NM

Question:

Greetings. Can you give us some more information about the Second Free Choice Planet? Does it have a name? Where's its location in the Universe? Does it have humanoids? Do they work with the same negativity we're working with? And will we be visiting them in the near future or far-flung future?

The group:

Oh, we love it when you lay it all out like that. It is so human to want to put everything in a box. We have purposely not spoken of the Second Planet of Free Choice, but we will give you some hints, some ideas of what it is like. We have purposely not spoken about this as there was little need. It will be a while before your world fully intersects with theirs. Others will also be coming forth with this information, and we ask the Keeper not to be an expert in everything. Let us explain it in another way: We will simply say to you, much of what you see in and around you exists within a specific vibrational range. Yet, even though you hold your finger up in front of your face, you perceive your finger only because the atoms in your finger are vibrating at a rate your eye can see. Your human brain will tell you nothing exists between your finger and your eye, yet we tell you that is not true. Entire worlds and universes may exist in the infinitesimal space between your finger and your eye.

The Second Planet of Free Choice is on a different timeline than you are at this moment, so a year for you at this moment could be twelve thousand years for the Second Planet of Free Choice. Therefore, there is much that is very different with the relationship with them, for even though they were in the amoeba stages only a short time ago, you will begin to see evolution. This is part of the reason why you have actually created the vortices you have on planet Earth, for we have even told you they will turn into inter-dimensional time portals. You immediately went to thinking that this was going to be for outer space beings who were coming to visit you. We tell you, they are inter-dimensional beings. That is where you will begin to understand the Second Planet of Free Choice.

Will they be coming to visit you? Oh, we hope so. You will see them very clearly for, as you advance first out of the human form into the Human Angel form, you begin taking responsibility for yourselves and your powers of creation, and you are there to help other angels up when they fall. You are there to help empower someone in your field. You are there to help in any way you can because you start understanding Unity Consciousness, as each one of you becomes the Human Angel who helps the other people around you, and all of your elevations rise very quickly. That is the first lesson, and will take some time. You can see resistance to that lesson even now, so it will take time, yet you are right on target.

The second part will be when you start understanding you have contracts that you will make with beings on the Second Planet of Free Choice, much the way we made a contract with the Keeper twelve lifetimes ago. No, we ask the Keeper not to chastise himself; he was not stupid. In fact, he has played this part with us several times. He simply does not re-member. However, much the way we have made contracts with him, many of you have contracts that are about to enact. Of course, all of these are contingent upon free choice. If you choose, you will take a place just over their shoulder. You will watch and be there to help when asked. There will be times when you will yell with all your might, "Turn right. Turn right." And you will watch as they turn left. And we will laugh hysterically, for we have experienced that with you.

Where is it in the Universe? It does not exist in a place where your own maps can see. It exists in the space between your finger and your eye, and you will see it. You will see it in the blink of an eye because of the choices you are making. When you become multidimensional beings, your vision will give you answers to many of the questions you have been asking. We also say, we cannot tell you when exactly that will happen. The reason for this is that when the collective vibration of humanity hits a harmonic vibration with itself in another timeline, the doors of multidimensionality magically open for all humans everywhere.

What are your contracts? Your contracts are only what you choose. What do you need to do to be there for them? You just need to experience your passion. You just need to play in your joy. How on Earth are you going to teach them how to do that until you do that? That is why we are here. And we thank you for asking the question.

SOUND AND MUSIC

Vibrational Healing

Crystal Walk-Ins, #D041202, San Diego, CA.

Question:
Could the group talk to us about the place of sound and music in the evolution of our consciousness?

The group:
We have told the Keeper before that you are a collective vibration as humans but additionally each one of you is a vibration, with vibrational signatures. We have spoken about vibrational integrity, which has four lines: what you speak, what you think, what you act and what you believe.

Most of you on this planet, especially those bound to third-dimensional thinking, have been walking around with two or three of those lines very much in integrity with you and the fourth one canceling everything out [laughter], for you often walk, act and think what you do not believe. Now you also send out an exact match into the Universe. This is the vibration you feel before you walk into a door, before you pick up a phone, before you walk into a meeting, before you handshake with other people and get a vibration from them. You are learning to trust those vibrations. That is the collective vibration each one of you has.

From a physical standpoint, each one of the organs within your body vibrates at a separate rate, or its vibrational signature. So overall, you have a collective vibrational signature. Music or sounds that harmonize with your vibrational signature will add to you just by listening. Since there is a natural wide variance in vibrational signatures, one man's music is another man's noise. [laughter] You are learning to introduce an overall vibration that varies enough in tone and in heart energy for it to encompass the possibility for many of you to reset your own vibrational signature. Vibrational healing will become part of the key on all future healing modalities on this planet.

Any time you are able to create a vibration from the heart, it will allow others to reset their vibrational tones. Understand and watch for opportunities to work with vibrational healing, for it will work in many areas. There are also those of you here in the room who work in different areas, for most of you are healers. We tell you, as healers, you will work many areas, some with your hands. By placing your hands on someone, you can make a difference. Or you can send energy from across the room with your hands.

Some of you work with words, and are counselors, seminar leaders or authors, for you can reflect other people's energy very clearly and you are magical. Some of you heal with tones and, even if you do not sing, people will listen to the tone of your voice rather than the words you actually speak. Others of you heal with your touch, or with your love. They are healings through vibration.

So please understand that your traditional medicine and the opportunity to introduce genetically altered herbs, which you call prescription drugs, into the body is actually a way of altering the vibration. You will find much simpler ways and many new opportunities to do things very quickly, for you are now in the higher vibrations of the New Planet Earth. Now you can make a difference with your own vibration. Enjoy the ride.

Power of Music

The Color Clear, #D051902, St. Louis, Mo.

Question:

Many of us are aware of the power that music has to affect our emotions, whether it's positive or negative, and I was wondering if you had information about music and how it can affect us. How it can help us?

The group:

As you move from one vibrational level to the next, you find your vibrations rise and your body becomes less dense. As that happens, you become more susceptible to vibration. We tell you to watch the area of vibrational healing, for it will no longer just be a song that makes you feel better. It will no longer be simply something that makes you melancholy or takes you to a state of memories. It will be a way to heal yourselves.

All of your senses are capable of entering energy through vibration into your field. You have a new relationship to vibration since you stepped into the fifth dimension and you will be more susceptible to it. You will also need to choose your reality very carefully. You will need to choose carefully where you live, who you are around, and who is in your field at all times.

As you do, you will find that each organ of your body has its own set of vibrational standards and basically has a vibration that vibrates at a healthy rate. Overall your entire physical body has what we term a "vibrational signature," and if you find that vibration, or a harmonic of it, it will help your overall body reset its vibrational signature.

The days ahead will reveal much. You will see so much opportunity to work with other people. The master healers here in this room are honored beyond your understanding. You are the ones who have been here time and time again to offer your services.

In the higher vibrations of the New Planet Earth, all healing must be requested, so you literally had to wait for the collective vibration of humanity to get high enough to request your work. That is the reason so many of you are waiting for this time.

Many of you also will experience the seed fear, for you came from the days of Atlantis as healers and much vibrational healing happened during those times. You have worked so hard to keep things from yourselves and you said, "If ever the collective vibration of humanity gets high enough to where it can support the return of those choices, we will all come back en masse and work together to make different choices this time." And as the trigger started happening, you all flooded back into the planet Earth and said, "It looks like we may make it this time. Let us go back in and see if we can make a difference this time, if we can take our power."

You all jumped in at the same time and made a huge difference. You went through your childhoods with some difficulties, some misunderstanding, and then came the time when you started to awaken as young adults. You looked into each other's eyes, you felt the heart connection and you recognized each other from the days of Atlantis. You had a great party you called the Sixties. And now, here you are, past the seed fear. Here you are as the healers, asking questions about vibrational healing. You see our excitement. Glad this is back, dear ones. You are here at the same juncture of time and space, the same stage of evolution, and you are taking your power. It looks very good on you. Enjoy the ride.

SYMBOLS AND NUMEROLOGY

Threes

Portals of Lemuria, #D032403, Kona, HI.

Question:

For myself recently, I noticed that numbers are always coming up in triplets and I'm curious about that. Even my hotel room had it.

The group:

It is very interesting that each one of you will pull different master numbers into your view, yet three is the number that has created time and time again, for all of what you see before you is base three. You all have a new relationship to that which you call the trinity as you begin unfolding the numbers. They are in your scriptures and other writings over and over again. They have been brought into your reality time and time again, through those of you who hold the information. They will help you understand the new relationship with the trinity as you move into a field of Triality.

The threes themselves are magical numbers, and many of you hold information that shows up in the master numbers you see on the clock face. Yes, you think that is interesting, and it is no secret to tell you that those numbers will show on the clock, and it is your own higher self that is using them as a trigger. As you walk through your home, your higher self says,

"Okay, look at the clock right now." You look and see '11:11' and exclaim, "Oh, it must mean something."

It does. It means you are evolving, and that your own DNA is re-connecting because you are purposely listening to your higher self.

Many of you will see the master numbers because it is inside of your own physical evolution. Those of you who see the number three over and over again, please understand, you are being tempted with the mark of a teacher. And that is who you are. It is only the re-minder of that, for that is the true dream.

Sacred Geometry

Tag—You Are It, Las Vegas, NV, 09/08/02

Question:

A lot about sacred geometry is coming up, and it is such a big attraction. Can you tell us more?

The group:

Yes. The rise in the collective vibration of humanity has made it easier for individuals to begin seeing this is just a Game, something that is not part of what you would call nature. You understand that much like you would put props on a stage, there are things that have no illusion to them. But there are actually props in your own field, and when you look at something as real, you are starting to doubt if it is really real. "What is real, anyway?" you are beginning to ask. As your vibrations rise, the veil begins to thin.

What you call 'sacred geometry' is your beginning of see-ing behind the stage. All things that make up the Gameboard are based in numbers. That is the basis of the sacred geometry. Throughout the history of your Gameboard, some of you have used those sacred numbers intentionally, even centuries old architecture. They have been based upon sacred geometry, much the way that you yourselves built the Gameboard and the props on the stage – the same sacred geometry. Right now, you are looking around and seeing all the things through nature. We have spoken of the Golden Mean. The Golden Mean is actually the base key of which all things upon the Gameboard are built. Ah, but what is real? "I can touch this," you say, and, "This is mine, this is here in this moment." We say, "Do not believe it."

Your highest purpose here as humans has been to take ethereal things, run them through your physical being, and bring them into your reality. There is actually a tube that travels up and down your body that controls that process. You take things out of the ethers, bring them in through your physical being, and create them in your three-dimensional world, as what you call real. Look around you; everything you see in front of you is what you would call man-made. We love your human phrases. Everything you consider to be man-made started first as a thought form, did it not? When you built the Gameboard, it was based on sacred geometry.

There will be other planets you will discover, including two within your own system. You will discover other races of beings who will contact you and you will find they are not based upon that same sacred geometry. They are all based upon some form of sacred geometry, yet, those forms differ for different games.

Many things you did not think were there before will start showing up as sacred geometry. Those will be the cosmic winks and much will happen here. Soon, you will begin to uncover the reason behind the geometry as it has been used on your Gameboard. Then the props and disguises become less opaque, you will see the transparency on the other side of them, as the veil thins.

Enjoy this ride, dear ones. Above all, do not take it too seriously, for there is a problem with reality and humans. You think it is real. Ah, but what is real? This is real (touching heart), and that is the connection point, where all things intersect between you and consciousness. That is real. The rest is illusion. We thank you for asking the question.

TIME AND SPACE

Visiting Other Dimensions

The Small Step, #029, Atlanta, GA.

Question:

I sometimes drift off and have a hard time coming back into this reality, and recently it is happening more and more frequently. I have no remembrance of where I'm going, just a feeling. Is this happening because of the energy changes or is this something I need to develop?

The group:

Part of what you are experiencing is actually experiencing a conscious time hole and a new relationship to time and space to which you are not fully adjusted as a human being. You are an inter-dimensional being who has been accustomed to being in one dimension at a time. You are now beginning to float between dimensions. It is an interesting process, for it is going to cause your medical and psychological sciences to re-evaluate many of their definitions.

What we do through the Keeper used to be called schizophrenia,[laughter] but what you are talking about is an opportunity for you to move inter-dimensionally between one dimension and the other.

Questioner:

I do not want to come back.

The group:

You and your own higher self have set these experiences up. You are someone who has taken the time out to allow yourself to move into another dimensional reality, to refresh, to feel whole, to re-member who you are in just that moment. The fact that you come back means you are not finished here and have work to do. You are a teacher from way back, and you will find opportunities to teach. But the physical body and its magnetics must be in alignment. That is what is happening as you move into these other dimensional realities. Enjoy the rest, enjoy your time, and come back.

Time Holes

Portals of Lemuria, #D032403, Kona, HI.

Question:

My question deals with time and experience. The Keeper said earlier how his marriage of so many years was really several marriages, and it's easy to notice how many children today have double sets of parents. I'm wondering if we're experiencing more lifetimes in a lifetime than ever before.

The group:

You have felt the speed of time and space quicken. It is real. Many of you have felt there are only twenty hours in the day, and we tell you to get ready for eighteen. It is not a problem, but only a new relationship to time and space you are now experiencing. In fact, you have been living in three dimensions.

The easiest way we can put this is to complicate it just enough for you to understand, for it is too simple for most of you to comprehend. You have been living in three dimensions – height, width and depth. You now have a new relationship to the next two, which are time and space. So time and space will now have a new relationship to what you are experiencing. You will see where they flow together and blend and where they stand alone.

Many of you have recently fallen through what we term "time holes." You are driving down a road you have been on three hundred times in the last two years, so you know how long it takes to get down that road. Suddenly you find yourself twenty miles farther down the road than you thought you were. You just went through a new relationship with time and space – what we call a time hole. Or the opposite may happen, where you experience yourself farther back. Many of you will change and fall through time holes. Also, there is the opportunity for some of your physical representations of energy to also fall through time holes. Yes, we love it when you walk in the door and put your keys in the same spot every time, and then suddenly they are gone ... for six months. And then they show back up in the same spot. These are time holes you will be experiencing.

Please do not think too much of them. Do not give them too much power, for they are a "cup of coffee" to enjoy. But they illustrate your new relationship to time and space. In fact, you have control over time and space, but you just do not know it yet. It is perfectly easy for you to bend time when you choose, and many in this room have been doing that for years. On your way to work, you look at your watch and see you only have five minutes to get to there, so you intentionally warp time and get there five minutes early!

There will come a time when you begin stretching time further and further. You will understand that through the linear hallway of time, it is possible for you to take a right-angled turn and to move through an alternate reality of time and space, and to even return with some of the beautiful things you picked up over there. By knowing which hallways to turn in, and which directions to go, always at right-angles, time travel is possible. And boy, your stock markets will be in a mess then.

In the meantime, many of your new relationships to time and space will be causing you opportunities to experience many strange phenomena. We have only begun to show you some of the very beginnings of this. As time goes forward, two of you here in this room will have an understanding that will trigger you, for you have taught this very thing before. You will jump into place, and will understand from a previous lifetime how to work it. In fact, that is why you are still here. You will understand more of what this is about, and you will play with it. And we thank you for asking.

Expanding Time

OverLight, #010, Oostamalle, Belgium.

Question:

I have a question about time. You are always talking about time becoming shorter but my time is doubling and tripling, and one week looks like one month to me.

The group:

Is that not wonderful? The default answer to uncontrolled time is to shrink. If you do not control it, the default answer is to shrink. But, in reality, it is only a perception of time that you are changing. Your own perception of time and your own rise in vibration have created a possibility for you to experience it in reverse and expand time.

When you do, take control of your life and the time in which you play the Game of pretending to be human. When you understand more of the mechanics of it, share it with others, for it is possible. It is entirely possible to manipulate time to your own choosing. You are just at the verge of getting off the first step of this wondrous staircase that now stands before you. By the time you get half way down, you will be time-traveling with no problem whatsoever. By the time you get all the way down, you will find it is not necessary to go anywhere. We thought we would just plant the seed to tickle you a little.

TRANSITION

Good Grief

The Small Step, #029, Atlanta, GA.

Question:

In this lifetime, I am playing a lot with grief, as people I love keep kicking over. I know there are more coming up, and I would like you to give us an idea of dealing with grief in a new way. I don't want to keep dealing with it in the old, pain-based way, because I know it's a glorious thing that's happening for people, for souls who are completing, and I want to honor that while I honor my process as well.

The group:

You humans have the most interesting expressions. "Kicking over" is a new one to us. We see you sometimes coming into this world kicking and screaming, but we have not quite thought of it as "kicking over" when you leave. Interesting.

You are working with grief because you have done that many lifetimes in a row. You happen to be an expert at it and it is quite humorous to us that you are asking us this question for, in fact, you are the one who will probably end up writing the book that will help open the doors to working with grief.

There are several stages of grief humans must go through in order to assimilate the changes in the spiritual realm into the physical body. It is a physical event and a change one must go through and experience. It happens first through the emotional bodies, but it is a physical event, and when you experience that event, it leads you through the process of grief, and you will never be the same physically again. Your physiology changes to encompass this new part of you, because the one who caused you this grief is actually a physical part of you. They are actually a piece of your physiology, so when they leave you behind, your physiology must actually adjust and that takes you through stages that accomplish this.

It is very frustrating, particularly for you, for you know so much about it that you want to go right through the stages very quickly, but most humans cling desperately to those stages and refuse to move from one level to the other, for they think they are healing and not growing when, in fact, a grief process is an opportunity to not only grow emotionally and spiritually, but even physically. It is not a wound that needs to be healed but an opportunity for growth, and to incorporate the energy of the one who left.

If you stop and think about it, grief is one major event almost all of you will work through at some point in your life. Dear ones, this is a subject that should be taught in schools so everyone is prepared.

You humans get comfortable in your pain, because pain is associated with most things in your Game on your planet. It is a very unique human experience, for only when you are finite in expression can you experience what you call pain. The reality is that pain is experienced only because of your separation from one another.

Also, please re-member, even though pain is the great motivator for you in all areas, when you get Home, you are going to re-member that pain as the most beautiful human experience. You are going to say, "Was that not wonderful, that we sat and cried together and moved to the next level together? Was that not wonderful? It was hard at the time and, boy, we thought we were just about done, but was that not wonderful?" Yes, you will re-member the human pain as the most beautiful, bittersweet experience, and it will be the great motivator for you.

The process of grief that becomes difficult for most people is when they do not deal with the frustration of mismatched energy. This is where you typically go through the grief stage of anger. Your life has been altered and, after you go through the earlier stages, you then get to anger. It is too difficult to understand that the anger is actually caused by the person who left so, instead, you generally place the anger on someone who is safe. Or you hold it within, and it becomes a frustration which builds and suddenly shoots out at other people at inappropriate times. It is appropriate that you would go through wide swings of emotions, so allow your clients to do so with foreknowledge of the process so that they can move through it.

That is the process of grief. The challenge you have personally with it is that everyone in your field sees your vibration. You vibrate out there as one who understands grief, that your a grief counselor and a grief facilitator. Even though you never mentioned the words, that is the energy you send out in your vibration. So when people experience it, they automatically attract you, they magnetize to you and they find you in the strangest circumstances.

When you have had enough, complete the energy by teaching it to someone else and then release it. And that will do it, for you have other healing work to do. You are ready to move to the next level and draw different students into your field. Play the game of tag. "You are it. Pass it on."

The reality is, the transition team members who work with grief, who work with the families to release the soul, do a tremendous job. Many in this room will choose willingly to step into a role and be taught by a person like this and take it on.

You will derive great joy from being able to help people but you do not understand the ultimate implications of what you do. For it is not about helping a person or a family process through grief; it is really about the soul who has left and is in the Seventh Stage of life. That stage is an acclimation period where they review all that they experienced and all the things they came to do in this lifetime. Then they decide which ones they are going to incorporate into their core personality, which ones they are done with, and which ones they are going to release.

It is a lengthy process, although, of course, time is different on the other side of the veil, yet even from their perspective, it is a lengthy process, not something that happens overnight. And during this time in particular, they are vulnerable to be pulled back to Earth by a grieving family, by those who will not let go, by those who think the person is an inseparable part of themselves that they cannot let go, by those who feel the loss so much, they refuse to feel the anger, refuse to feel the resistance.

If you can work with the soul to go to the next level, you do a tremendous deed not only for the family but also for that soul's advancement, as he or she is no longer hampered and can move very quickly. Likewise, you do a huge deed to the collective consciousness of All That Is, for that stops the impedance of forward movement. The door is then open and people can flow readily.

Others of you here will work as a transition team member with the soul after it has left the body, for the moment the soul steps out of the body, it may not immediately go into the Seventh Stage of life. Some of them are confused and do not know where they are going. These are what you call "ghosts." Some of them get stuck in an earthly reality for, the moment they step out of the body, they are in an enhanced state of creation and can create a reality that makes them believe they are still alive. If they become attached to a human emotion, they can create a reality that makes them think they are still alive. Sometimes they simply need to know they have died. Other times, they need help releasing the emotion that has them earthbound.

Some of the tragedies you have seen that are large in scale have opened doors to these realities. The events of 9-11 opened doors for souls to go through, not only from that tragedy itself but also souls trapped since the Civil War. You heard the call and many of you jumped right into action and helped some of these souls move forward. And as you did, you opened the door for not only these but for many dimensional realities to create the same thing, and it was a wondrous thing. The possibilities were beyond your understanding at that point. Not only did you help at that level for those souls to move forward, but the collective consciousness also took huge strides as a result of that. Look for these opportunities and jump in when you feel it, for many here in this room will work with souls after they leave.

Some of you in the room will also work with families after they leave. Some of you will feel the transition team pull to work with people as they are leaving, which is a beautiful job, too, for in the lower vibrations of who you used to be, your primary motivation was survival. It is, therefore, very difficult for you to leave when you are fighting for life. Oh, what a strange concept, for you never need to fight for life; you simply allow it to move through you, to be part of it.

When many are in the process of leaving, they will fight, because of their primary motivation in the lower vibrations of who they have been. They may find it very difficult to let go because most have not the training or the knowledge you have. Many of you here cannot wait to go Home. In fact, you look forward to it, knowing we will embrace you with open arms. When you do finally come Home, we will be waiting and you will know a hug like you can only find here.

There is a special moment when someone in the dying process goes into survival mode. When they are fighting for breath, a magical person lovingly touches them with the touch of an angel and says, "It is okay. You can go if you like, you did a good job and it is all right to let go."

When you give them permission to go, it is a magical event, for it immediately allows them to step into the next stage and experience the Seventh Stage of Life. The Sixth Stage of Life is required so that you become childlike in order to make that transition. And those who refuse to become childlike are pushed into it through what you call Alzheimer's, for example, or what you call "dementia." We love the titles you come up with to describe these things.

If you refuse to become childlike during the Sixth Stage of Life, you cannot make the step into the seventh stage of life. And we tell you, it is a difficult step for you to make, a scary step indeed, but not nearly as scary as the birth canal. That is much more frightening to us all. You have already made that step, which was the hard one. Going Home, the moment you step out of your body, you look around and often see your body lying there on the bed or operating table. Or you may see it amidst a twisted heap of metal you used to call your car. As long as you are not confused or attached to human emotions, you go Home.

If you have been able to become childlike, you can go Home. If you are not trying to think in a thought process the whole time, you go Home. When you do, you step into the Seventh Stage of life. Sometimes, that is a difficult transition, when people in the family actually pull you back because they cannot grieve, it hurts. A soul may not know how to deal with it.

Can you now see the importance of what she has been doing? It is a big deal. Teach it well, dear one. You have already touched many souls with your work. Teach responsibility as well, for humans get wrapped up in their emotional pain. There is a comfort to that pain but rather than change, many will choose to experience the pain, for the thought of change seems worse than the pain itself. Help them. Take them by the hand. Touch them with the touch of an angel with your love and understanding.

Transition teams will become more important as time goes forward and we thank you for bringing this up, for it allowed us to say something we are passionate about. It is a joy to see this work being done. That is the work of angels, and you do it well.

No Rest Between Lifetimes

Crystal Walk-Ins #D042102 San Diego, CA

Question:

Earlier you spoke about people who are very tired all the time because they didn't rest in between lifetimes. I'm wondering if you might have some suggestions about how to do that now or get some energy now?

The group:

What happens in this situation is that you saw opportunities to be here at exactly this time, and you did so without regard for yourself. We honor that, but also know that to do your work, you must have the energy, and to be effective, you must feel good. You deserve to feel good and to be abundant in all areas, including health. Abundance is simply the definition of having more than is minimally needed. Currently, you have exactly enough energy to carry your body from one place to another and not a lot extra, so we will work on you on abundance. For part of what you have come in with is a stress.

Many of you have come in with energy difficulties from birth because you did not get ample time to rest in between incarnations. And yet some of you who have come in and had that struggle have rectified it because you took care of yourselves and placed yourselves first. Know it is not possible to give to another until you fill your own cup first. Yet some of you have had life lessons that have led you into a different direction, making you think you must come last.

Understand, you must take care of yourself. Over long periods of time, you have placed yourself under stress. There are many opportunities to help you with your energy disturbances. For some, it is a simple case of reversed polarity. However, it has been with you for so long that your body believes this is its normal position. You were born in this energy. For those of you who carry this type of energy, it will be necessary to release fully. Even some of your belief systems have placed you here. Open the door to try new things and dare to have the courage to place yourself first in the energy flow so you can feel better.

When you feel good, not just minimally, when you really feel good, you have more to give to everyone. That is when you can find your passion, when you attract others around you that vibrate the same. That is when others bring healthy relationships into your field. You have so much you can do with this. All it takes is to ask.

Visits from the Other Side

The Magic Wand, #D110203, Waginengen, Holland.

Question:

I would like to ask a question about when I was twenty-five and a good friend died. Last month, he came in way more close from the other side of the field, and I had that feeling yesterday and today. In a way, I have the feeling he wants to give me something. I do not know if it is true but it's the feeling I have. It's quite a strong bond we had and I would like to know if I can do something with it now.

The group:

In all passing, whether it be a transition of a soul coming from Home into the life experience through the birth process, or whether it be a soul leaving the birth process going back Home through the death process, there is a gift. When you find the gift, it releases the soul to move forward. Finding and incorporating that gift in your life is the key effective grief work. Many people miss the gift. They get so wrapped up in their own loss that they do not see the gift at first.

The gift can sometimes be very simple, very plain. When anyone dies, everyone gets spiritual for a least a few minutes. That is a gift and there are times when a soul comes in with the main intent to leave early and give that very gift. When someone dies at the age of ninety-two, you say, "She lived a full life." But when someone leaves early, everyone who is touched by that knowledge becomes spiritual, if only for five minutes. You become aware that you are more than the physical body.

You accepted the gift. That is why he was able to connect with you in other ways that he could not before then. And yes, there was an important connection between the two of you that you were not able to complete and that is why he is talking with you. The energy was not complete. You had an important contract with him – to give him permission to say good-bye and let go. But you were not able to do that, and he did not get the opportunity to say good-bye to you. He is completing the energy now.

There will be messages you will get much clearer than this from him directly for we are translating, in a way. You know what we mean and the best way to do that. Your heart was not fully expressed as you held a space for others to heal. Express it now. Give it now and you will have all of the gift. We thank you for sharing.

Daughter Crossed

The Magic Wand, #D110203, Waginengen, Holland.

Question:

My daughter went to the other side five months ago. She told me it had to be this way. It couldn't go any other way. I do not understand.

The group:

Of course, you do not. Of course, your heart is torn in two at this point. You miss your daughter so much, it is hard to see she is over your right shoulder.

Question:

I know she is.

The group:

She is there talking to you. She has appeared twice to you in dreams already, only once that you re-member. But she has spoken to you as clearly as we are speaking to you now. But we tell you, she knew since the age of three she would be leaving early. She knew what her contracts were, what her setups were, and why she came in here.

Even though she went through childhood and many difficult times here, she was a very old and balanced soul. She gave gifts of touching people's hearts all throughout her life. And when her time came, she had a choice of whether she would complete that contract or not, and she did so willingly. And she is working with you all of the time, because of all the gifts that were given, she was not able to give you the full gift.

You were the one who took the big hit here. And we know it is difficult. We know you cannot see the higher perspective of things, but let us tell you this. Not only is she very, very happy, and very comfortable, but she was a last timer. Because of her willingness to go through and complete this energy, it is not necessary for her to come back here ever again. She completed. She had a unique opportunity to bring in seeds of Crystal energy and leave early. Hers was a short, bright life with a very big wake left behind her that will touch many lives. It was a very important role to play and the timing of this contract had to be perfect. She is done.

Question:

She's Home?

The group:

She is Home, all the way Home. The interesting part is she probably will come back, for you two were sisters once and there is an opportunity to play that role with you again and she probably will do it. Thank you for sharing that.

VORTICES AND PORTALS

Playing with Portals

Amor—The Emerald City, #D041402, Bemidji, Mn.

Question:

I would like to know what the connection is between the portal I saw in the sky and the portals that are in the lake.

The group:

One portal you see in the lakes is inter-dimensional, having to do with the Earth energy. The portals through the Earth energy are quite different than what you would see in the sky, but one has to do with inter-dimensional realities within the same time and space as the Earth Herself, and the other has to do with portals used simply for what you call space travel. Both will eventually connect but in the interim, you will be able to see them as separate, for many of the portals are just now forming.

Your own vortexes that you sometimes start when you do your own ceremonies create the birthplace for these portals to happen, and create the potential for a portal to be activated. In doing so, you have created many that are just now becoming awakened, for the time is right to activate these portals. And as they are starting to be activated, many connections are being made at one time, yet not all of them are connected. So you will see portals that will start out and begin connecting.

You will see them in the sky, in the Earth, and in your dreamtime, which may seem strange to you, but it is part of what you will understand here as time goes forward. And even in that energy, you will have an opportunity to play with the portals and use them, for if you bless them and open them up, you have literally given permission for entities and energy to come through the portals, and that is what you are looking for, dear ones.

You will find out you are not alone, and when you understand that, you will be much, much more tolerant of each other. You now look at each other and see differences with yourselves, with your religions, with your energies and with your looks. You fight wars over this, and we cannot wait to see what you react with when you start seeing space beings from other places because, to them, you all look alike. [laughter] Have we answered your question?

We will add simply that you hold a space, for you are the guardian of a very important portal on land. You know where this place is. You do it well and we thank you for that.

What to do with a Portal

A Day of Rain, Oostmalle, Belgium, 05/21/05

Question:
Hi. I have a question about vortexes and portals. We had an awesome dialogue session yesterday about them. We either formed a vortex or a portal, I don't know. And I read about it also in Beacons of Light I brought with me. And I'm trying to grasp what you can do when you put an object through the portal. And then it works backwards in time? And I'm sort of trying to grasp what I can do with it.

The group:

At this point, it is best just to simply play with it. Do not worry about healing the Earth or opening portals to other worlds. A vortex has its own activation schedule. Rather, play with the portals so you can become accustomed to them and understand them. Then, when something really strange happens somewhere, at least one person has an inkling of what might be going on. That is the greatest thing we have asked you to do.

A vortex is very simple. If you were to blow a breeze through this room at this moment from that direction to here, it would catch the bodies and form a circular motion, because there is a circular energy in this room from the humans sitting in a circle. So therefore, the energy of the breeze or of the air would start moving in a circle. Whee.. That is a vortex. Energy in a circular motion. You have seen them in the way of tornadoes; those are drastic, out-of-control vortices. But the reality is, a vortex is simply energy moving in a circle.

You can easily create that with your mind by simply thinking of a circle and doing some of the fun little exercises the Keeper has done by having people hold hands and intentionally move energy in a circle. That is a vortex. At a trigger-point, with a certain intensity of human experience and Higher Self connection, you can turn that vortex into a portal. A portal is the connection between all dimensions of time and space in that physical space. For instance, if you are to create a portal right here – which by the way we have just done –you may find that you put something in that space and it will disappear. You can watch it if you like, but typically it will not happen until you look away or leave. When you come back, it will have gone.

There are times when energies will go through the portal, and other times when physical attributes will go through it. In your not-too-distant future, you will go through those portals. There are eleven dimensions of time and space, therefore, there are eleven of you. And all of you are doing something very similar but a little bit different, sometimes due to slightly different choices. A portal connects all of those for a time, which is partly why we have suggested walking backwards in time and playing with the portals.

Every time you see a very magical place, take a small piece of it. Take a small stone and intentionally recreate that same portal in your own backyard. Then nurture it and flow with it.

Question:

And put a stone there.

The group:

Yes. If you do, watch what happens in the general vicinity. Your own spirits will probably have to distract you a little bit because if you watch closely and you see something pop up, your own mind will try to categorize it in such a way that you will actually negate it. Suddenly, what popped up will disappear. It is much simpler if you are simply distracted, leave and come back to it. But you have the capabilities of intentionally creating portals, so play with them and have fun.

There are many portals that will create for a lot of different reasons. One simple one was created recently by some of the stones taken from Mt. Shasta where we showed the portals. The person brought back a piece of Glass Mountain and placed it on a desk because it was a very beautiful rock. The energy of Mt. Shasta was placed on a desk, although the person did not think anything of it. One day, the rock disappeared. A few weeks later, the person came back and found a camera, although was not sure whose camera that was. Since then, five or six different things have popped up on the desk in roughly the same spot as the stone that disappeared. This is happening because you are playing with the portals, not just in this dimension but in eleven. Play, Work, Plurk.

Question:

How do I make sure my other dimensions don't want my jewelry?

The group:

You don't. Enjoy.

Vortex of a City

Smile of Spiritual Confidence, #013, Edmonton, Alberta, Canada.

Question:

Greetings. I have known for a while that Edmonton, or near Edmonton, is a "hotspot." I have been drawn to it, and figured that my energy was needed here. I am really curious about the energy particular to this area. What can you say about that?

The group:

If you look at an aerial view of this city and see where rivers come down and turn into lakes, you can almost understand where the vortex is centered. The draw of this natural vortex is why this city has manifested itself in that particular location. There is generally some physical property that draws people to a location to begin building a city, and from there, it just sprouts out.

Edmonton, however, does not have that. Edmonton is a ley line crossing-point and that is what has the pull to people. This energy is also why it is the capital of your province. Part of this is an energy vortex, which has been here from day one and has pulled people, magically, almost like a magnet, to it. That is why the population is very dense in this particular area, while the surrounding areas are sparsely populated.

On top of that, you are not the only ones it has attracted. Although the activity is very minimal now, at one point in time, this area attracted tremendous numbers of what you call "space visitors." There is a history of energy being focused here from that, which is part of the magic.

Now, even though that energy is here, it still has to be activated by humans. And you have done that. You love your Home. It is a beautiful place, and in many ways, you have created that vortex and allowed it to blossom and be seen. You should be very proud of your Home, for it is marvelous. You have had a lot to do with creating that yourselves. We thank you for the question.

WATER

Water Emotions

Earth Changes, #054, Kona, HI.

Question:

There were two pods of dolphins in the bay this morning while we were having breakfast, sending amazing, amazing energy to all of us. My question is, I'm reading a book by someone named Masaru Emoto, who studies water and the ice crystals. I was wondering if you can comment on his work.

The group:

We would be thrilled to, for he is a channel. He has looked in a direction and listened to his own guidance through his own higher self. He is a thinking channel, for he calls himself a scientist, but he has been looking from the heart, not the eyes; therefore, he has seen things other people have not seen. What he has done is place a drop of water in a container, send energy to it, and watch the molecular structure of that water change. He believes he is actually changing the structure of the water to accommodate the energy. What we tell you is, this is close. We would describe it more as the water is the reflector, the mirror of his energy. He is looking for answers and he found them. More accurately, he created them.

It is that simple. For that is what the energy of water does. Now, if you understand that, think of the fact that you are about 70 percent water. Think of all the times you look in the mirror and say, "Oh. my goodness, I am fat." What happens to the water in your structure? It changes at a molecular level and says, "She says we are fat so we must produce this. Here we go." So you can stop eating and still gain weight.

However, it goes beyond that, for there is a collective thought pattern that is gathered through the vibration of all humanity which goes into this water right here. That is what the dolphins are the keepers of, which is why you saw the two pods today, and you will see no less than three pods this afternoon. They are here to balance your energy in connection with the energy of Earth known as water, and that is what you are working with. And when you see them, smile that beautiful smile you have, for that is the energy that fills their hearts. Espavo

The Matrix of Water

Earth Changes, #054, Kona, HI.

Question:

Thank you. Earlier you were talking about certain spots around the world that holds the matrix of the water. If you were to work with areas that are polluted, would it be better to work with that area, to charge that area, by connecting with those different spots?

The group:

You will find energetic ways to clean and clear water very quickly. There are only three problems humans have with water on Earth: too much, too little, and too polluted. You will find ways of dealing with all three of those. Many of you are from a place called Holland and have dealt with "too much" very well. You have learned to focus the channel of energy called water and create beautiful lands from it and adapt that which was claimed by water for your own practical use. Wonderful. You will see more opportunities for the talents you have.

You will also see sciences and biological sciences starting to uncover animals and microscopic creatures that will help to clean the water for you. They have been waiting in the wings and are here to start that evolutionary process. But please understand that your view of something good and bad may change as time goes forward. So you consider something to be polluted that is not drinkable or usable by humans, but many times, it is actually usable by the Earth. Enjoy the ride.

Let the River Flow

The Color Clear, #D051902, St. Louis, Mo.

Question:

Here in the heartland, we've got the wonderful rivers, the Missouri-Mississippi, and the possibility of flooding reminds us of their power. I feel particularly connected to the rivers and the spirits of the rivers, not just the big ones but also the small ones. It really pains me when you were talking about boundaries earlier today. It pains me to see the way in which our community destroys them, bulldozes them over in order to build houses and parking lots and so on. I'm wondering if there is a message from the rivers or from the group that can help us, help me, celebrate our connection and turn that problem into the positive force you referred to earlier.

The group:

What you perceive many times as natural disasters are only a result of something you yourselves have set into motion, and many times exactly what you have spoken of happens. As it unfolds, you understand there is something further upstream where you have made space or cleared the land. It is not "wrong" to clear the land, and also not "wrong" that you should have a physical reaction of it. But if you understand the correlation, you understand the Universal Energy, for every action there is a reaction. The idea is to understand the reaction first, so it becomes much less complicated. You are working not only with the energy of water but also, as you said so very nicely, the spirits you would call the oversouls of the rivers themselves. You have seen them in the animal kingdom and in the plant kingdom as the devas of the forest. You do not understand that a mountain also has an oversoul.

Many times, the Keeper goes to his favorite place in Arizona in the great painted deserts and valleys, and he looks up and sees the boulders that seem to be overlooking the entire valley. We have even called them the "guardians of the valley" and that is exactly what they are. That energy has looked over and guarded over, which is why that energy still exists today. In the areas where you have removed some of the guardians, you can feel the difference in energy. There is a hole in the energy field.

When that happens and man changes or attempts to restrict the flow of energy, the energy of water has no choice but to react.

The energy we know to be water is a form of energy you do not understand. It is one of the base energies that underlie all other energies and when you begin unlocking those secrets, you will be able to take one cubic centimeter of water and light your cities for years. You are on the verge of discovering something very soon that will lead to that discovery in the next forty years. Enjoy the ride, dear ones, for you are in for a thrill. You will see much of what you have called "devastation" on this planet is, in fact, repairable in the body. Do not fear your own powers of creation. You are good at it. Understand you are here in a very critical time. You are the right ones for the job. Thank you for asking the question.

WHALES AND DOLPHINS

New Roles?

Portals of Lemuria, #D032403, Kona, HI.

Question:
What will be the role of the whales and the dolphins in the new energy?

The group:
The dolphins have a particular energy to hold at this time. Like the whales, their contracts have recently changed. They have been the guardians of the Earth and the energy balancers, even though man was originally intended to hold the energy of the planet but was not able to do so. So the whales and the dolphins held the energy. You have recently been handed that torch, which is why there is such an influx of interest in the whales and the dolphins, and the energy.

Many of you know there is a connection, for it is no secret that dolphins are here to help you play, because you take life way too seriously. You have a problem with reality in that you think it is real. Watch them, the way they work and who they are. Watch their knowingness of who they are. Watch how they flow through things, for they are the epitome of Atlantis. They are so abundant that they need not carry anything with them. They have the dolphin flow, for they trip through the murkiest waters and nothing sticks to them. They know how to flow through energy, to be a part of the energy as it transforms from one to the next, so that they can go through. They will do so with a smile on their face and laughter in their heart, and you will even sometimes hear that laugh. You will all hear it very soon. Laugh with them. Carry the smile in your heart.

When you look upon a dolphin, it is much easier for you to really know what is important in your own life. Perhaps you will gain perspective. We tell you, the whales will hold a similar, but slightly different, energy for they will hold the ultrasonic resonance of your very beings. Without ever knowing it, they will communicate with you, for you are not only unable to hear their communication, most of you do not even feel it. It does not mean it is not happening.

Crystal Children and Dolphins

Portals of Lemuria, #D032403, Kona, HI.

Question:
Can you speak of the connection of the Crystal Children and the dolphins?

The group:
They are born four vibrational steps closer than you are, although many of you are very close. Now this may be disappointing to some when you take a Crystal out to connect with the dolphins, they may say, "So what?" for they are able to communicate on levels that do not require them to go out and get wet. They do not even need to be at the ocean's edge or to be playing with them, or to even intentionally set aside a specific time to talk to them.

We also tell you that the whales themselves have an opportunity to leave. Please understand, as your ocean temperature rises, they may choose to leave. Many of you will look for why, or think it is the mysterious sonar, water temperature or pollution. It may be all of those things, but they may just choose to come Home. It is okay; they have done a beautiful job and will be received with open arms.

You are stepping into the energy of becoming the Human Angels yourself, and there will be great celebration. Thank you for your question.

Dolphins

Earth Changes, #054, Kona, HI.

Question:

Can you tell me some more about the dolphins here in Hawaii? The other day we saw a gathering on the bottom of the ocean of a group of spinner dolphins. What happened back there?

The group:

Dolphins carry energy you are not accustomed to carrying. They carry a magnetic energy that imprints you every time you see them. The reality is, you are changed the moment you even look at a picture of a dolphin, which is why some of you are so attracted to them and have little statues all over your houses. It actually changes who you are and helps you become more centered as a being of Earth.

The dolphins are one of your original parental races. Dolphins and whales are of a class called cetaceans, and they came here to hold the balance of planet Earth. Now that humanity, their babies if you will, have grown to a level where they can hold that job themselves, they have turned it over to you. They are here now to hold your energy, not the energy of the Earth. They are here to teach you to play. Have you ever seen a dolphin work hard? Have you ever seen one who was not smiling? We rest our case.

The Tip of Lemuria

Earth Changes, #054, Kona, HI.

Question:

Can you comment on the connection between the whales and Mauna Kea?

The group:

Mauna Kea is the tip of Lemuria, the place of origin. It is the oldest of all history on Earth. Even though your geologists will argue that fact, the reality is, it has changed so much through the eruption of time. If you understand that the lungs of the planet are the volcanoes underneath the Pacific Ocean, Mauna Kea was once one of those lungs. But because of the buildup of material, even though somewhat dormant for a short time, she is now a marker and a central locating point for all whales everywhere. She is a central focus in much the same way your own airplanes and ships use compasses. Many birds also focus on those magnetic structures and simply glide along the magnetic pathways.

The whales themselves follow magnetic migration lines as they move back and forth. They follow the ley lines and the magnetics of the Earth, not the grid work of the planet. They also use Mauna Kea as a central spot, for it is the deepest of the life-breathing volcanoes of the planet, which is why it is so important. In a way, it can be considered the lungs of the planet.

We tell you also, there is a whale not too far from you who has purposely not migrated. Even though the season has passed, there is a whale out there, and you have seen her. She is waiting to connect with you, and you will connect energetically very quickly. Enjoy the ride.

RE-MINDER

Dear ones, we are so overjoyed that you made it in time. It was your greatest wish to place yourself in the Game and forget all you had planned to see if you could be here to help the miracle unfold. Despite all the distractions and side doors that appeared, here you are. You now stand at the pinnacle of humanity. It is time to take your place. Before you lies the greatest of possibilities. Yes, we know it is hard and your guidance is not always clear. If it were easy, everyone would want to be a human. But here you are, ready and willing to usher in the Age of Empowerment. Dear ones, it is our greatest honor to be there and be of service as you awaken from the dream. The first smile you see will be ours and we will dance in the Light once again.

Espavo, dear ones, Espavo.

We offer three simple re-minders:
1. Treat each other with respect,
2. Nurture one another,
3. Play well together.

The group

About the Author

Steve Rother was comfortably settled into life as a general building contractor in the San Diego area when, through a synchronistic series of events, he was placed firmly in the middle of his contract. Steve and his wife, Barbara, began shifting their focus on life and living on New Year's morning, 1995, when they found themselves unexpectedly expressing their intent for the coming year during a ceremony that took place as the sun rose over a California beach. From that day forward, their lives were never to be the same.

Soon after, Steve began receiving divinely inspired messages from 'the Group,' which he published monthly as the 'Beacons of Light.' These monthly writings from 'the Group' are about re-membering and accepting our own power, and living comfortably in the higher vibrations now on planet Earth. The Group calls Steve the 'Keeper of the Flame' or just 'Keeper' for short.

Steve never returned to his contracting business. Today, he and Barbara, his wife of 35+ years present empowerment seminars to Lightworkers throughout the globe. They have presented these in many countries, and are five time presenters at the United Nations on two continents. In April of 2000 at the UN in Vienna, Austria, Steve and Barbara presented a class on channeling, believed to be the first such class ever presented at a U.N. facility.

Barbara & Steve

Steve and Barbara make their base in Las Vegas, Nevada, where they work together in Love and Lightwork. They have formed the nonprofit corporation of Lightworker and, together with the volunteers and staff, plant seeds of Light through personal empowerment on a global basis. More information about Steve, Barbara and the Group, including their seminar schedule, can be found at the web site: http://www.lightworker.com.

Connect with spiritual family:

http:// www.Lightworker.com

'The Beacons of Light Re-minders from Home'
monthly messages from the Group, are available online or as a free e-mail service by request.

http://www.Lightworker.com/Schedule

Connect with original spiritual family on the message boards and in the chat rooms. Set your creations into motion in the 8 Sacred Rooms. Lightworker is a large site where the Groups information is translated into 20 languages. Come spend time creating Home.

Re-member… You are not alone… Welcome Home

Check the schedule on the web site at:
http://Lightworker.com/Schedule

You will receive notification of events in your area by adding your name to our mailing list at:
http://Lightworker.com/Signup

Paths to Empowerment Seminars
from Lightworker

Paths to Empowerment Seminars provide practical applications of the information for living in the higher vibrations of the new planet Earth, based on information from the Group. All gatherings include practical techniques for evolving as empowered humans, together with a Live channel from the Group through Steve Rother.

One-day informational seminars

Designed to connect family and introduce a new way of thinking ad living as empowered humans.

Two-day Interactive seminars

Experiential seminars over two days that apply practical applications of the material being covered. Each workshop is desdribed in greater detail on the web site.

Four-day OverLight Trainings

Three days of working with one of the OverLight modalities for healers shows the applications of the specific modality. Certified trainings. Several OverLight modalities have been adapted for a three day intensive. More on the OverLight modalities including a detailed description of each can be found at http://Lightworker.com/OverLight

Six-day OverLight Facilitator Trainings

Spiritual Psychology, Transition Team Training, Spiritual Communication, Human Angel Harmonics and Inverse Wave Therapy are th first of these with more added each year. The six day trainings are for those wishing to have a complete understanding of this material and its uses in daily life or for facilitators who wish to offer these modalities in their own work as facilitators. These are Lightworker certified courses.

Re-member: A Handbook for Human Evolution

This book will re-mind you how to:

- Discover and step into your 'Plan B' Contract.
- Purposefully craft your own reality and create your own version of Home on Earth.
- Adjust to the new levels of vibration affecting your biology.
- Master the arts of Time Warping and moving between Alternate Realities.
- Re-discover your gifts and tap into your own guidance and Re-member your power.
- Play "the Game" to the Highest Outcome and enjoy the journey.
- Prepare for the next phase of our evolution and the Crystal Children who are coming.

It's an exciting time on Planet Earth. In this enlightening book, Steve Rother and the Group offer a look at Higher Truths that will change the paradigms and the way we perceive ourselves. We Humans have just won the Grand Game of Hide-and-Seek and are now moving the Game to a new level!

"Mankind is evolving. We are moving from a motivation of survival to a motivation of unity. We are reaching for 'Higher Truths' in all areas as a quiet revolution is taking place. This transition does not have to be difficult. This book documents not only profound information for the planet, but also the LOVE journey of two enlightened and high-vibrational people."

– LEE CARROLL, author of The Kryon Writings

"This book will remind you of why you are here on the planet at this time. Peace is real now, and Steve's work will help you find that magic place within yourself."

– JAMES TWYMAN, author of Emissary of Light, The Secret of the

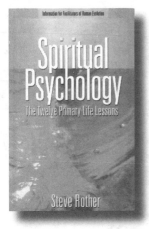

Spiritual Psychology:
The Twelve Primary Life Lessons

Have you ever wondered why it is that one person can grow up with every conceivable advantage, and yet seem incapable of mastering even the simplest things in life?

Have you ever known someone who, despite being highly intelligent, keeps on repeating the same mistakes over and over again?

It is only when we begin to view the human experience as the evolutionary process of a soul that we can begin to understand all these strange forces at work in our lives.

We see ourselves as human beings searching for a spiritual awakening when, in fact, we are spiritual beings trying to cope with a human awakening. But what causes us to seek these experiences in the first place? What is it, precisely, that sets certain life patterns into motion? Why do these patterns emerge in our own behaviors repeatedly? More importantly, what would happen if we could find ways of identifying this higher purpose and in so doing transform seemingly destructive patterns into positive attributes?

Spiritual Psychology offers a radically different view of life and the human experience. This book offers a view of humanity from the higher perspective of our own spirit.

"This book gives us help for our bodies, sanity for our minds and food for our Souls."

> – CHARLES L. WHITFIELD, MD, author of Healing Your Inner Child
> and The Truth about Mental Illness
> – BARBARA HARRIS WHITFIELD, RT, author of Spiritual Awakenings

"The word 'psychology' originally meant 'study of the soul' (psyche). After exploring far afield, we are returning full circle to encompass an understanding of ourselves as spiritual beings into our understanding of human health and behavior. Steve Rother's remarkable pioneering work is a cornerstone in challenging us to expand our knowledge and skills as empowered and empowering healers."

> – PAULINE DeLOZIER, Ph.D., Clinical Psychologist

Welcome Home:
The New Planet Earth

Welcome to the 5th dimension. Did you feel the ascension? The world we knew is rapidly evolving. Life on planet Earth is becoming increasingly unpredictable. The old rules no longer function. According to 'the Group,' these changes have greater implications than we imagine. As unexpected as recent events have been, they merely mark the beginning. The evolution of mankind has begun.

The Group's purpose is to prepare us for what lies ahead. In *Welcome Home*, they otter us keys to unlocking the secrets of developing our full power as creators, and using them in our lives now.

Welcome Home is divided into four sections:

1. Current Events: A cosmic view of where we are, how we got here and where we are heading.
2. The New Planet Earth: The new attributes of life in the 5th dimension and how we can apply them right now.
3. Questions and Answers on a wide range of topics taken from live presentations.
4. Where do we go from here? Prepare to be surprised!

"Steve Rother has tapped into the root of a new consciousness blossoming in the hearts of Humanity. Re-Member offered practical step-by-step instructions on how to awaken to the Pathway of the Soul. Welcome Home is the next step ... useful, loving, wise, and beautifully engaging – another tremendous book for the 'enlightened seeker.'"

– ISHA LERNER, author of Inner Child and Power of Flower cards

"Steve and the Group present an exciting new way to look at our world. This book provides a deeper understanding of the power and miracles that are now available to us."

– Ronna Herman, author and messenger for Archangel Michael

"Did anyone notice that life has changed? Perhaps you also feel that time has sped up and the spiritual rules are getting overhauled. Are you asking the question, 'What's next?' If so, you have the right book in your hands! Join Steve, Barbara and the Group for more loving insights into one of the greatest energy shifts our planet has ever seen."

– LEE CARROLL, author of The Kryon Writings

Greetings from Home

The contents of this book were given to Steve Rother over ten years as divinely inspired monthly messages by a collection of warm and loving spirits that he simply called 'the Group.' In the spirit of true empowerment, they refused to identify themselves because they do not want readers to give up their power to titles, labels or an image of superior beings. They say: "It's not about us; it's about you, the masters of the gameboard of free choice. It is our task to help you remember who you really are."

"Humanity is stepping from an experience of duality into a field of Triality where light and dark selves are balanced by a new connection to the higher self. It is an exciting and sometimes scary time for humans for it means taking your power as conscious creators. We are here to offer you an empowered view of the human experience. That view is not right, nor is it wrong for, in a field of Triality, you no longer have the need for those contrasts. We ask that you do not follow us, for the game of follow the leader is now ending and the game of follow yourself is just beginning. When you return home, you will be greeted as heroes for playing the game of free choice and you will then understand that ascending into spirit is not nearly as important as having a wondrous human experience."

ESPAVO

the Group

Each month Spiritual Family Gathers for the **VirtualLight Broadcast.**

Lightworker presents a 3-hour international broad-cast free of charge on the internet to connect spiritual family on the new planet Earth.

_____

Each month see:

Special guests each month, leaders in Lightwork.
2 minute readings from Steve & the Group
Lightworker events and attractions.
The "Beacons of Light" message from the Group presented live.

_____

Watch it live on the internet at http://Lightworker.com
or
Attend in person in Las Vegas, Nevada
or
Watch the shows at your convenience in their entirety:

http://VirtualLightBroadcast.com